The School Library Program in the Curriculum

THE SCHOOL LIBRARY PROGRAM
IN THE CURRICULUM

Ken Haycock

1990
LIBRARIES UNLIMITED, INC.
Englewood, Colorado

Readings selected from the journal *Emergency Librarian*
published by
Dyad Services
Box C34069, Department 284
Seattle, Washington 98124-1069
and
P.O. Box 46258, Station G
Vancouver, British Columbia V6R 4G6

The School Library Program in the Curriculum is copublished with Dyad Services.

LIBRARIES UNLIMITED, INC.
P.O. Box 3988
Englewood, CO 80155-3988

Library of Congress Cataloging-in-Publication Data

The School library program in the curriculum / [selected by] Ken
  Haycock.
   xi, 169 p. 22x28 cm.
   Selected articles, originally published in Emergency librarian.
   Includes bibliographical references.
   ISBN 0-87287-776-0
   1. School children--Library orientation.   2. School libraries-
-Activity programs.   3. Libraries and education.   4. Curriculum
planning.   5. Teacher-librarians.   I. Haycock, Ken.
[Z675.S3S359   1990]
025.5'678'223--dc20   89-49590
                                                              CIP

Contents

Part 3
PROGRAM PLANNING AND DEVELOPMENT

Part 4
INFORMATION SKILLS ACROSS THE CURRICULUM

Part 5
SECONDARY SCHOOL APPLICATIONS

Part 6
ISSUES AND CONSIDERATIONS

Preface

Over the course of the past ten years I have clarified my thinking on the role of the teacher-librarian and the school library program. This has come through professional research and reading, dialogue with colleagues and most especially through the in-depth programs offered through more than 50 professional associations, school boards, universities and departments of education across the United States, Canada and Australia. There is nothing quite like three days of intensive training with committed, professional teacher-librarians and administrators to challenge your philosophical positions and directions for effective professional practice.

This work was summarized at the request of the International Association of School Librarianship through the keynote address to their 1984 conference in Honolulu, Hawaii. The speech was subsequently published in more than a dozen professional journals in four countries. "Strengthening the Foundations for Teacher-librarianship" brings together basic beliefs on a solid premise aimed at deep structure for the program and significant infusion into the school beyond simple public relations and advertising glitz. *Information Power*, the new guidelines for school library media programs, calls the speech "an important statement on the role and change of directions for the library media center." I hope that you agree.

In this book, readers may note some inconsistencies in spelling, usage, and referencing styles. These differences are due to the nature of these readings, taken from previously published articles and written by a variety of authors of different nationalities.

Part 1
THE SCHOOL CONTEXT

Twenty years ago a bright new age dawned for school librarians when the school library became the "heart of the school." A wide range of educational planners and thinkers bought into this new and pervasive philosophy of teaching and learning, and many school principals and school librarians failed to grasp the sophistication and underlying tenets of resource-based teaching and learning, whether modes of inquiry or independent study. In fact, too many school librarians failed to grasp even that it was educational change and innovation that was necessitating support for school libraries rather than a simple recognition of the inherent "good" of school libraries. Sadly there are still too many of our colleagues who decry the lack of understanding of principals and teachers of the importance of school libraries, while not recognizing that of far greater significance is their lack of understanding of the place of the library in the school context and their lack of commitment or skill in redressing the issue. Michael Marland provides an overview of the school context and major issues facing school librarians from the perspective of a secondary school principal in London; we know that many, many principals in North America and elsewhere share these perspectives and challenges.

School libraries are different from other types of libraries and have more in common with other learning laboratories in the school than with other types of libraries, if one were forced to choose. School libraries are in fact resource centers for the instructional program and this is the term we prefer and use consistently throughout *Emergency Librarian*. Most libraries focus on effective access to information and the efficient delivery of information by and to users. School resource centers, however, while recognizing the importance of the management and service considerations to support good access and delivery, focus far more on information handling and processing. It is more important in the context of the school to ensure that students can process and use information effectively and efficiently than it is to make it easy to get at or to provide it. Once the material is in hand, can the student acquire, organize, and use the information? The integration of school learning resources with classroom teaching requires more than a librarian to provide support for teachers; it requires a highly skilled and experienced classroom teacher with additional training in the selection, management, and use of materials, a *teacher-librarian* if you will. This term we also use consistently to designate a teaching role first and foremost and an emphasis on cooperative program planning and team teaching as an equal teaching partner with colleagues.

The research base for teacher-librarians and resource centers is quite strong, but it is not well known and not used to best effect with colleagues. *What Works* stirred great reaction from the education community when issued by the U.S. Department of Education but little examination by the school library community. We include the summary here since it is still valid and warrants closer examination. Certainly the conclusions drawn about the importance of teacher collegiality, study skills, speaking and listening, reading aloud, independent reading, storytelling, student assessment, and others, have implications for the role of the teacher-librarian. We extend this with our own approach to the research in teacher-librarianship through summaries of doctoral studies and the implications for professional practice. A different research finding is highlighted in each issue of *EL* and we urge teacher-librarians to use these with school administrators, teachers and trustees.

The school context is the teacher-librarian's world and affects every part of the job from program aims, professional role, program development and emphasis, and program advocacy.

1

Libraries, Learning, and the Whole School

Michael Marland

THE CONTEXT

The school library resource center has generally appeared uncontroversial; the only issue has been "more"—more money, more space, more staff—but a greater pedagogical rigor is required, particularly with regard to the relationship of libraries to learning in the context of the whole school, and especially the planned curriculum.

THE SITUATION

What is the present situation? Individuals have an increasing need to be able to find things out; never before have lives depended so much on the ability to handle information successfully. We all, therefore, need to search out what we require, to assess it critically, to examine the ideas and facts offered and then to make use of the findings. This "learning to learn," which begins at school, continues throughout adult lives, and yet the paradox is that schools, concerned with learning above all else, seem to find it very difficult to teach students how to learn. Although some students are able to use the full range of resources, most are not; and yet it is the central responsibility of the school to help its students cope with learning. There has been a growth in "the Project Method," a love affair with projects which starts when children are about seven and are told to find a topic, to find out something about it and write it up. It goes on every year until they are about 17, with no noticeable increase in skill apart from the cover pages which are rather more carefully done by the 17-year-olds.

This learning to learn is rarely stated as a specific overall aim. It seems to be presumed by those planning school curricula that the process will be assimilated while subjects are being studied; while you are being taught math, you will learn "learning." As students meet the middle years of secondary school the burden placed on them by the sheer quantity of facts and concepts increases, then the emphasis moves from the process to the product and hard pressed teachers start short-circuiting this by just getting over the information in the quickest possible way. All the evidence suggests that when "how to write a paper" is taught, it is taught separately, without conceptualized lessons on the use of the index or use of reference sources and it is not put in context. In many schools it is not even taught at all. Most research shows, what is painfully obvious to all teacher-librarians, that the use of books and other materials at all levels is disappointingly inefficient. And new demands that schools should plan their curriculum as a whole give no hint as to how this should be done nor do they as much as mention the fact that learning how to learn, study skills, and information handling, are among the most important "whole school" curriculum issues.

There is often too much stress on charisma in the teacher-librarian's role. There are, instead, five conditions for any educational activity to flourish. First, there must be a fair definition of aims; second, an expectation of its value; third, specific teaching—research has shown that when you teach, students may not learn everything but they do learn more than if you did not teach it; fourth, a suitable range of materials; and fifth, opportunities to practice. Even in those schools where there are good facilities and a reasonable budget many of those five conditions are not present. There is not a fair definition of the aims of information handling skills; there is not an expectation of its value on the part of the teaching staff; there is little teaching and precious few opportunities for practice. Of course in many other schools there is not a suitable range of materials either.

Do resource centers deserve more money? Do they have a right to go to government for more money when in many schools there are shelves of books, but they constitute some of the most expensive wallpaper known, because they are so ineffectively used? If you were to go into a school and ask a 14- or 15-year-old to find a resource in the library, the youngster could very well say, "I'd ask Miss, Sir", because asking "Miss" is the main information strategy that we have managed to teach.

THE CAUSES

That is the situation, so what are the causes? Even when the resources are available, programs are still not doing very well. Ten rather dismal causes follow, for only by looking at why these are problems can any solutions be developed.

The first is a disparity of specialists. One can study the teaching of reading, the teaching of the less able, the teaching of English, even how to be a teacher-librarian. But on the whole, library schools don't teach about the teaching of reading, because that is someone else's job. And indeed, the specialist in the teaching of the less able, is not taught about libraries or how to make effective use of the resource center.

Second, education is seen as an aggregate of courses. A well-educated person has added math to history to social studies to something else. That additive method of curriculum planning is at the heart of the problem because it does one of two things. It either leaves library "user education" out completely, or it makes it yet another subject on its own, struggling forcefully to try and be a separate subject but not, in fact, illuminating all other activities.

The third problem is the perversion of the recent emphasis on learning methods. The stress on practical work is fine until it produces science lessons in which looking quizzically at fuming test tubes is regarded as the only thing that real scientists ever do; until it produces craft design and technology lessons in which drawing and making is assumed to be the only thing a technologist does. Another aspect of this perversion of modern teaching methods is the idea that a textbook is some fiendish invention of commercial authors who do not understand children and it is used only by teachers who want to dominate children. This was a convenient belief when it became obvious that many students could not read the textbooks. This was presumed to be the author's fault and the publisher's fault and part of the capitalist plot for bringing the wrong kind of writing into schools. Probably there is some truth in this for many of the books placed before children in this way were not suitable, but it totally ignored an alternative hypothesis that students had not been taught how to read these books and as a solution to this the allegedly child-centered worksheet arrived.

The worksheet is something that a teacher has typed out somewhat inaccurately late one night; it is presumed the student can read it more easily because the teacher typed it. This worksheet simply extracts a paragraph and gives it to a student—it is the most teacher-centered learning material there is, because the student has been denied the opportunity to select from the book, never mind select the book itself. It is relevant that there is no way that students brought up on pre-selected paragraphs will ever be able to properly use a library.

Some learning approaches in themselves are good—more practical work, more individualized work, but it is too easy to lose some important central skills.

The fourth problem is simply to stress that the non-fiction book is a complex tool and the practice in many secondary schools of teaching reading only through the study of literature is not a preparation for the utilization of the book as a learning tool.

A fifth problem is that surface detail becomes more important than underlying intellectual problems. For example, in a 9th grade English or language arts lesson which is concentrating on the research paper, the teacher may be teaching foot-noting. Now that's fine, but foot-noting (to take the small example) is a surface detail of a much deeper and fundamentally more difficult problem—when do you require support for a point you are making? That is not taught. When you are in fact having information searches and need to write up your findings, you have to work out that which is obvious, that which requires support and that which is contentious and the whole paraphernalia of bibliographical reference is really only the surface detail to that. While the teaching of the surface detail has its place, this fifth problem is that we do not teach the fundamentals on which this detail lies, and you cannot teach these fundamentals in a library lesson or a language arts lesson because they are not library issues, and they are not language arts issues. They are intellectual issues that have to be taught in the specific subject area.

The sixth problem is teacher training, which is particularly weak in the use of studies, resources, and personnel.

Seventh is the lack of quality resource-based programs as examples.

Eighth is the inadequate resources in many parts of the world. Many U.K. secondary schools for example do not have libraries that are retained as resource centers throughout the week. They are often timetabled for teaching for any subject that has to be jammed in there.

And the ninth problem is the inherent intellectual difficulty of what we are really concerned with, which is the intellectual task of deciding what it is you want to know. That is the most difficult thing. We are facing a great problem because of the wastage of public money on Ph.D's which never get completed. If you read the study of uncompleted Ph.D's or talk to people who have given up their Ph.D's the usual reason is the same reason that a 15-year-old fails with a research paper—they find that the question they set out to investigate is too vague to pin down, or impossible to research. The inherent intellectual difficulty in the task of information searching is too easily glossed over.

The tenth and final problem is the difficulty about the role of the teacher-librarian in the educational system. Just check out where "the librarian" is listed in the faculty list. Many schools provide a list of teachers, office staff, janitor, and librarian. Few have thought out why there is a teacher-librarian in a school. Is the librarian there to select materials, to maintain the collection, to teach library skills, to be a general propaganda guru—or be part of curriculum planning and team teaching? That is the final problem because the school library movement is floundering on this failure to define the role of the school librarian. In other words, problems are not primarily involved with resources, with staff, with persuading "those damn teachers," but with something much more fundamental. It is a failure to produce a coherent school policy which defines the role of the teacher-librarian. (My favorite definition is that a librarian is a teacher whose subject is learning itself.) And the feelings described here are not limited to poor schools, to the lazy, or the ill-trained. They are endemic even where professionals are working very hard indeed.

THE TEACHER AND TEACHER-LIBRARIAN

Two relationships become critical: that between the teacher and the teacher-librarian, and that between the curriculum and library resources.

First—get the school library out of the area of resources and under the label of curriculum. Resources are secondary as a problem; the key problem is relating the resource center to the curriculum.

Second, develop the concept of the teacher-librarian's role. We need a close working relationship between the teacher-librarian and other teachers. With a clear definition of why there are teacher-librarians and what the job is, the gap could be closed. The teacher-librarian is part of the curriculum planning team. (This is less difficult in those countries where the school librarian is qualified as teacher, but more difficult in the U.K. where few professional school librarians are qualified teachers.)

The teacher-librarian should be a leader of teachers, an adviser and guide to teachers, rather than one who is primarily looking after materials or even working directly with students. One cannot generalize the expertise of "the librarian" throughout the entire student body. If teacher-librarians expect to work on a one-to-one basis with the whole student body, they will never complete the job. Nor will this produce "library impelling instructors." The second aim then would be to reconstruct the concept of the teacher-librarian's role as a primarily inservice training and curriculum planning person.

The third aim is to actually *have* curriculum planning in our schools. That's easy to say and difficult to pull off. Even where there are small curriculum planning teams, they are still working in pre-determined divisions and those matters which go across the divisions are still difficult to plan. Start with the overall curriculum aims first, within which the separate segments, sectors, or focuses are planned. Fourthly, there should be a reading curriculum so that there is continuity in reading development. I would wish there to be, fifthly, a research and study skills continuum. Labels are less important—study skills or information handling skills—the important thing is that there has to be a continuum and a framework.

The sixth aim deals with the setting of assignments. Hard work in the resource center counts for little if teachers are setting impossible assignments or assignments for which there are no resources. Similarly, there is a lack of communication between the teacher and the teacher-librarian over the preparation of reading lists. The specification of reading lists in lessons needs very great care.

Seventh, the functions of the resource center require different sections for studying, teaching, searching. These are incompatible tasks. Yet in many schools the same geographical space and architecture is being used for all these different tasks.

The selection policy too often seems to cover the entire field of human knowledge at every level possible. Now there will never be enough resources for that, so the result is that most students learn most of the time when they go into the resource center to find a book that they will not be able to find it. We all need experience of success, but we have such experience of non-success in school resource centers because of our selection policy. There may be whole sectors of human knowledge not stocked in the school; for these, refer students to the public library because the school cannot do everything. Eighth, then: there should be good material on key topics, at all ability levels, all reading levels, in the resource center rather than an unsuccessful attempt to cover the whole of human knowledge.

Ninth, there must be a good relationship between book and non-book material.

Tenth, the catalog should be a focus, but really thought out from the student's point of view. There are too many schools where the jargon of teachers is not compatible with the jargon of the catalog. There should be access to reasonable on-line bibliographical searches available in schools. It is fatuous to teach children about the computer revolution and not provide this experience.

Eleventh, there should be a close relationship between the resource center in the school and bookshops and other libraries outside. It is a peculiar thing that we take children on visits to the theater, exhibitions, and sports events, but rarely to the public library or bookshops. There should be a very close liaison, advertising each other's services, having displays of each other's wares. Perhaps in some schools there should not even be a library—one high school is so near the public library that they don't have their own resource center but *do* still have their own teacher-librarian.

Twelfth. The library could assist teachers with bibliographical control and ordering.

And thirteenth, there must be more in-service training for teachers in this whole area.

THE MAJOR ISSUES

These fall within the context of some major issues:

Curriculum Planning. The main difficulty of teaching information handling is to relate this to different subjects. Time is precious in schools; therefore, programs have to be a vehicle for carrying the subject content and at least one, if not several, skills. This requires good curriculum planning. It also requires whole school policies. Just ask: what does each student by the age of such and such need to know in terms of facts, concepts, and skills and attitudes on this facet of the curriculum?

Now one facet of the curriculum will be concerned with information handling and study skills for which there needs to be a school outline. This should start at a high level of generality working down to quite small details. This is not something taught and left, because there are important things which keep coming up again as we get older. Within this overall curriculum, one can begin to divide out the aspects.

All teachers have responsibility here, but this can mean that no one is doing it. Without adequate planning, some students are taught how to use indexes all day, while others go through five years without having been exposed to indexes at all.

Then a good teacher of history could be a good teacher of library use in history. A good teacher of science could be a good teacher of information handling skills in science. Then ensure that any assignment in those areas has the double payload of the skills and the content simultaneously.

Overall Resources Policy. This is very difficult. It means at its least the putting right of the problems mentioned earlier—the mismatch between books recommended in the classroom and the books available in the resource center. There should be a policy for all resources in a school to ensure that they relate one to another, they relate book to non-book media, they are balanced from the point of view of having a world view and not a locally centered view of the world, that they relate clippings and journals to bound books. Now this requires leadership and control which is very difficult to achieve.

Underlying Skills. One of the problems is teaching the surface and not the underlying foundation. When teaching "library use," we have started too late—intellectually too late. We have started with how the resource center is laid out—the orientation. However, a technological design problem, a scientific problem, or a historical research problem, basically have similar intellectual stages and, as an educational institution, the school has to help students analyze those stages and see that they are in fact analagous one to another. An information search is like a design problem.

Every single assignment, from the short piece of written work that the six-year-old does, to the major piece of research, has to proceed through the same kind of sequence and teaching should ensure that specific skills are taught.

Reading Curriculum. Not only should there be practice in vocabulary building, in essential structured reading, in the analysis of paragraphs, in selection of material, in the pace of reading—knowing where to pause, where to go back, where to focus—there should also be *time* for reading.

Recent research findings have shown that for:

- science teaching in high schools, only 9 percent of student's time was spent reading, and

- in humanities for 15-year-olds, the amount of time spent reading was in bursts of 40 seconds.

So, a reading curriculum should be planned and integrated as a sequence up the years.

Information Skills Program. This could be a kind of index to the curriculum, a check list that could be drawn on by all other subject teachers. It would have in it the start of topic definition, which of course is the most difficult part. Students are lost in most school resource centers because they have not defined what is being searched for. It would go on to search strategies, to selection, and rejection. We give students a whole battery of books and say choose the right one, but we rarely give them an extract sheet with paragraphs, one of which is totally irrelevant and all they have got to do is strike it out—easy exercises seeing the irrelevance, but of course as you get to higher levels seeing the irrelevance is a very hard part of the study. Then one could go on to the apparatus of a book, how to judge whether it is covering the field or not. The simple details of bibliographical data aren't taught often enough. Then it is important to teach how to go through and judge the parts of the book and decide how to get out of it what you want. Even that great human invention, the index, is too often taught at the level of surface skills. It is critical to understand the function of an index, which literally disorganizes a book, and by disorganizing it makes it available for the reader to reorganize it. The index needs to be taught at all levels of the curriculum using more and more difficult examples. It cannot be left entirely to chance nor can it be left entirely to exercise. It has to be a mixture of the specific and the disseminated.

Then there are all the other study skills of note-making and references. When is the student allowed to copy? What about the use of visual evidence? How many schools teach the reading of a photograph? A photograph is too often regarded as an artifact that is totally un-problematic. It is evidence, just straight evidence. But if the student is going to use a photograph as evidence, there is a need to know how to judge, to see how it came to be, and the effect the photographer had on it.

This curriculum is a two-way flow as skills feed back into the subject curriculum to provide context for the items in the research and study skills continuum.

Assignments. The most important part of a resource center is neither the resources nor the staff, but the assignments set by the teachers. One thread of a student's schooling is a series of things to do. From short tasks to complex ones— "look it up," "find out"—are frequent injunctions we throw to students. But very often these apparently easy assignments

prove to have unexpected snags, as many a parent has found out.

Perhaps more than that are the massive assignments which are so huge that when the teacher reads the ultimate report and is unhappy about it, it is difficult to know where the student has gone wrong. Was it in the first stage of defining the topic; or finding the resources; or having found them, understanding them; or having understood them selecting from them; or having selected from them, making their notes; or whether having made their notes writing it up?

Too often teachers give "unmodulated assignments." We start by giving mechanical assignments—look up the date of someone or an event. When we have given two or three weeks of exercises we then say, "right, you've now learned how to find things out. Now here is a library of 3,500 volumes and you can choose anything that interests you or which you feel is important to write about and you've got three weeks to do it. If you have any problems come and see me." That is an unmodulated assignment. We go straight from the small mechanized, to the huge amorphous, and then when we get an unhappy result, we can't pin down where they have gone wrong.

The key to study skills is the setting of assignments and we have to break down these assignments into stages so that everything is not thrown at students simultaneously. Sometimes they might be concerned only with search—accept a pile of books as the end of the assignment. They don't have to read them or make notes. Other times they would be given all the references collected together for them. They might be given the specific pages. At that point, their task is the end only—the notemaking and writing.

Teachers need to be taught to set assignments. First they must work out the purpose and context of the assignment. Sadly, assignments are too often just time-fillers.

Relate assignments to the skills program. Don't throw in too many skills at once. Ensure an adequate range of material, otherwise students use the same information source year after year after year. Make sure they have to use a videotape, an audiotape, and they have to use the clippings collection. Finally, the teacher has to know the point of assignment reinforcement, that is to say they absolutely have to make sure that in setting the assignment, they give the crucial advice at that particular time. One of the snags of having lots of good teacher-librarians in a school is that the teachers clear off. I have sat in an American school staffed with three teacher-librarians—therefore, divide the class into three and what does the teacher do, goes off to read *Beautiful Homes and Gardens* in the corner. In the U.K., the school librarian often complains that when the teacher brings the class to the resource center he slips off to the staffroom to do a bit of marking. What we have to ensure is that when the teacher sets the assignment, the teacher gives the specific piece of advice that will be helpful for that assignment. Essentially, we need to pull the whole issue from resources and staffing to the curriculum.

FOR THE FUTURE

For the school, requirements include an adequate definition of the role of the teacher-librarian, emphasis on the planning of the curriculum as a whole, a reading and research and study skills continuum, with more trained student assistance.

Resources must match specific curriculum needs, and other libraries and bookshops be promoted. Material must be more accessible through student-oriented catalogs.

Close collaborations between teacher and teacher-librarian of an equal status provide the best approach to effective library use and resource-based learning.

What Works

RESEARCH ABOUT TEACHING AND LEARNING FROM THE U.S. DEPARTMENT OF EDUCATION

The Home

Curriculum of the Home

Parents are their children's first and most influential teachers. What parents do to help their children learn is more important to academic success than how well-off the family is.

Reading to Children

The best way for parents to help their children become better readers is to read to them—even when they are very young. Children benefit most from reading aloud when they discuss stories, learn to identify letters and words, and talk about the meanings of words.

Independent Reading

Children improve their reading ability by reading a lot. Reading achievement is directly related to the amount of reading children do in school and outside.

Counting

A good way to teach children simple arithmetic is to build on their informal knowledge. This is why learning to count everyday objects is an effective basis for early arithmetic lessons.

Early Writing

Children who are encouraged to draw and scribble "stories" at an early age will later learn to compose more easily, more effectively, and with greater confidence than children who do not have this encouragement.

Speaking and Listening

A good foundation in speaking and listening helps children become better readers.

Developing Talent

Many highly successful individuals have above-average but not extraordinary intelligence. Accomplishment in a particular activity is often more dependent upon hard work and self-discipline than on innate ability.

Ideals

Belief in the value of hard work, the importance of personal responsibility, and the importance of education itself contributes to greater success in school.

The Classroom

Getting Parents Involved

Parental involvement helps children learn more effectively. Teachers who are successful at involving parents in their children's schoolwork are successful because they work at it.

Phonics

Children get a better start in reading if they are taught phonics. Learning phonics helps them to understand the relationship between letters and sounds and to "break the code" that links the words they hear with the words they see in print.

Reading Comprehension

Children get more out of a reading assignment when the teacher precedes the lesson with background information and follows it with discussion.

Science Experiments

Children learn science best when they are able to do experiments, so they can witness "science in action."

Copies of *What Works*, the complete 65 page report, including commentary and sources, are available on request from *What Works*, Pueblo, Colorado 81009. Prepared by the U.S. Department of Education Office of Research and Improvement.

Storytelling

Telling young children stories can motivate them to read. Storytelling also introduces them to cultural values and literary traditions before they can read, write, and talk about stories by themselves.

Teaching Writing

The most effective way to teach writing is to teach it as a process of brainstorming, composing, revising, and editing.

Learning Mathematics

Children in early grades learn mathematics more effectively when they are physical objects in their lessons.

Estimating

Although students need to learn how to find exact answers to arithmetic problems, good math students also learn the helpful skill of estimating answers. This skill can be taught.

Teacher Expectations

Teachers who set and communicate high expectations to all their students obtain greater academic performance from those students than teachers who set low expectations.

Student Ability and Effort

Children's understanding of the relationship between being smart and hard work changes as they grow.

Managing Classroom Time

How much time students are actively engaged in learning contributes strongly to their achievement. The amount of time available for learning is determined by the instructional and management skills of the teacher and the priorities set by the school administration.

Direct Instruction

When teachers explain exactly what students are expected to learn, and demonstrate the steps needed to accomplish a particular academic task, students learn more.

Tutoring

Students tutoring other students can lead to improved academic achievement for both student and tutor, and to positive attitudes toward coursework.

Memorization

Memorizing can help students absorb and retain the factual information on which understanding and critical thought are based.

Questioning

Student achievement rises when teachers ask questions that require students to apply, analyze, synthesize, and evaluate information in addition to simply recalling facts.

Study Skills

The ways in which children study influence strongly how much they learn. Teachers can often help children develop better study skills.

Homework: Quantity

Student achievement rises significantly when teachers regularly assign homework and students conscientiously do it.

Homework: Quality

Well-designed homework assignments relate directly to classwork and extend students' learning beyond the classroom. Homework is most useful when teachers carefully prepare the assignment, thoroughly explain it, and give prompt comments and criticism when the work is completed.

Assessment

Frequent and systematic monitoring of students' progress helps students, parents, teachers, administrators, and policymakers identify strengths and weaknesses in learning and instruction.

The School

Effective Schools

The most important characteristics of effective schools are strong instructional leadership, a safe and orderly climate, school-wide emphasis on basic skills, high teacher expectations for student achievement, and continuous assessment of pupil progress.

School Climate

Schools that encourage academic achievement focus on the importance of scholastic success and on maintaining order and discipline.

Discipline

Schools contribute to their students' academic achievement by establishing, communicating, and enforcing fair and consistent discipline policies.

Unexcused Absences

Unexcused absences decrease when parents are promptly informed that their children are not attending school.

Effective Principals

Successful principals establish policies that create an orderly environment and support effective instruction.

Collegiality

Students benefit academically when their teachers share ideas, cooperate in activities, and assist one another's intellectual growth.

Teacher Supervision

Teachers welcome professional suggestions about improving their work, but they rarely receive them.

Cultural Literacy

Students read more fluently and with greater understanding if they have background knowledge of the past and present. Such knowledge and understanding is called cultural literacy.

History

Skimpy requirements and declining enrollments in history classes are contributing to a decline in students' knowledge of the past.

Foreign Language

The best way to learn a foreign language in school is to start early and to study it intensively over many years.

Rigorous Courses

The stronger the emphasis on academic courses, the more advanced the subject matter, and the more rigorous the textbooks, the more high school students learn. Subjects that are learned mainly in school rather than at home, such as science and math, are most influenced by the number and kind of courses taken.

Acceleration

Advancing gifted students at a faster pace results in their achieving more than similarly gifted students who are taught at a normal rate.

Extracurricular Activities

High school students who complement their academic studies with extracurricular activities gain experience that contributes to their success in college.

Preparation for Work

Business leaders report that students with solid basic skills and positive work attitudes are more likely to find and keep jobs than students with vocational skills alone.

RESEARCH AND STUDY SKILLS

Research Finding: **The development of student competence in research and study skills is most effective when integrated with classroom instruction through cooperative program planning and team teaching by two equal teaching partners – the classroom teacher and teacher-librarian.**

Comment: Minimal gains in research and study skills can be achieved through instruction by the classroom teacher or the teacher-librarian (TL) alone. Effective instruction depends on the cooperative effort of both teacher and TL; stated another way, scheduled library skills classes taught solely by the TL are not as effective as integrated, cooperatively planned and taught programs.

Students in flexibly scheduled schools believe that the resource center is more useful in their school work than students in scheduled schools. Flexibly scheduled resource centers provide greater academic benefits.

The TL and school resource center can have a significant effect on student achievement in information skills development and content areas when used effectively.

The use of the TL to provide spare periods or preparation time for the classroom teacher negates the possibility of a successful school program.

The term "library skills" is misleading since many of these same skills are taught by classroom teachers in various areas of the curriculum but are labelled differently (information skills; research and study skills; problem-solving skills; etc.).

Educators of TLs need to provide more leadership and instruction for TLs in cooperative program planning and teaching and in articulating and teaching research and study skills. TLs should have teaching qualifications and classroom experience prior to further training as a TL.

References: Becker, Dale Eugene. *Social Studies Achievement of Pupils in Schools with Libraries and Schools without Libraries.* University of Pennsylvania, 1970. 172 pages. Ed.D. dissertation. (2411-A – #70-22,868)

Hodson, Yvonne D. *Values and Functions of the School Media Center as Perceived by Fourth and Sixth Graders and Their Teachers in Compared School Settings.* State University of New York at Buffalo, 1978. 188 pages. Ph.D. dissertation. (39:3-4, 1172-A – #7817042)

Smith, Jane Bandy. *An Exploratory Study of the Effectiveness of an Innovative Process Designed to Integrate Library Skills into the Curriculum.* George Peabody College for Teachers, 1978. 1974 pages. Ph.D. dissertation. (39:8, 4569 – #7902510)

Volume, issue, page and document numbers are from *Dissertation Abstracts International.* The terms teacher-librarian (TL) and resource center are used in descriptions for consistency even though they may not have been used in the original research study.

THE IMPACT OF RESOURCE CENTERS ON READING/RESEARCH SKILLS

Research Finding: **Students in schools with well-equipped resource centers and professional teacher-librarians will perform better on achievement tests for reading comprehension and basic research skills.**

Comment: There is a positive relationship between the level of resource center service available and student scholastic achievement.

In schools with good resource centers and the services of a teacher-librarian (TL), students perform significantly better on tests for basic research skills, including locational skills, outlining and notetaking and the knowledge and use of reference materials, including the use of a dictionary and encyclopedia.

In schools with good resource centers and full-time TLs, students perform significantly better in the area of reading comprehension and in their ability to express ideas effectively concerning their readings.

The greatest predictor of student achievement (of the school resource center collection size and expenditure and public library collection size and expenditure) is school resource center collection size.

Students in larger population centers and in larger secondary schools have a higher level of resource center service available to them, in terms of collection size, than students in smaller cities and in smaller schools.

References: Greve, Clyde LeRoy. *The Relationship of the Availability of Libraries to the Academic Achievement of Iowa High School Seniors.* University of Denver, 1974. 130 pages. Ph.D. dissertation. (4574-A — #75-1870)

McMillen, Ralph Donnelly. *An Analysis of Library Programs and a Determination of the Educational Justification of These Programs in Selected Elementary Schools of Ohio.* Western Reserve University, 1965. 250 pages. Ed.D. dissertation. (330-A — #66-8017)

Yarling, James Robert. *Children's Understandings and Use of Selected Library-Related Skills in Two Elementary Schools, One with and One without a Centralized Library.* Ball State University, 1968. 210 pages. Ed.D. dissertation. (3352-A — #69-4202)

COOPERATIVE PROGRAM PLANNING AND TEACHING IN SECONDARY SCHOOLS

Research Finding: **Teacher-librarians in secondary schools are not as involved in cooperative program planning and team teaching with classroom colleagues as equal teaching partners to the extent that principals, teachers and teacher-librarians themselves believe that they should be.**

Comment: If the teacher uses the resource center and consults with the teacher-librarian (TL) about planning student work, then the use of the resource center is greater. In fact, students rate schools more highly when there is agreement and communication among principal, teachers and TLs regarding program objectives and where there is planned, consistent and integrated instruction in library use. Student perceptions are valid indicators of program quality and, when carefully documented, can guide expenditures for resource center support. Districts should seek program evaluations annually from graduating students.

Important factors which affect TL involvement in curricular issues include the principal's attitude towards the TL's role, teacher preference for TLs with successful teaching experience and a teacher's frame of reference, the amount of support staff, lack of teacher understanding of the role of the TL and the potential of the resource center. The evidence is inconclusive as to the extent to which the personality of the TL makes a significant difference.

Qualified TLs rate curricular tasks as more important to their role than those without additional qualifications.

Since principals, teachers and teacher-librarians all agree on the importance of cooperative program planning and teaching, all three should be involved in resolving issues mitigating against substantial involvement. TLs need to organize more in-service training for colleagues; and educators of TLs need to revise programs to include courses which foster cooperation and understanding between teachers and TLs.

References: Corr, Graham Peter. *Factors That Affect the School Library Media Specialist's Involvement in Curriculum Planning and Implementation in Small High Schools in Oregon.* University of Oregon, 1979. 183 pages. Ph.D. dissertation. (40:6,2955−A, #7927234)

Hartley, Neil Britt Tabor. *Faculty Utilization of the High School Library.* Vanderbilt University/George Peabody College for Teachers, 1980. 199 pages. Ph.D. dissertation. (41:09, 3805, #8105512)

Scott, Marilynn Stewart. *School Library Media Center Programs: Student Perceptions as Criteria for Library Media Program Funding.* University of Southern California, 1982. Ed.D. dissertation. (43:01, 40−A, not given)

RESOURCE CENTERS AND THE CURRICULUM

Research Finding: **Secondary school resource centers are more effective when designed according to the needs of the instructional program and of the student population.**

Comment: Educational specifications developed through the cooperative efforts of teacher-librarians, teachers and administrators result in a well-planned program, and working with the architect, a physical facility designed to support this program.

Secondary school resource centers should be planned for greater flexibility. There is no optimum design for resource centers; each situation presents different problems; there are basic kinds of spaces necessary, however, regardless of the uniqueness of the school philosophy.

There has been a growing awareness of the need for instructional areas for independent study in the secondary school.

Three separate areas are required for effective programs: a general study and reading area, an animated (activity) area, and supportive work spaces for resource center staff. The general study area should constitute 50 percent of the total space, the animated areas 25-30 percent, and supportive areas 20-25 percent. The general study and reading area should be capable of seating 10 percent of the student population and additional spaces such as media and conference rooms, 5 percent of the study body. A minimum of 30 square feet per student accommodated is recommended. Space for aural and visual instructional techniques is vital.

The resource center should be located on the main floor of the building and adjacent to the majority of instructional areas but removed from areas which create excessive noise.

Greater care should be taken in planning facilities. More attention should be paid to spatial relationships. The use of color, natural and artificial lighting and architectural lines are important elements. The resource center should be equipped and furnished with those amenities which are appropriate for the physiological and psychological needs of teenagers rather than adults. This includes optimum thermal environment, furniture and color schemes.

While facilities are important, students are less concerned with the physical features of the resource center−size, location, furniture and attractiveness−than with academic relevance, accessible high quality materials and approachable and effective teacher-librarians.

References: Herald, Wayne Homer. *Planning Library Facilities for the Secondary School.* Stanford University, 1957. 178 pages. Ph.D. dissertation. (#23,174)

Kelsey, Anne Peyton. *A Study of the Criteria for the Effectiveness of Secondary School Libraries as Perceived by Selected Student Clients.* Miami University, 1976. 175 pages. Ph.D. dissertation. (4024-A−#77-1003)

Rutland, John Thomas. *A Study of the Basic Physical Facilities and Educational Roles of Secondary School Libraries.* University of Tennessee, 1971. 201 pages. Ed.D. dissertation. (#71-29,490)

Trotter, Charles Earl. *A Fortran Computer Program Designed to Identify the Physical Facilities for Public Secondary School Instructional Materials Centers.* University of Tennessee, 1964. 172 pages. Ed.D. dissertation. (#64-11,150)

PERSONALITY FACTORS IN SUCCESSFUL RESOURCE CENTERS

Research Finding: **Teacher-librarians who are less cautious and more extroverted tend to be more successful.**

Comment: Teacher-librarians tend to be responsible, emotionally stable, cautious, intellectually curious, energetic, non-assertive, and less trusting of colleagues.

TLs in exemplary resource centers are extroverted and independent; as leaders they have "tough poise."

The best set of predictors of high circulation of materials in the resource center is a high extroversion score and a high degree of curriculum involvement by the TL.

There is a significant negative correlation between cautiousness and curricular effectiveness.

High role conflict scores are significantly associated with low cautiousness, responsibility and emotional stability; high role ambiguity scores are significantly associated with low responsibility and emotional stability.

TLs differ significantly from librarians as a group as measured in 1957; they are more extroverted, demonstrate less neurotic tendency, and are more sociable.

References: Charter, Jody Beckley. *Case Studies of Six Exemplary Public High School Library Media Programs*. Florida State University, 1982. (43.02, 293-A – #DA8215239)

Hambleton, Alixe Elizabeth Lyon. *The Elementary School Librarian in Ontario: A Study of Role Perception, Role Conflict and Effectiveness*. University of Toronto, 1980. (41:06, 2338-A)

Madaus, James Richard. *Curriculum Involvement: Teaching Structures, and Personality Factors of Librarians in School Media Programs*. University of Texas, 1974. 123 pages. Ph.D. dissertation. (5436-A – #75-4965)

TEACHER-LIBRARIANS AND THE PROFESSIONAL LITERATURE

Research Finding: **Teacher-librarians need to assume more responsibility for writing about teacher-librarianship and school library programs for professional journals read by teachers and administrators.**

Comment: An accepted means of communication with teachers, that of writing in professional journals, is not being used to its fullest potential in communicating the contribution of teacher-librarians and school resource centers to education.

Articles concerning teacher-librarians tend to be accurate only when written by teacher-librarians themselves or those intimately involved with good programs. Teacher-librarians are occasionally described in disparaging terms by others.

General journals in education tend to mention teacher-librarians and media more than curriculum and association journals.

Simple identification of the resource center appears much more frequently than discussion about teacher-librarians and the resource center program.

Where articles do appear about the teacher-librarian and resource center they are more generally directed to the general aspects of teaching than to the needs of specific subject areas. The area of curricular emphasis has tended to be language arts rather than social studies, science and other core areas.

Education is emphasizing research and development but these are virtually missing in articles about library programs which appear in journals for administrators.

Acceptable levels of financing resource centers are seldom mentioned in journals aimed at school administrators. Where finances are discussed they concentrate on expensive facilities but not the ongoing expense of operation.

The cause and effect between the resources necessary for a good program and good service is omitted from journals for administrators.

Education articles in journals for administrators which mention the library program dropped from 224 in 1954-1955, to 95 in 1960 to 61 in 1969.

Information about the teacher-librarian and resource center, when included in journals for teachers and administrators, does not emphasize the curricular role of the teacher-librarian.

References: Holzberlein, Deanne Bassler. *The Contribution of School Media Programs to Elementary and Secondary Education As Portrayed in Professional Journals Available to School Administrators from 1960 to 1969.* University of Michigan, 1971. 262 pages. Ph.D. dissertation. (6466-A—#72-14,896)

Mack, Edna Ballard. *The School Library's Contribution to the Total Educational Program of the School: A Content Analysis of Selected Periodicals in the Field of Education.* University of Michigan, 1957. 389 pages. Ph.D. dissertation. (1442—LC Card No. Mic 58-1431)

Van Orden, Phyllis Jeanne. *Use of Media and the Media Center, As Reflected in Professional Journals for Elementary School Teachers.* Wayne State University, 1970. 243 pages. Ed.D. dissertation. (293-A—#71-17,324)

MEDIA DIRECTOR HAS POSITIVE EFFECT

Research Finding: **The school library media coordinator/director has a positive effect on school library program development in the school district but suffers role conflict in his/her work.**

Comment: The existence of a library media director results in significantly higher implementation of professional guiding principles for personnel, budget, purchasing, production, access and delivery systems, program evaluation, collections and facilities.

The higher the director's position is placed in the hierarchy, the wider the range of activities that can be performed in the development and regulation of school library programs and services.

The director suffers role conflict due to differences of expectations and perceptions of performance among and within principals, teacher-librarians and the supervisor of the director.

The director suffers conflict in realizing the organization's objectives due to the real, practical job world; teacher-librarians are aware of a gap between the real and ideal role behavior of the director insofar as the organization's goals are concerned, also resulting in conflict for the director.

The director finds that "the real world" makes it more difficult to attend to human needs than one ideally believes that one might be able to; teacher-librarians believe there exists a very evident gap between the real and ideal world insofar as human needs factors that they want the director to display toward them, again creating more conflict for the director.

Perception of performance is uncertain among the groups. The director works most closely with: principals, teacher-librarians and the director's supervisor.

References: *A Comparison of Perceptions and Expectations for a Central Administrative Leadership Role of Library Media Director as an Indicator of His/Her Role Behavior.* Andwood, Donald Edward. St. John's University, 1984. Ed.D. dissertations. (45/03-A. p. 693)

The Organizational Structure for State School Library Supervision and the Functions, Duties, and Activities of State School Library Supervisors. Esther Mary Carter. Ph.D. dissertation. Indiana University, 1971. (2719-A. Order No. 71-29,562)

Perceptions of "Guiding Principles" in "Media Programs: District and School." John Gordon Coleman, Jr. Ed.D. dissertation. University of Virginia, 1982. (43/07-A. p. 2206)

Role Expectations of the County School Library Supervisor and Their Perceived Fulfillment. Ruth Becker Newcombe, Ph.D. dissertation. Florida State University, 1968. (529-A. Order No. 69-11, #317)

PRINCIPAL HAS KEY ROLE

**Research
Finding:**   **The role of the principal is the key factor in the development of an effective school library program.**

Comment: The attitude of the principal to the role of the teacher-librarian (TL) affects the TL's involvement in curricular issues.

Exemplary school library resource centers are characterized by strong administrative support.

Principals in schools with exemplary resource center programs establish evaluation procedures, integrate the resource center in instructional programs, encourage student and teacher use and provide flexible scheduling.

TLs continue to view the support of the principal as critical to program improvement.

Principals may serve as a barrier to the improvement of resource center programs if they do not perceive the need for change and do not have the necessary expertise on which to base improvement decisions.

References: Anderson, Edward Lawrence. *The Educational Media Building Coordinator: His Role as Perceived by School Administrators.* Michigan State University, 1970. 163 pages. Ph.D. dissertation. (4374-A, #71-2019)

Charter, Jody Beckley. *Case Study Profiles of Six Exemplary Public High School Library Media Programs.* Florida State University, 1982. 321 pages. Ph.D. dissertation. (43:2, 293-A, #DA 8215239)

Corr, Graham Peter. *Factors that Affect the School Library Media Specialist's Involvement in Curriculum Planning and Implementation in Small High Schools in Oregon.* University of Oregon, 1979. 183 pages. Ph.D. dissertation. (40:6, 2955-A, #7927234)

Guise, Benjamin R. *A Survey of Public School Library Resources in Arkansas.* North Texas State University, 1972. 152 pages. Ed.D. dissertation. (33:4, 4444-A #73-2904)

Hellene, Dorothy Lorraine Ingalls. *The Relationships of the Behaviors of Principals in the State of Washington to the Development of School Library Media Programs.* University of Washington, 1973. 161 pages. Ed.D. dissertation. (3835-A)

Shields, Dorothy McDonald. *A Fault Tree Approach to Analyzing School Library Media Services.* Brigham Young University, 1977. 203 pages. Ed.D. dissertation. (2392-A, #77-23,174)

Walker, Carol Chism. *The Role of the Principal in the Provision of Effective Library Services in Selected Indiana Elementary Schools.* Indiana University, 1982. 107 pages. Ed.D. dissertation. (42:11, 4683-A, #DA 8209883)

LIBRARIES COMPLEMENT RESOURCE CENTERS

**Research
Finding:**   **Students generally use libraries as a complement to school resource centers and prefer books to other resources.**

Comment: TLs believe that students are more aware of resources and services than they really are.

Only a small percentage of students use the resource center regularly and these tend to be better students.

In order of frequency, students use books (through the card catalog) as the medium of choice, periodicals (through the *Readers' Guide*) second and encyclopedias third. Periodicals used tend to be in the resource center.

Students have a more positive attitude to the resource center when there is a full-time TL.

Most students use the public and/or college library as a complement to the school resource center.

References: Ducat, Mary Peter Claver. *Student and Faculty Use of the Library in Three Secondary Schools.* Columbia University, 1960. 302 pages. DLS dissertation. (LC Card No. Mic 60-2449)

Durand, Joyce Jenkins. *A Bibliometric Study of Student Use of Periodicals for Independent Research Projects in High School Libraries with Implications for Resource Sharing.* Georgia State University, 1985. 140 pages. Ph.D. dissertation. (46/08-A, 2115)

Geppert, Alida L. *Student Accessibility to School Library Media Center Resources as Viewed by Media Specialists and Compared to Students in Southwestern Michigan Secondary Schools.* Western Michigan University, 1975. 134 pages. Ed.D. dissertation. (#76-8463)

Stroud, Janet Gossard. *Evaluation of Media Center Services by Media Staff, Teachers, and Students in Indiana Middle and Junior High Schools.* Purdue University, 1976. 186 pages. Ph.D. dissertation. (37/08-A, 4674, #77-1783)

MORE CONTINUING EDUCATION NEEDED

Research Finding: **More and more varied continuing education opportunities need to be provided for teacher-librarians in order for them to pursue their own professional growth.**

Comment: Teacher-librarians respond more to professional development opportunities which are of high quality and which offer new and creative ideas applicable to the job site.

Time, location and inferior quality detract TLs from attending professional development programs.

Programs should be offered by school districts on serving specific client groups, such as special education teachers and students.

University continuing education programs should reflect the expressed needs of TLs, such as microcomputer applications to their role and the resource center.

Workshops presented at conferences can provide effective continuing education by effecting changes in knowledge and attitudes toward a particular topic.

Continuing education opportunities need to be provided in a variety of formats and approaches.

References: Bell, Geraldine Watts. *Determining a Job Performance Basis for the Development of an Individualized Staff Development Program for School Library Media Specialists.* University of Alabama, 1977. 183 pages. Ed.D. dissertation. (DA 39:3-4, 1904-A)

Buckley, Cozetta White. *Media Services for Exceptional Students: An Exploratory Study of the Practices and Perceptions of Library Media Specialists in Selected Southern States.* University of Michigan, 1978. 239 pages. Ph.D. dissertation. (5781-A)

Cantor, Phyllis Fine. *Role Expectations for Library Media Services Held by Library Media Specialists, School Administrators, and Teachers.* Columbia University, 1975. 211 pages. DLS dissertation. (#76-12,728)

Davie, Judith Fields. *A Survey of School Library Media Resources for Exceptional Students in Florida Public Schools.* Florida State University, 1979. 220 pages. Ph.D. dissertation. (Volume 40, Number 09, 4786-A)

Hawley, Catherine Agnes. *An Examination of Management/Communication Perceptions of Library Media Managers.* University of Colorado, 1982. Ph.D. dissertation. (Volume 43, Number 04, 962-A)

Schlieve, Paul Lynn. *Perceived Microcomputer Professional Development Needs of Wisconsin Public School Library/Media Specialists.* Southern Illinois University, 1981. 146 pages. Ph.D. dissertation. (Volume 42, Number 10, 4413-A)

Stone, Elizabeth W. *A Study of Some Factors Related to the Professional Development of Librarians.* The American University, 1968. Ph.D. dissertation. (Volume 29, Number 04, 1240-A)

Tassia, Margaret Rose. *Conference Programs as a Vehicle for Continuing Education: A Case Study of an Educational Gains Workshop Presented to School Library Media Specialists.* University of Pittsburgh, 1978. 214 pages. Ph.D. dissertation. (Volume 40, Number 02, 514-A)

In Search of Effectiveness

Ken Haycock

During a recent discussion session with school principals regarding the implications of research related to the effective schools movement, one school administrator stated categorically that there were only three ways to develop and improve programs school-wide:

- In a new school, the principal selected teachers carefully with a view to planning and implementing a coordinated curriculum, building on the enthusiasm and team spirit of a new professional adventure.

- In an existing situation, the principal and teachers might recognize a serious problem which all agreed has to be addressed for the benefit of all; school-wide discipline standards and improving penmanship were mentioned as examples.

- Other than these two unusual or extreme circumstances, the only other method with any chance of success was to hire an enthusiastic teacher-librarian with a well-defined role as a teaching partner who was committed to planning jointly with teachers and team teaching units of study!

It's not hard to imagine how difficult it was not to ask that it be shouted from the rooftops!

In reviewing the literature on effective schooling, it is apparent that the teacher-librarian can play a key role in school improvement. Since teacher-librarians and school resource centers are barely mentioned specifically in this literature, it becomes imperative that we draw conclusions and connections ourselves and make sure that these are understood in our schools and school systems. This latest trend in professional concerns and interests (one need only browse the professional journals of administrators to see how pervasive it is) can be one more discussion point for the teacher-librarian and association concerned about the broader implications of what could become narrower thinking on educational issues. (The focus of much of the literature is on raising achievement scores on standardized tests but the research does not suggest more drill and practice and more testing necessarily.)

The effective school has a well-coordinated curriculum. We know that the teacher-librarian is often the catalyst for this by starting the process of a school-based continuum for information skills, a process which can then be transferred and applied to other areas as well, whether writing or science. The effective school has a staff committed to these sorts of goals, a staff which is cohesive and plans and works together. The teacher-librarian, with that continuum, can encourage cross-grade planning of resource-based units of study, and can engage in cooperative planning in staff rooms and faculty lounges to promote a tone of "talking teaching." This is part of the quality interactions among colleagues referred to in the literature. The effective school then makes sure that resources are used effectively to support these goals.

As a member of a school staff, the teacher-librarian works toward clear and attainable goals and objectives and a climate conducive to learning. The program emphasizes learning with clear specification of skills and processes and careful monitoring and regular evaluation. Planning with other teachers helps to clarify thinking and make objectives much clearer; this leads to more efficient use of instructional time and, of course, the enormous advantage of two teachers (classroom and resource center) working with the same group of students. This integration of information skills in cooperatively planned and taught programs is a *proven* and *effective* teaching method. Where there are difficulties in explaining or developing the necessary support to work well together, one might note that the effective school provides in-service programs for all teachers on a regular basis.

An effective school, as any teacher-librarian knows, has strong leadership from a principal with a sense of direction and a commitment to instructional excellence. With good staff relations and the promotion of a positive school tone, the principal can support and enhance resource-based programs just by *presence* and moral suasion, let alone a strong action orientation.

Read the effective schools literature. Have a staff in-service program on it. Effective schools have effective teacher-librarians and resource centers! Let the word go out!

Part 2
THE ROLE OF THE TEACHER-LIBRARIAN

It is important for readers to recognize that the readings included in this section are more than ten years old. We include them because we think that they are important and have a validity that is timeless. Ken Haycock's paper on the role of the teacher-librarian as a professional teacher was written in 1976 and published in 1981 in *Emergency Librarian*. While some of the components could be revised and the citations updated it does nevertheless outline the basic arguments for teacher certification and experience.

More than ten years ago the Canadian School Library Association started to define what it meant by a "qualified school librarian," since certification standards and the quality of programs educating teacher-librarians varied considerably from area to area. In keeping with the great traditions of professional associations, it established a national task force toward that end and "What is a school librarian? Towards defining professionalism" is the result. Readers are also referred to *Education for School Librarianship in Canada* (Canadian Library Association, 1982, 0-88802-177-1) which includes a model curriculum for educating teacher-librarians, based on nine critical areas of competence, both in faculties of education and faculties of library and information studies.

Teacher-librarians need to be educated in a manner which builds on their teaching qualifications and experience, rather than simply supplementing it with library courses. Only then will there develop a common process of professional socialization, resulting in a well-understood and commonly supported role for the teacher-librarian. As Alixe Hambleton relates in the summary of her doctoral dissertation, there is "static in the educational intercom" resulting in conflict for the teacher-librarian, since principals, teachers and teacher-librarians do not agree on a preferred role. Perhaps understandably, teacher-librarians are the most confused of all. However, if we don't understand our role, and stand up for it, others will define it for us. The findings and conclusions from Alixe's study have been replicated by others, suggesting a universal problem which requires attention.

It may indeed be a time of "hard times ... hard choices"—the future lies in working closely with teachers within the context of a clearly defined role, understood and advocated not only by teacher-librarians but also by administrators, teachers, and the community.

The Role of the School Librarian As a Professional Teacher: A Position Paper

Ken Haycock

INTRODUCTION

In the last fifteen years changes in education have been rapid and decisive. The traditional lock-step methods of teaching in small, enclosed classrooms using limited instructional resources—mainly textbooks—have developed into more innovative approaches based on research related to children, teaching and learning. Due to changing environments and the information explosion, instruction now centres more on the process of learning itself than on subject content. It is becoming far more important that the student understands factors which contribute to a given situation than to memorize data describing it. The method of the subject specialist is of concern but specific knowledge of the field is less necessary. Discovery and inquiry methods of teaching are becoming increasingly common and contribute to the development of independent, disciplined learners who can recognize problems, formulate hypotheses, ask important questions, locate, analyze and evaluate information and reach valid conclusions.

Students are treated on a more individual basis as it is finally accepted that everyone does not learn in the same way or at the same rate. Each child is not necessarily following an individual program but efforts are made to correlate expected performance with individual ability levels to ensure realistic goals. Grouping of students is used to an increasing extent to match what is to be taught to those who need to learn it, whether it is a large group lecture to introduce facts or a small group work session to reinforce skills. These trends have also led to more independent study programs at all levels of education. The three Rs (reading, writing, arithmetic) are still among the basic skills of schooling but the three I's (inquiry, individualization, independent study) represent an improved approach to teaching and learning.

School resource centres have been a vital part of these changes in education. Indeed, many innovations would not be possible without the services of a resource centre. As a reflection of these changes, emphasis has shifted from the traditional library base of selecting, organizing and circulating books to the more pronounced educational and teaching services of planning for the effective use of book and nonbook media through program planning and cooperative teaching. If the resource centre has any validity whatever in the school it must be on this firm theoretical and educational foundation. Libraries per se are not seen as particularly significant in a formal education context; the planned use of learning resources is, however. The development of the school library to a resource centre then represents more of a change in function than a change in name. The implications of educational research and the implementation of new programs have led to a need for a vital integral resource centre. With a strong movement towards more effective team work, professionals in schools need a common base of concern and understanding to exploit the full potential of instructional methods.

TEACHER-LIBRARIANS

Traditionally, the person in charge of the school library has been called the school librarian; today, however, since all roles in education are being redefined in light of new trends and priorities and, since the term "librarian" should include professional library qualifications, school "librarian" is less acceptable to many. The school librarian is usually not a professional librarian in education, training or outlook; indeed, perhaps it was a mistake to ever use the terms school library and school librarian. The school librarian is, or should be, an outstanding or master teacher with specialized advanced education in the selection, organization, management and use of learning resources, and the school library, a resource centre inseparable from the instructional program. For the sake of clarity and simplicity the terms "teacher-librarian" and "resource centre" are used here. Teacher-librarian clearly denotes a teaching role with a library-related specialization. A teacher-librarian is not an unqualified or "under-qualified" librarian but a professional learning resources teacher who may also be a professional librarian. The term refers to a single unified teaching/librarianship role and not to the amount of time spent in the classroom or the resource centre.

Teacher-librarians are increasingly involved in curriculum development and in cooperative teaching situations where each teacher—classroom and resource centre—prepares for instructional responsibilities based on areas of expertise. Teachers accept teacher-librarians as equal partners in the school when they witness competence in the planning and implementation of curricula. With increased attention to the needs of individual students communication must be particularly effective between the classroom teacher and the teacher-librarian; the same professional language and education as well as the same core of experience—classroom teaching—go a long way toward reaching this goal.

PROGRAM PLANNING

In the development of any specific unit of study in a school certain factors predominate. Societal needs and influences determine the direction mandated by a provincial government, the curriculum followed by a local board of education and the program implemented by a school within its community. The curriculum designer brings to the task a theoretical knowledge of teaching and learning supplemented by subject content, tested with practical classroom experience. The foundations of society and of education in conjunction with the implications of individual differences, group relations, growth, motivation, teaching methods, learning processes and evaluation are examined and considered. Although it is far too narrow to categorize youngsters by specific characteristics at definite ages it is recognized that mental and physical development generally proceeds on a continuum. The characteristics of varying levels of this development can be identified and do have significant implications for appropriate teaching methods and the resulting use of the resource centre.

In order for learning resources to have validity in the instructional program, their use must be carefully planned through integration with this curriculum. As a specialist in the selection, organization, management and, most important, the utilization of all manner of book and nonbook media, the teacher-librarian is most concerned with the quality of use of reference and research tools and learning materials. The subject specialist has an intimate knowledge of an academic discipline or content whereas the teacher-librarian's "subject" is learning itself. There is no teaching content to a library or resource centre, only the process of unlocking knowledge and critical thinking, the process of learning. As a learning resources teacher, the teacher-librarian is concerned with those skills which are necessary to the development of motivated independent learners who can locate, analyze and evaluate information in all media formats.

The following psychological principles (19:311-312) have been identified by the National (U.S.) Council for the Social Studies as essential for undergirding a developmental skills program:

1. The skill should be taught functionally, in the context of a topic of study, rather than as a separate exercise.

2. The learner must understand the meaning and purpose of the skill, and have motivation for developing it.

3. The learner must be carefully supervised in his first attempts to apply the skill, so that he will form correct habits from the beginning.

4. The learner needs repeated opportunities to practice the skill, with immediate evaluation so that he knows where he has succeeded or failed in his performance.

5. The learner needs individual help, through diagnostic measures and follow-up exercises, since not all members of any group learn at exactly the same rate or retain equal amounts of what they have learned.

6. Skill instruction should be presented at increasing levels of difficulty, moving from the simple to the more complex; the resulting growth in skills should be cumulative as the learner moves through school, with each level of instruction building on and reinforcing what has been taught previously.

7. Students should be helped, at each stage, to generalize the skills, by applying them in many and varied situations; in this way, maximum transfer of learning can be achieved.

8. The program of instruction should be sufficiently flexible to allow skills to be taught as they are needed by the learner; many skills should be developed concurrently.

In planning for the implementation of a program based on these principles the teacher-librarian joins with the classroom teacher to form a horizontal team of two equals working toward established objectives. This dyad cooperatively plans what is to be done and the most effective way to accomplish the task. The classroom teacher and the teacher-librarian each bring different backgrounds and strengths in teaching but they do understand the potential of various approaches to learning and recognize common goals. Through planning with other teachers the teacher-librarian is also a source of ideas for program development.

If the use of learning resources is intended, the teacher-librarian is involved in preplanning before a unit of study begins. In this way the teacher can at least ensure that appropriate materials are available. Since the teacher-librarian will be working with a class, group or individuals, it is important to know what the preliminary objectives of the teacher are. The teacher decides on a unit of work and outlines its scope. General teaching strategies which may be conducive to resource centre use are considered. The teacher meets with the teacher-librarian to select and plan the use of materials and services. The teacher and teacher-librarian determine the sequence of content on the basis of the availability of materials and necessary personnel.

The dyad or teaching team redefines objectives and determines the skills to be stressed in relationship to local curricula, student needs and available learning resources. These may be subject skills, study and critical thinking skills, reference and research skills or listening and viewing skills. The teacher and teacher-librarian then set up a series of learning experiences involving individual students, small and large groups or whole classes. Selected materials may be kept in the resource centre or moved elsewhere, whichever is most appropriate. At this point the unit is introduced by a team member. The students work on the unit in the resource centre and the classroom with the classroom teacher and teacher-librarian stressing skills related especially to the program unit. The teacher-librarian may teach a short integrated skill lesson, develop a series of related lessons, offer an enrichment lesson or give a book talk on the theme.

When planning with one teacher, a group or committee of teachers, or a teaching team, the teacher-librarian *cooperatively*:

determines the contribution that the resource centre is to make to the overall teaching plan

determines specific teaching objectives to be accomplished through the use of learning resources and guidance

identifies basic concepts and skills to be introduced, reinforced, or extended

structures learning guides; reading, viewing, listening checklists; summary forms; reaction charts; critical evaluation cards

determines appropriateness of proposed assignments and the availability of suitable materials

sets target dates for each phase of the resource centre role in the program

designs specific teaching strategies requiring resource centre support

designs specific learning experiences and activities requiring learning resources

designs specific unit and support activities

designs strategies for meeting student needs, interests, goals, abilities, progress rate, concerns, and potential

identifies specific media uniquely appropriate for each of the teaching and learning designs

programs for the most logical use of media in progressive, sequential order

designs appropriate culminating teaching and learning activities

designs appropriate evaluating activities to determine the effectiveness of the resource centre role

COOPERATIVE TEACHING

In this cooperative teaching situation the teacher-librarian may work with a group of students over an extended period of time while the classroom teacher works with another group in the classroom. The contribution of the teacher-librarian extends to the specific needs of the student. This means that the teacher-librarian may be offering remedial teaching, leading novel study, managing behaviour or teaching in other ways suitable to the particular level, subject, unit and objectives related to resource centre use as determined cooperatively by the team. Throughout the project, the teacher and teacher-librarian evaluate the growth made by students in planned skills, the effectiveness of the materials as well as the effectiveness of the unit itself.

With the movement from an insular school library to an integrated resource centre the skills for using libraries effectively have been better integrated with the curriculum.

Scheduled library science classes are inappropriate and no longer offered where effective programs predominate. These classes were not based on the principles of learning and psychology outlined. They were not seen as relevant by the learner, were not necessarily given when needed and were generally ineffective. Scheduled classes on a regular timetable persist only where the principal has little notion of the educational foundation of the resource centre, where the classes provide spare periods for teachers—an expensive and dubious practice—or where the teacher-librarian is not prepared to become actively involved in program development and curriculum implementation.

COLLECTION OF MATERIALS

Although a professional librarian, given a knowledge of curriculum content, can obviously select materials to support units of study from appropriate reviewing tools, the criteria for previewing and reviewing learning resources involve additional factors often not included in selection for a general or public library audience. The teacher-librarian needs to know not only the community and users, the nature of the existing collection, general and specific criteria for different types of subject material and sources of bibliographic and review information but also needs to have a professional knowledge of other teachers, of instructional strategies used for specific units of study, of the instructional design of products examined, of the intended audience in grade and ability levels, of curriculum relationships and of the principal and potential uses of the material. Learning resources must have a planned purpose or at least the possibility of such and this means a more complete integration with teaching/learning processes.

The balanced collection found in many public libraries is a mistake in the school resource centre. To select material on all topics, a financial impossibility at best, is to neglect the context of the service. If one country is studied using Socratic approaches and the textbook and another is studied using inquiry approaches and learning resources then little should be purchased on the former since the teaching method does not necessitate material and a great deal more purchased on the latter since the strategy here means that support will be necessary for a specific number, usually at least class size, of users. Similarly, when organizing resource centre information the nature of the users and elements of the school curricula are taken into account. The subjectivity of the selection and organization of materials can become more precisely defined in the school setting.

INTERAGENCY COOPERATION

With increasing demands on learning resources, coupled with decreasing tax dollars, there should be improved cooperation among schools and among schools and other libraries. Such cooperation is based on a clear understanding of the role of each agency and a commitment to sharing materials and services where mutually beneficial. Each agency serves a quite different purpose with specific criteria for attempts at combining services (16). Librarians must recognize the unique expertise of the teacher-librarian and be knowledgeable about the role of the resource centre. The development of the resource centre as an integrated learning centre to provide the skills for self-realization means that public library use will increase tremendously; if the public library is relatively untapped by students as a community resource, this can be overcome through cooperation. The school must also be aware of the services of the public library and actively promote its use with both staff and students.

DESIGN AND PRODUCTION OF MATERIALS

Should suitable material not be available in the resource centre, not available on loan from another school or agency, and not available from commercial sources the teacher-librarian has the ability as a media specialist to determine the instructional need and design a product based on theories of learning and educational technology. The appropriate medium is matched to the instructional purpose and message to be conveyed. The teacher-librarian then produces or supervises the local production of needed learning resources. Too often the production of materials is seen as a purely technical matter but in the resource centre the instructional design function is an important factor in the development of media. The unique characteristics of a filmstrip, for example, with its fixed sequence and visual qualities might be much more justifiable for the intended purpose and audience than a sound recording which can require a higher level of motivation and improved listening skills.

PROMOTION OF READING

Reading continues to be of prime importance to the teacher-librarian and numerous methods of motivating voluntary reading are common in resource centres. In conjunction with fellow teachers, the teacher-librarian works toward broadening horizons, increasing language proficiency and resolving student problems through storytelling and book talks as well as improved reading guidance (which can approach bibliotherapy), creative dramatics, puppetry and related programs.

INFORMATION SERVICES

Information services are offered to students and teachers with the reference interview becoming a professional teaching situation in many cases. Since the teacher-librarian is familiar with individual units through advance planning the student may receive precise information immediately or have skills introduced or reinforced depending on defined individual objectives. Teachers gain the ability to ask questions at a variety of levels, from the recall of information to the evaluation of abstract concepts, through professional education and classroom experience. These techniques are necessary in the resource centre to gauge the precise information needs of the student and the level of specific skill attainment at that time. Reference and research skills are taught as an integrated part of the instructional program in each subject on a continuing sequential basis. Where desirable and valid, however, some skills may also be reinforced and extended as a short unit themselves. For example, a cooperative unit may be planned for a senior commercial class where the student will need to know a variety of specific skills such as how to use a dictionary as an aid in typing, how to locate quotations for speeches, the correct form of address to be used in given circumstances and how to file information for easy retrieval in order to function effectively and efficiently in a business office. Evaluation of learning always takes place in the context of classroom teaching and its extensions.

MEDIA SKILLS

The teacher-librarian is also actively engaged in teaching students the effective use of nonbook media and equipment; this includes the skills necessary to report research in many and varied ways other than the traditional essay format. The student of today must be knowledgeable about the electronic environment outside the school. We know that by the time a student completes secondary school more time has been spent watching television than has been spent in school — it would be gross negligence to overlook the skills necessary to evaluate this and other nonbook sources of information or to relegate these learning skills to a single separate course in screen education. Graphic analysis and visual and aural literacy are necessary components of a student's education; as a media specialist, the teacher librarian works with other teachers to integrate these learning skills with appropriate areas of the curriculum.

PROFESSIONAL DEVELOPMENT SERVICES

Two of the most important areas of competence in school librarianship are professional development services to teacher and strategies for change, both of which necessitate teacher education for maximum effect. Educational information services for staff members are necessary and useful if the teacher-librarian considers the specific interest, time and energy of the user. An even more fundamental professional development service is in-service education. As a curriculum developer and educational leader the teacher-librarian has a professional obligation and responsibility to lead seminars and workshops on the effective use of the resource centre. Topics range from the operation of audio-visual equipment to the implementation of effective teaching strategies. In-service education is carefully planned and pursued. It demands a critical analysis of need based on relevant educational principles, a real reason for teachers to attend, effective teaching by the teacher-librarian and involvement by participants. Evaluation of the session itself and how well it met the need originally identified provides guidance for future workshops. Only through increased knowledge of resource centre services as necessary components of teaching methodology will the potential of teacher-librarians and resource centres be realized.

A parallel consideration is the area of strategies for change in which in-service education programs are one part. Through perspective as a teacher plus an intimate knowledge and understanding of the institutional framework within which the resource centre operates, the teacher-librarian can identify areas of potential support and hindrance more easily. By exploiting political realities and building on aspirations of administrators and the goals of teachers the teacher-librarian can not only integrate services better but also develop a well-supported program.

The debate over faculty status for community college and university librarians has raged for years but is not a concern in schools. The teacher-librarian has full faculty status and is recognized as an equal partner in education in terms of salary, working conditions and vacation leave. This status was gained by the most obvious means possible—the same basic qualification to be in the school in the first place followed by a similar role through specialization within the field. Indeed, most school districts have defined the role and expectations of the teacher-librarian as a master teacher and have granted additional responsibility allowances for department headships and educational leadership.

Collegiality is a characteristic of the teaching profession that cannot be ignored; just as the professional with a Master of Arts or Master of Science degree has a teaching certificate so too does the professional with a Master of Library Science degree. Professional roles in a school, other than peripheral or support positions, begin with teacher education and classroom experience followed by additional qualification for specialization. Whether one agrees or not, it is a fact of life in a school that teachers do not extend their privileges, rights and status to noncertified personnel, regardless of position or qualification. Familiarity with curriculum design and particularly successful experience in the classroom provide a respectability that cannot be achieved by academic qualifications alone.

STANDARDS

Comparison of libraries is often done by examining quantitative data but in a school the number of personnel, book and nonbook materials, equipment and square feet per student are relatively meaningless for determining the level of development and value of resource centre services. Numbers are significant only when establishing new resource centres to equalize tangible products and potential. Much more useful but more difficult to measure are qualitative considerations. The resource centre can be distinguished from a library by its specialized curriculum implementation (program development and cooperative teaching) services; the teacher-librarian and resource centre represent a variety of teaching strategies found to be educationally effective. The school which practices inquiry-centred approaches to learning requires much more personnel, resources and space for the same number of students than a school which stresses textbook-oriented Socratic methods. The resource centre must be essential to the instructional process if it is to have significance or even to survive. With budgetary restraints the resource centre is using money that could mean smaller classes, more counselors or more remedial assistance. Unlike an integrated resource centre, a children's or young adult library added to the school could not and would not outlast financial cutbacks and the setting of priorities. Perhaps a more reasonable method of informal evaluation would be to close the resource centre for a

month to see if teaching and learning continue as before. If a teacher can teach and if the student can learn without the resource centre and the teacher-librarian, the service as it exists in that situation is merely a beauty spot on the body politic, an expensive and doomed educational frill. The following problems have traditionally prevented the full implementation of a planned program for facilitating independent learning using the resource centre:

1. lack of a school district K through 12 developmental study skills program that mandates the integration of independent learning skills with all aspects of the program

2. limitation of instruction in the use of the resource centre to a brief orientation session

3. failure to include in provincially or locally developed courses of study, specific learning experiences requiring resource centre support and specific reference to the necessity of integrating instruction in the use of the resource centre within the framework of the teaching-learning program

4. isolation of the teacher-librarian from curriculum study and revision activities

5. failure of teacher education institutions to include in basic programs an adequate understanding of the function of the resource centre as a learning laboratory and the role of the teacher-librarian as a fellow teacher

6. failure of the teacher to expand class knowledge beyond textbook content and classroom confines

7. reluctance of the teacher to preplan with the teacher-librarian for the effective use of the resource centre media, facilities, and services before a unit is introduced to the class (or, unfortunately, the reluctance of the teacher-librarian)

8. lack of sufficient staff—both professional and paraprofessional—to support adequately a comprehensive, diversified instructional program in the use of the resource centre—methods which effectively utilize resource centre personnel and services.

The resource centre will never be really necessary until students are unable to do satisfactory work without access to the professional teaching and library media services which it provides.

EDUCATION FOR TEACHER-LIBRARIANS

Although it is possible to define the role of the teacher-librarian as a teacher and as a librarian it is most unwise to do so. Indeed, this is a common mistake made by educators of teacher-librarians. There are essential competencies necessary from teacher education, classroom experience, library and media education but it is the fusion of these that leads to excellence, not dual qualifications in themselves. Until programs which educate teacher-librarians, whether faculties of education or library science, recognize, require and develop these areas of competence, there will continue to be a chronic shortage of teacher-librarians who understand this specialized teaching role and have the necessary skills to implement it. The time is long overdue for instructors in school librarianship to examine the basic research (1, 2, 3) and get on with the job of developing the necessary course components. A specialized Master of Education degree in school librarianship would provide sufficient scope at the appropriate level to build on a teacher's background and experience. It would also provide a suitable framework for the components which are too often missing: instructional design, program planning, cooperative teaching, human relations, selection of learning resources in all formats, the institutional setting, design and production of media, developmental reading. For too long we have paid lip service to a specialized teaching role and translated it into courses in administration, cataloguing and literature.

CONCLUSION

The school must examine its own program in order to determine the type of service that it requires from the resource centre. If the only concern is the circulation of materials, then parent volunteers or a clerical assistant may be sufficient. If selection and organization warrant increased attention as well as children's and young adult services and programs then a library technician or librarian should be employed depending on the scope and quality of service preferred. If the utilization of learning resources through valid, planned experiences leading to independent learning is of prime importance then a master teacher with advanced education and training in school librarianship is required.

Teacher-librarians have progressed from the days when it was all too common for refugees from the classroom to be placed in charge of school libraries to a time when outstanding specialist teachers head vital resource centres. School libraries have moved from their position outside the mainstream of education to resource centres at the physical and philosophical heart of the school. This development is a direct result of changes in education and, more specifically, changes in teaching strategies. Instruction in learning skills is integrated with all aspects of the curriculum and taught together by the classroom teacher and the teacher-librarian. The direction of teaching and learning focuses increasingly on learning how to learn so that students will have the necessary motivation and the skills to examine their own environment, evaluate it and perhaps even reform it.

What Is a School Librarian?
Towards Defining Professionalism

Ken Haycock

At the Annual General Meeting of the Canadian School Library Association in Edmonton in June, 1978 a motion was passed to the effect that the C.S.L.A. define a "qualified school librarian." Subsequently, a committee on qualifications was established to report to the Executive Council of the Association. This committee was chaired by Ken Haycock who is Coordinator of Library Services and a Supervisor of Instruction with the Vancouver School Board and included both elementary and secondary school librarians. All committee members have faculty of education courses in school librarianship/media services and half also hold accredited library degrees.

The committee consulted a variety of sources listed in the selected bibliography but the basis of the first draft was primarily a document on minimum qualifications for school librarians developed by the Vancouver Chapter of the British Columbia School Librarian's Association in consultation with the Vancouver School Board Coordinator of Library Services; this document was adopted by the Vancouver School Board on March 2, 1979. The Vancouver chapter granted permission to use their work as a basis for a national report. Several revisions were made in the course of the development of this report and it was revised further for the purposes of the Canadian School Library Association.

Since the committee was local in composition and since the document could be important for school librarianship in Canada a "reactor panel" of 75 leaders in the field in Canada was selected. Invitations were sent to all provincial supervisors, all instructors in school librarianship in Faculties of Education and Library Science, all deans of library schools, all presidents of provincial school library associations and a representative sample of personnel at the school and district levels. Approximately one-third of those invited to serve as reactors were elementary and secondary school librarians, one-third were library educators and one-third were district coordinators/supervisors.

All reactors were invited to involve their colleagues in the review process with the result that one hundred and fifty reactors offered more than two hundred and fifty pages of reaction to the draft document. The breakdown of the reactor panel by province is as follows:

Province	Invited	Actual
British Columbia	15	40
Alberta	12	12
Saskatchewan	5	5
Manitoba	6	31
Ontario	20	45
Quebec	3	2
New Brunswick	2	1
Nova Scotia	6	10
Prince Edward Island	3	1
Newfoundland	3	3
TOTAL	75	150

Substantial revision was made as a result of this feedback.

Criticisms and/or recommendations from reactors were dealt with in detail and at length. Each committee member received copies of all correspondence from reactors and areas of agreement and disagreement noted. There was strong and near unanimous support for teaching qualifications and experience, specialized advanced education in school librarianship and professionalism and leadership. Areas of disagreement among reactors provided a useful overview of issues in school librarianship today and these will be explored in future issues of *Emergency Librarian*. It would be fair to say that the final report has the general and specific support of leaders in school librarianship across Canada.

The committee report was introduced to the general membership of the Canadian School Library Association at a presentation at the annual conference in Ottawa on June 15, 1979. Participants had an opportunity to make their views known to individual members of the Executive Council of C.S.L.A. following that session; all comments were favourable. At the Annual General Meeting on June 17, members requested that this document be approved as soon as possible. Only one delegate (from Nova Scotia) voiced any reservations, and this was about the well-documented need for a teaching certificate for school librarians. On June 18, 1979 the report was accepted and endorsed by the Executive Council of the C.S.L.A. and recommended as a high priority for wide disemination.

THE CANADIAN SCHOOL LIBRARY ASSOCIATION STATEMENT ON QUALIFICATIONS FOR SCHOOL LIBRARIANS
(approved by the Canadian School Library Association on June 18, 1979)

Prepared by:
Liz Austrom, Teacher-Librarian, Killarney Secondary School, Vancouver, BC
Dave Boettcher, Teacher-Librarian, Waverley Elementary School, Vancouver, BC
Stan Copland, Head of English, Churchill Secondary School, Vancouver, BC

Gerry Gibb, Teacher-Librarian, Kitsilano Secondary School, Vancouver, BC
Ken Haycock, Coordinator of Library Services, Vancouver School Board, Vancouver, BC, Convener
Debbie Porteous, Teacher-Librarian, Strathcona Elementary School, Vancouver, BC

INTRODUCTION

During the past two decades, our schools have been struggling to adapt to the changing needs of society. What has emerged is an institution which focuses on the development of individuals who are prepared to think rationally and logically for themselves and to assume responsibilities. To develop students of this type has meant that schools have had to emphasize learner-oriented methods such as guided discovery and inquiry as well as traditional teacher-oriented methods.

This broadening of educational methodology has had a great impact on school libraries. Many school librarians have been leaders in understanding and focusing on the expanding variety of teaching approaches and student experiences which the changing needs of society require. It is fact, however, that the inclusion of inquiry, individualization and independent study programs has placed many additional demands on the library and on the librarian. The need today is for the learning resource teacher to be a highly skilled teacher, able to function on the school team as a professional with competencies from teacher education and classroom experience as well as competencies from school librarianship and media services. Similarly, the library has moved from being a subject and merely a place to a service and a concept, a learning resource centre for teachers and students. We attempt to identify those competencies which are essential to the success of a learning resource teacher. In each case competencies are listed and have been developed and defined through multiple indicators of quality.

Expectations for learning resource teachers are very high. It is expected that a learning resource teacher will be in the forefront of curriculum and professional development services, will be familiar with the full range of instructional strategies and learning styles, will be able to organize time, personnel and materials to maximize utilization of each and will be active in professional concerns within the school and the district.

For the learning resource teacher to achieve these expectations, adequate support staff is essential to free the professional from clerical and technical tasks. School districts must recognize this need if the potential of the learning resource teacher and resource centre is to be realized.

It should be noted that successful completion of formal course work will not guarantee success as a learning resource teacher. Personality factors, interpersonal relations skills, creativity, flexibility, professional commitment, and willingness to participate in continuing education, should be major factors in evaluating a learning resource teacher.

Recent advances in education make it essential that the learning resource teacher demonstrate the competencies outlined if the resource centre is to offer an educational service which is vital to the school's instructional program.

AREAS OF COMPETENCE

Although learning resource teachers have competence in the areas listed, services are offered on the basis of the school program and the availability of personnel, materials and facilities. Priorities are determined by the individual school since not all services will be offered in every school or to the same extent in all schools. Different approaches to evaluation are available to administrators, school staffs and learning resource teachers and several of these are outlined in the Winter, 1974 issue (Volume 17, Number 2) of *Moccasin Telegraph*, the journal of the Canadian School Library Association.

1. **Competency: Administration of the Learning Resource Program**

    Administration includes the ability to manage resource centre programs, services and staff in order that these services may contribute to the stated educational goals of the school.

    Indicators of Competence:
    The learning resource teacher is able to:

    a. Establish rapport with school staff, students and community.

    b. Establish short and long range goals in terms of district guidelines and school objectives.

    c. Select, supervise and plan for the effective use of resource centre professional and support staff.

    d. Recruit, select, train and motivate adult and student volunteers.

    e. Invite and accept suggestions from teaching staff about the services the program provides.

    f. Develop resource centre facilities to support the objectives of the instructional program.

    g. Plan for efficient use of space and equipment and for appropriate security for learning resources.

    h. Plan and manage a flexible budget which reflects the instructional program.

    i. Organize and develop staff, collections, budget, facilities and services to achieve objectives.

    j. Maintain an inventory of materials and equipment.

    k. Prepare oral and written reports on the resource centre program.

    l. Provide an environment conducive to learning.

    m. Apply technological advances such as automation to resource centre services.

    n. Involve school staff in the evaluation of the effectiveness of resource centre program in terms of district guidelines and school objectives.

2. **Competency: Selection of Learning Resources**

    The selection of learning resources includes the ability to apply basic principles of evaluating learning resources for the purpose of developing a collection which will support the instructional program in the school.

    Indicators of Competence:
    The learning resources teacher is able to:

    a. Develop and implement criteria for the evaluation and selection of a wide range of resources.

    b. Develop policies and procedures for the selection of learning resources which meet curricular informational and recreational needs.

    c. Build a collection of bibliographic and evaluative sources to provide current information about learning resources and equipment.

    d. Organize teacher involvement in the preview, evaluation and selection of learning resources.

    e. Develop extensive "consideration for purchase" files of book and nonbook media.

3. **Competency: Acquisition, Organization and Circulation of Learning Resources**

    The acquisition, organization and circulation of learning resources includes the professional tasks of classifying and cataloguing information and of organizing circulation procedures and the *supervision* of efficient and systematic technical and clerical support services.

    Indicators of Competence:
    The learning resource teacher performs, organizes systems and/or deploys trained assistants to:

    a. Implement procedures for ordering, receiving and processing learning resources.

    b. Classify and catalogue learning resources as necessary and according to accepted standards.

    c. Maintain an accurate catalogue according to established rules.

    d. Develop an efficient system for lending, renewing, reserving and recalling needed learning resources and equipment.

    e. Route curriculum resources and professional materials.

    f. Establish procedures for, and encourage the use of, interlibrary loans.

    g. Select commercial cataloguing services appropriate to school needs.

4. **Competency: Reading, Listening and Viewing Guidance**

    Guidance in reading, listening and viewing includes the ability to assess student needs and interests and to provide resources which satisfy a given situation. Through this guidance students develop attitudes, appreciations and skills that motivate and stimulate the improved selection of appropriate learning resources.

    Indicators of Competence:
    The learning resource teacher is able to:

    a. Work with individuals and groups of students to provide direction, improve selection, and develop critical thinking.

    b. Provide guidance for students and teachers during the school day and before and after school.

    c. Share with students and teachers the joy of reading.

    d. Promote appreciation and interest in the use of learning resources by giving book/media talks.

    e. Develop storytelling, storyreading and other resource-centered programs for language development.

    f. Assist students and teachers in the effective use of media.

    g. Recommend to teachers learning resources in various formats which may assist in the accomplishment of specific learning objectives.

    h. Advise teachers of medium appropriateness for particular instructional purposes.

5. **Competency: Design and Production of Learning Resources**

    The design and production of learning resources includes the ability to plan, design and produce materials for a specific instructional purpose, such as to improve communication effectiveness skills where appropriate commercial materials are not available.

    Indicators of Competence:
    The learning resource teacher is able to:

    a. Advise students and teachers in media design and production through instruction and in-service programs.

    b. Supervise the production of materials such as cassettes, slides, transparencies, talking books, video and slide/tape presentations.

    c. Assist in the evaluation of media produced.

6. **Competency: Information and Reference Services**

    Information services include the ability to use reference materials in seeking answers to questions. The learning resource teacher also acts as a liaison between the resource centre/school and outside agencies for information services and resources.

Indicators of Competence:
The learning resource teacher is able to:

a. Answer, or obtain answers to, questions from teachers and students.

b. Provide guidance to teachers and students on locating information.

c. Develop a working relationship with public libraries, specialized libraries, other resource centres, community organizations, resource people and district resource services.

d. Locate specific information and resources found outside the school.

e. Participate in cooperative and coordinated projects within the district which involve the sharing of ideas, experiences and learning resources.

7. **Competency: Promotion of the Effective Use of Learning Resources and Services**

    The promotion of the effective use of learning resources and services includes the ability to alert users to the full range of available resources.

    Indicators of Competence:
    The learning resource teacher is able to:

    a. Communicate effectively with teachers and administrators.

    b. Develop an informational and public relations program for staff, students and the community.

    c. Capitalize on themes through special promotions and media celebrations.

    d. Develop bulletin boards, displays, and other publicity materials.

8. **Competency: Cooperative Program Planning and Teaching**

    Cooperative program planning and teaching include the ability to participate as a teaching partner in the accomplishment of identified learning objectives through a knowledge of recommended resources and appropriate teaching/learning strategies.

    Indicators of Competence:
    The learning resource teacher is able to:

    a. Develop cooperatively with teachers a sequential list of media, research and study skills for cross-grade and cross-subject implementation.

    b. Plan and develop units of work with teachers from the setting of objectives to evaluation.

    c. Integrate media, research and study skills with classroom instruction for independent and continued learning.

    d. Pre-plan with teachers and teach skills integrated with classroom instruction to large and small groups and individuals.

e. Integrate the planned use of learning resources with the educational program.

f. Provide leadership to develop programs which integrate the promotion of reading with the total school program and with individual teacher programs.

g. Initiate specific teaching units to encourage the acquisition of skills and the effective use of learning resources.

h. Provide curriculum-related book and nonbook media talks and celebrations.

i. Compile bibliographies, resource lists and book and nonbook media lists as needed.

9. **Competency: Professionalism and Leadership**
Professionalism and leadership include the ability to develop and promote the use of the human and material resources of the school resource centre and its facilities through cooperative professional activities.

Indicators of Competence:
The learning resource teacher is able to:

a. Develop a strong team approach with other teachers.

b. Lead in-service education programs on the effective use of the resource centre: criteria for selection of materials; designing resource-based units of study; using audio-visual equipment; promoting voluntary reading; media, research and study skill development; cooperative teaching; community resources.

c. Share techniques and strategies for using learning resources.

d. Involve students and staff in establishing learning resources policy and service guidelines.

e. Plan strategies for developing, presenting and securing support for learning resource services.

f. Serve on local and district curriculum committees.

g. Keep abreast of current developments in school librarianship, library and information science, media services and related fields.

h. Participate in the school's educational program by serving on advisory groups and committees and working with the student extra-curricular program.

i. Take advantage of opportunities for continuing education and professional development.

j. Apply specific research findings and the principles of research to the development and improvement of resource centre services.

k. Maintain membership and participate in professional education and library associations at the local, provincial and national levels.

Guiding Principles for Education for School Librarianship

Although there is little consistency in provincial requirements for learning resource teachers, the Canadian School Library Association believes that programs for the education of learning resource teachers should reflect the areas of competence outlined. Further, the following basic principles should form the foundation for formal education programs:

- A valid teaching certificate and successful classroom teaching experience should be required of all candidates prior to entry.

- Programs should be offered at the post-baccalaureate and/or graduate levels only.

- Courses should reflect the general framework of teaching and learning in elementary and secondary schools.

- Programs should reflect an integrated approach to "library" and "audiovisual" services.

- Programs should be a minimum of one academic year or equivalent.

- Access to programs should be improved through part-time and summer session study and continuing education opportunities.

New and revised programs for the education of learning resource teachers should be based on required competencies. These programs and provincial requirements should be developed as soon as possible by agencies involved in education for school librarianship in consultation with the appropriate professional associations.

SOURCES

American Association of School Librarians. Certification of School Media Specialists Committee. *Certification Model for Professional School Media Personnel.* Chicago: American Library Association, 1976.

American Association of School Librarians. School Library Manpower Project. *Behavioral Requirements Analysis Checklist; A Compilation of Competency-Based Job Functions and Task Statements for School Library Media Personnel,* by Robert N. Case and Anna Mary Lowrey. Chicago: American Library Association, 1973.

American Association of School Librarians. School Library Manpower Project. *Curriculum Alternatives; Experiments in School Library Media Education*, by Robert N. Case and Anna Mary Lowrey. Chicago: American Library Association, 1974.

American Association of School Librarians. School Library Manpower Project. *Evaluation of Alternative Curricula: Approaches to School Library Media Education*, by Robert N. Case and others. Chicago: American Library Association, 1975.

British Columbia School Librarians' Association. Vancouver Chapter. *Minimum Qualifications for Teacher-Librarians in District 39 (Vancouver)*. Vancouver: Vancouver School Board Library Services, 1979.

Canadian School Library Association. Education for School Librarianship Committee. *Education for School Librarianship in Canada; Proceedings of a Workshop Held at Jasper Park Lodge on Saturday, June 8, 1968.* Sponsored by the Canadian School Library Association, Alberta School Library Council and the Saskatchewan Association of School Librarians. Ottawa: Canadian Library Association, 1970.

Chisolm, Margaret E. and Donald P. Ely. *Media Personnel in Education: A Competency Approach.* Englewood Cliffs, New Jersey: Prentice-Hall, 1976.

Davies, Ruth Ann. *The School Library Media Centre; A Force for Educational Excellence.* Second Edition. New York: R. R. Bowker, 1974.

Haycock, Ken. "The School Librarian as a Professional Teacher." *Moccasin Telegraph*, Volume 19, Number 3-4 (Spring-Summer, 1977), pp. 2-6 + .

Haycock, Ken. *Services of School Resource Centres: A Discussion and Planning Guide.* London, Ontario: Dyad Services, 1975.

Media Programs: District and School. Prepared by the American Association of School Librarians and the Association for Educational Communications and Technology. Chicago: American Library Association, 1975.

Resource Services for Canadian Schools, edited by Frederic R. Branscombe and Harry E. Newssom. Prepared for the Association for Media and Technology in Education in Canada and the Canadian School Library Association. Toronto: McGraw-Hill Ryerson, 1977.

Static in the Educational Intercom: Conflict and the School Librarian

Alixe Hambleton

For the past twenty years many excellent, rational and resounding professional statements have stoutly proclaimed the potential of school library programs. Liberally sprinkled through these statements are phrases which assert that the school library of today is the keystone of the educational program, a "force for educational excellence" and the "heart" of the school. Unfortunately, these phrases remain only clichés, and often the school library is still regarded as an adjunct or auxiliary service, and often, in times of fiscal restraints, is a prime target for cuts in both staff and resources. There is obviously static in the communication system between sender and receiver. The message is not getting through or, at best, is being distorted.

Research in school librarianship has attempted to discover the source of this static, and a trend in the research literature since the early 1960s has been continuing concentration on role perception studies, with a major focus on the school librarian's role as viewed by other members of the educational system.

Many of the findings of these studies have negative connotations. In the numerous studies carried out in the past twenty years, a number of conclusions are common: that the school librarian's perception of that role differs significantly from that of others in the educational system, that the school library seems to play only a marginal role in the total educational program, and that the low regard for the school librarian militates against a direct involvement in the instructional program of the school.[1]

Role theory suggests that when differing perceptions of a role are present, the person performing that role is placed in a conflict position, resulting in a loss of effectiveness, both for the individual and for the organization.

In order to investigate the implications of such theory on the operation of school libraries within a school system, the writer carried out a research project in the elementary schools within an areas of central Ontario. The objectives of the study were to determine the perceptions of principals, teachers and school librarians of the role of the school librarian; to test the relationship between the extent of role conflict and effectiveness in the performance of the curricular teaching role; and, finally, to explore the relationship between personality and the extent of role conflict.

Eighty-four elementary schools from nine school boards in central Ontario were surveyed. All respondents were asked to complete a role inventory questionnaire consisting of sixty items. Principals also completed an effectiveness questionnaire dealing specifically with the curricular-teaching role of the school librarian. The school librarians responded to a role conflict questionnaire and to a personality inventory. Responses were received from 90 percent of the principals, 80 percent of the teachers and 98 percent of the school librarians.

It is not possible, within the scope of this article, to present a complete analysis of the data. Rather, the intent is to discuss some of the findings which may be worth consideration as possible contributors to that "static" which seems so persistently evident in the school system.

The role inventory questionnaire dealt with seven roles performed by the school librarian: materials specialist, curriculum development, teacher, technical services, administration, extra mural activities and the sub-professional role. Analysis of the distribution of scores indicated differences in perceptions among the three groups on all of the seven categories of the librarian's role. Of particular interest was the fact that for the items related to the materials specialist role (which one might expect to be the particular expertise and responsibility of the school librarian), there was a significant difference among the three groups. Also, there was no agreement on any of the items relating to the sub-professional role, indicating that the concept of the school librarian as a professional member of the school staff is not yet universally accepted. Though it may be tempting to explain this finding by citing the lack of clerical help in the schools, it is nevertheless true that this situation is not likely to change as long as the present perceptions of the librarian's role exist.

For all groups, the majority of responses fell most often in the preferential (Preferably Should or Preferably Should Not) categories, a further indication of a lack of definite role expectations. This is a safe response, one carrying little commitment, and is also a response which indicates a reluctance to delineate priorities.

Distribution scores did not present the total picture. It was necessary, as well, to look at agreement or disagreement within each of the three groups. Variance scores for each item of the questionnaire calculated for each of the respondent groups provided results which also indicate another serious source of the static which is perhaps prohibiting successful communication. Variance scores computed for the group of principals showed that there was low agreement within that group on 43 percent of the items. Within the teacher groups, a low level of agreement was found for 53 percent of the items. For the librarian group, a low agreement was found for 55 percent of the items.

These variance scores were also categorized by the seven types of librarian's roles. It was found that principals are more consistent in their perceptions than teachers or librarians, and that they have a more "professional" view of the librarian's role. They agree on more of the items making up the materials

specialist, teacher, and administrative roles, indicating that principals may be expecting more of the librarian in these areas than many librarians assume. However, principals are confused, as a group, about the technical services and sub-professional roles, and in view of the lack of agreement on the part of the librarian group, they will likely continue to be confused unless some direction is forthcoming.

Teachers, as a group, are generally in agreement on the teacher role of the librarian, but do not agree on the curricular involvement role of the librarian. The majority of responses to the items in these categories were in the preferential rather than mandatory category.[2] Teachers seem to see teaching of individual classes as part of the role of the librarian when this is possible, but they do not see the librarian as being involved in overall curriculum development. Teachers do not agree on the materials specialist role of the librarian. Also there is little agreement among teachers as to the administrative role of the librarian and much less agreement on the technical services and sub-professional role. Although the scores for items making up the extra-mural role indicate agreement of this role, 36 percent were undecided as to whether the librarian should act as a community resource person.

Librarians as a group are in agreement on less than one-half of the sixty items. There is low agreement within the group on 47 percent of the items comprising the materials specialist role, 50 percent of the items making up the curricular role, 50 percent of the administrative role, 75 percent of the technical services role, and 92 percent of the sub-professional role. They agree, as a group, on the majority of items making up the teacher and extra-mural role. A larger percentage of their responses fall in the mandatory category than is the case with principals and teachers.

The high incidence of low agreement within the librarian group suggests that librarians themselves are not prepared to communicate a definite role to principals and teachers.

Librarians' response to the role conflict questionnaire indicated they experienced conflict as a result of unclear guidelines, a realization that different groups serviced by librarians may operate quite differently, a too heavy work load, a lack of adequate resources or manpower, and the necessity of having to work on too many assignments at one time.

If role theory is to be borne out, as differences in perceptions are great, role conflict should also be great. In statistical terms, a high correlation should exist between conflict and differing perceptions. However, when the data were analyzed on an individual school basis, a different picture emerged. When conflict scores were correlated with scores representing the difference in perception between the school librarian (the role receiver) and principals and teachers (the role senders), this expected correlation was not evident. Surprisingly, the correlation, although not statistically significant, was negative, indicating that in schools where the highest discrepancy in role perceptions exists, the conflict scores tend to be low. Unsure themselves of their role, school librarians may neither recognize nor respond to the conflicts that are present in an individual school. If conflict is not recognized, no positive attempt will be made to resolve it, and the future role of school librarians may continue to be in jeopardy.

Principals were asked to assess the degree to which their school librarian participated in tasks related to the curricular role since this has been considered one of the more controversial and less agreed upon roles. They rated their school librarian's performance on a five point scale which ranged from Almost Always to Almost Never.

In the Almost Always/Frequently group were found those items related to selection of resources, library assignments, the location of resources, the publicizing of resources to teachers, and curriculum planning. In the Almost Never/Rarely group were found those items most closely related to the teaching role including team teaching, planning and carrying out workshops, participation in staff meetings, acting as an information source for teachers, and providing innovative instructional help for teachers. School librarians were doing most frequently those tasks that have a specific connection with resources and library programs. Those tasks that require the school librarian to perform in a teaching role were not being carried out to any appreciable extent.

School librarians are seen by the majority of principals as performing "library type" tasks, as opposed to "teacher type" tasks, in spite of the fact that 91 percent of the principals felt that all were tasks that *should* be carried out by school librarians.

Data on eight personality characteristics were also collected, and scores were determined for the librarians on the traits of ascendancy, responsibility, cautiousness, original thinking, personal relations and vigour. Librarians' mean scores were lower for personal relations, ascendancy and sociability than for the other traits. In a comparison of the librarians in the sample to other groups for whom norms are available (college women, female low level managers, college men), it was found that, with the exception of the cautiousness and sociability scales, the school librarians scored equal to, or significantly higher than, comparable groups on the other scales.

Paradoxically, perhaps, the school librarians rated high on both original thinking and cautiousness. School librarians with the potential for creative and innovative ideas may, in practice, be too cautious to implement these ideas. This cautiousness may also be partially responsible for the lack of cohesiveness within the librarian group, the lack of response to possible areas of conflict, and the tendency to perform most often those tasks that relate to library expertise rather than those which involve the librarian in the teaching program.

The correlation between curriculum effectiveness scores and cautiousness scores was significant and negative. Low cautiousness scores are associated with high effectiveness scores. Correlations between conflict scores and three of the personality factors were significant and negative. High conflict scores were associated with low cautiousness, low emotional stability and low responsibility scores. Since the scores on these three traits were generally high, it can be assumed that the recognition of conflicts is restricted to a relatively small group of librarians. The majority of librarians scored high on cautiousness, emotional stability and responsibility and low on conflict scores.

The findings relative to the presence of differing perceptions provide ample proof that static does exist between librarians and the school staff. The lack of agreement on the role of the librarian within the librarian group itself is certainly one of the factors contributing to such static. If a message is to be transmitted without distortion, that message must be clear and also clearly stated. If there is a confusing message, it is not surprising that the receiver of that message is also confused. The school librarian must build a relationship with teachers and the principal that is based on strong, professional expertise—an expertise that is a necessary part of the educational environment. That expertise must be defined, and defined in terms which can be understood by educationalists. Then, and only then, can a strong, clear, professional message be communicated effectively to principals and teachers.

The reluctance or the inability to recognize or resolve conflict where it does exist is another factor contributing to the static and interfering with effective communication. Here again, a firm conviction concerning role and an equally firm commitment to that role become prerequisites. Once the role is defined and is communicated effectively, it becomes easier to develop the ways and means of carrying out that role.

Communication without static will not take place in a school system without a realization on the part of all three groups that both teaching and learning go on in a school library, that the school librarian makes an important contribution to the intellectual and social growth of the student, and that this contribution is possible because of an expertise which effectively blends librarianship and teaching skills. This will be realized only when that expertise is both practised and effectively communicated in such a way that it becomes recognized as a necessary part of the educational enterprise.

As the study revealed, school librarians may be too cautious and too unsure of their role to provide the clear message that is necessary if school libraries are to fulfill their potential. This barrier to effective communication must be removed and soon, for in times of fiscal restraint a clear message becomes crucial to survival. Conflict may, indeed, be a source of static in the educational communication system; but until the nature of this conflict is realized, and until school librarians recognize their responsibility to resolve it, the school librarian role will likely continue to be marginal, and any hope of providing a "force for educational excellence" will continue to be unrealized.

NOTES

1. See for example, doctoral theses by E. F. Tielke, E. H. Daniels, L. E. Olson, B. A. Hull, C. J. Anderson.

2. The two responses, *Definitely Should* and *Definitely Should Not* were considered *Mandatory*, while the *Preferably Should* and *Preferably Should Not* were considered *Preferential*.

Hard Times ... Hard Choices

Ken Haycock

In times of declining financial support for public institutions and services of all kinds it is perhaps useful to remind ourselves of the basic principles on which school library services thrive and prosper and the major issues confronting the profession. Too often we deal well with the symptoms but ignore the causes, resulting in an inevitable rematch, as symptoms, like weeds, keep coming up.

The research and the experience of those developing support for teacher-librarians and school resource centres, is quite clear. The single most important role of the teacher-librarian is cooperative program planning and teaching with classroom teachers. This major shift for the teacher-librarian from determining what the student is to do, to cooperatively determining what the student is to learn, has resulted in the teacher becoming the primary focus. Cooperative planning and team teaching not only provide better opportunities for purposeful use of library resources and the integration of media, research and study skills with classroom instruction but also provide better opportunities for classroom teachers and administrators to learn first hand the role of the teacher-librarian as a teaching partner, something quite different from a teaching adjunct. The need for *flexible scheduling* of facilities and services is obvious if integration is to take place. Furthermore, it is downright foolish for the school's librarian to provide planning/preparation time for teachers if the first priority of the teacher-librarian is to be available to plan with that teacher. Some school districts have policies defining clearly the role of the teacher-librarian and mandating flexible scheduling of resource centres. (There *are* cheaper ways to provide spare periods for teachers!) Teacher-librarians need a defined role, the integrity and confidence to stand by it and a willingness to take risks in initiating planning with colleagues.

Needless to say, teacher-librarians need the skills of *program advocacy*. It is essential that both school and district personnel and decision-makers understand the "newer" role of the teacher-librarian and its importance for teaching and learning. Every teacher-librarian should be able to articulate the aim of the program (see *Emergency Librarian*, 8:5), the best means of achieving that aim, the role of principals and teachers in a *cooperative* venture, and the confidence to talk to parent and community groups, professional groups and individuals about these. Put simply, if the teacher-librarian doesn't sell the program, nobody will and it *is* a given that teachers have no idea of the role of the teacher-librarian at the beginning of their careers.

And how well prepared is the teacher-librarian for these roles? *Education for school librarianship* holds the key to both success and survival in school librarianship but where are the courses (not a single class) in cooperative planning? It isn't good enough any more to direct prospective teacher-librarians to work with teachers—how do you do it? What are the curricular entry points? the strategies for involvement? the skills to work with professionals you dislike? the scope and sequence of research and study skills K-12? the process for developing school-based policies? Where are the courses in cooperative teaching in elementary and secondary schools? When are the professional skills of in-service education for teachers taught and applied? Where are the strategies for implementing innovation dealt with? Since new courses are unlikely to be added, teacher-librarians will have to continue to argue for a restructuring of existing programs to better meet needs identified by both the profession and research.

It's time to stand up and be counted as a professional with integrity, confidence and skill. The management of newer materials and technology, while important, will not save or even necessarily enhance the status of the teacher-librarian if undertaken outside this framework. The future lies in working closely with teachers within the context of a clearly defined role, understood and advocated by teacher-librarians and thus by administrators, teachers and the community.

Part 3
PROGRAM PLANNING AND DEVELOPMENT

With all of the emphasis on inquiry, individualization, and independent study for all these years, why is the task so difficult? Jean Brown clarifies the world of the classroom teacher for teacher-librarians who have forgotten or who missed this essential experience. Changing teaching practices in order to meet current expectations is much more complex than some imagined, particularly since the expectations are fairly clear in newer curriculum guides but a lack of support for change makes classroom practice much slower to change. Further, those same curriculum guides often imply the presence of a well-equipped resource center and a skilled teacher-librarian but rarely is this explicit and specific.

James Henri points out that Australian teacher-librarians are facing the same dilemmas as North American counterparts and increasingly recognize the need for cooperative program planning and teaching as a means to develop an integrated approach to school library programming. Teacher-librarians are equal teaching partners—not "instructional consultants" but not handmaidens either, equals in the educational enterprise and equal as professional teachers, not teacher and librarian. Carol-Ann Haycock takes a systematic step by step approach to developing the resource center program with excellent suggestions for beginning and strengthening the program.

Often when planning with a teacher, the teacher-librarian simply doesn't realize that each is starting from a different perspective. Antoinette Oberg offers points of departure for the school librarian and the classroom teacher as partners in curriculum planning and clarifies the different "platforms" on which each begins this complex process. Carol-Ann continues with the specifics of cooperative program planning and a model that actually works—it's even been field tested by hundreds of teacher-librarians and teachers. The significant strategies, questions and information are included together with the admonition to record units of study for future adaptation and use with the same or different teachers. Build on your work from year to year rather than starting fresh and leave a legacy for your successor.

Cooperative program planning and teaching and flexible scheduling go hand in hand and they do have the necessary ingredients to last. The educational approach is sound; it's grounded in research; it's proven in practice as workable and as having an impact on teaching and learning. It does, however, require considerable training and skill and "deep program structure." It too often falters because teacher-librarians overlook this or don't know how to establish the necessary foundation.

Ron Jobe is a master at strategies for effective influence and teacher-librarian collegiality—you may not feel comfortable with all of his suggestions but there will be something of value for most everyone. Barbara Howlett extends these strategies to communication skills generally and has more ideas for teacher-librarians. We conclude this section with a short piece on maximizing learning in small groups as a reminder by Igor Kusyszyn.

SERVICES OF SCHOOL RESOURCE CENTERS

A PLANNING GUIDE*

PHASE III

CURRICULUM IMPLEMENTATION

Curriculum Planning and Development
Cooperative Program Planning and Team Teaching
Professional Development Services to Teachers

PHASE II

CURRICULUM ENRICHMENT

Promotion of Materials and Services
Guidance for Readers, Listeners, Viewers
Information Services
Design and Production of Materials
Cooperation with Outside Agencies

PHASE I

CURRICULUM SUPPORT

Administration of Resource Center
Selection of Materials
Acquisition of Materials
Organization of Materials
Circulation of Materials

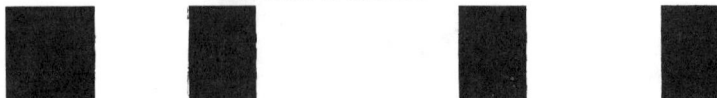

*Services are offered on the basis of the school program and the availability of personnel, materials and facilities. Priorities are determined by the individual school since not all services will be offered in every school or to the same extent in all schools.

© Ken Haycock, 1973

Emergency Librarian, 13:1

Changing Teaching Practice to Meet Current Expectations: Implications for Teacher-Librarians

Jean Brown

School library resource centers are an integral and essential part of the school's instructional program, at least in theory, with teacher-librarians involved as teaching partners with classroom teachers. However, in actual practice many school libraries are viewed as frills, or as merely a storehouse of recreational reading materials, existing on the periphery of the school's instructional program. Rather than seen as essential, the teacher-librarian is often seen as dispensable, a rather expensive clerk or technician, the first to be laid off in times of staff reductions. Why does the gap between theory and practice exist, and what, if anything, can be done about it?

Since it is generally accepted (again in theory) that a school library resource center ought to be an integral part of the school, an obvious place to begin in attempting to understand the problem is with the school itself. Since the school is part of a school district, and also part of the larger society, it is also necessary to examine conditions in the school district and to consider national concerns that affect the school. Since the major concern here is with the implementation of school library media programs, conditions and factors which affect this program are focused on.

THE WORLD OF THE SCHOOL

Interestingly, the gap between theory and practice does not exist in school library media programs alone. There is a considerable gap between theory and practice in all areas of the curriculum. Schools today, in spite of the literature which would make you believe otherwise, are very similar to what they were years ago. The many reforms which curriculum planners envision for the schools are, in actual fact, found in very few classrooms. Studies show that rather than a change in teaching *practice*, there has been a change in *expectations* for that practice. It is a situation which has caused many concerned educators to lament, "The more things change, the more they stay the same."

NATIONAL ECONOMIC AND SOCIAL CONDITIONS

The 1980s have not been a particularly good time for schools or teachers. It has been a time of major social and economic crisis. Unemployment rates have been high; inflation figures have soared. Although government measures have reduced the rate of inflation, the effects of the recession are still being felt. Many government workers, including teachers, have had to accept wage freezes. The threat of budget cuts and teacher layoffs has increased the insecurity of teachers. All these conditions have led to low teacher morale. On the national scene, teachers have been bombarded with negative reports on education. *A Nation at Risk*, the report of the National Commission on Excellence in Education, and approximately a dozen others that were published in 1982-83, expressed concern that standards seem to be falling, and placed most of the blame on the school system. The reactions to these reports are reminders that the schools are indeed part of the larger society. Block, a superintendent of education in Minnesota, angrily reacted to *A Nation at Risk*, which he called "a foul shot at American education."

> Mediocrity? Maybe—but we know the roots of it. We are a nation that has become so materialistic that we refuse to give up the second snowmobile or the second car or the bigger house or the speedboat so that we can pay for excellence in education.[2:183]

SCHOOL DISTRICTS

School districts have had to contend with declining enrollments and declining dollars. Elementary and secondary enrollments in Canada, for example, declined by 17 percent, from 1970-71 to 1983-84. This decline has occurred at the same time that governments have experienced the effects of the recession. The result has been that money allocated to elementary and secondary education has declined dramatically between 1970 and 1981, "from 22 percent to 16 percent, and the downward trend is continuing."[4:7] Faced with such restraints, many boards are unable to maintain the quality of education; Burke and Bolf, after surveying 3,724 educators, concluded that the school environment had deteriorated especially "when it came to the availability of funds for repairing or replacing supplies, equipment and buildings, for increased class size, or for professional development and supply teachers."[5:9]

At the same time as they are experiencing financial cutbacks, school boards have been faced with demands for new programs. Legislation has been passed requiring school boards to make special arrangements for the mentally and physically handicapped. Across Canada, parents have demanded and obtained classes in French immersion. In some areas, the needs of gifted students have been recognized through special programs: English-speaking classroom teachers are being laid off while French-speaking teachers needed for French immersion classes are being recruited. Other classroom teachers are being declared redundant due to declining enrollments. Boards who wish to hire new teachers with special expertise are often prevented from doing so by collective agreements requiring that teachers declared redundant be given priority.

Scarcity of funds and the reality of teacher layoffs have forced district offices to look at what is essential to schooling and what is not. Few districts have attempted to broaden their programs in such a climate. Many principals and superintendents feel that they are winning the battle if they can simply maintain their present staff and programs. Only positions and programs which are seen as essential have survived. How essential are school library media programs and teacher-librarians to education? To answer that question, it is necessary to examine classroom teaching.

CLASSROOM TEACHING PRACTICES

What goes on in most classrooms? There are an abundance of studies to provide glimpses behind the classroom door,[6,8,9,11,12,14,16] and show that, in general, "a school is a school is a school," regardless of location.

The classrooms observed generally looked much alike. The teacher was usually explaining or lecturing to the whole class or to a single student, often asking questions which required recall answers.

Teachers, when not lecturing, were usually supervising students who worked individually at their desks. Students were usually engaged in passive activities, involved with writing answers to questions asked by the teacher, listening to the teacher, or waiting and preparing for the next class. Despite curriculum guidelines which suggest that teachers provide for student individuality in learning rates and styles, there was little indication that individual differences were considered.

There was ample evidence that the many changes advocated by curriculum developers and recommended in curriculum guidelines are not being integrated into classroom practice. Goodlad concluded "Over the years, these ways of schooling have proved to be extraordinarily resistant to change, encouraging the view that nothing changes; there is only the appearance of change."[11:267]

In order to summarize the findings on teaching practice, it is useful to categorize them under the following generalizations:

Teaching is an isolated activity. Most teaching occurs behind closed doors in a self-contained classroom, and that is the way most teachers want it. In fact, some teachers said they could not work with another adult in the room and refused to use a teacher aide.[16] Most teachers have never observed a colleague teaching, they do not really know their fellow teachers' educational beliefs, teaching competency, or treatment of students. Teaching, it was revealed, is not discussed by many staffs, and most teachers work in total isolation.

Teachers perceive themselves to be autonomous in their classrooms. Most teachers guard the autonomy of their own classrooms, and feel threatened if their superiors make demands that reach into the classroom. Teachers recognize that they have to teach certain subjects, but how and when they do it is seen by them as their decision. Requiring teachers to plan in advance was perceived as a threat to the teacher's autonomy.[12] Visitors are not welcome in most classrooms, mainly because most teachers fear them as being critical or evaluative.

Teaching goals are vague rather than specific. Teachers, working in isolation in their own classrooms, are often vague as to their goals, and are uncertain as to whether or not they have realized certain objectives. What happens in the classroom may be radically different from the rational model: instead of a linear progression from objectives, to change, to evaluation of how objectives were met, teachers tend to allow action to precede goals. "We saw teachers begin to team teach, change their reporting procedures, create a totally new classroom atmosphere, and years later begin to talk about the goals of the school."[13:53]

Teachers work with groups, not with individuals. A reality of most classrooms is that goals must be met in a group context. Teachers are generally responsible for a class of thirty to forty students. The physical limitations imposed by such sizes force teachers to adopt certain instructional practices as a means of crowd control. Goodlad saw the classroom as "a crowded box"[11:175] within which teachers have little opportunity to work with individual students. He observed, "In the secondary schools no teacher could get to know many students well. Many students were not well known by any teacher."[11:126]

Teachers rely on textbooks and are concerned with coverage of all the content in it. Given the demands placed on today's teachers, Eisner asked, "Is it any wonder that many teachers—perhaps most—would welcome textbooks and other kinds of workbooks that in effect decide for them what children shall study, in what order, for what ends?"[8:27] The textbook provides security for both teacher and student, for it outlines the course, suggests activities, provides practice exercises and discussion questions, and even helps in the evaluation process. The trend in many schools seems to be that, "The textbook and its partner, the workbook, provide the curricular hub around which much of what is taught revolves."[8:27]

Reliance on textbooks has been shown to lead to concern with coverage of all the content in the textbook. Part of the reason for this is the way textbooks are organized. Packaged as a complete, sequential program, it conveys the idea that if children do not cover all the material, and use all the parts of the program (workbooks, practice sheets, etc.), then they are missing out on important learning activities.

Teachers have to control the class in order to teach. The important matter of classroom management, discipline, and control has been shown to exert influence on the delivery of curriculum content and the type of activities introduced in the classroom. Studies show that teachers are aware of better teaching methods than they employ, but the necessity for them to maintain control discourages the adoption of teaching strategies such as use of small groups and discovery learning. Certain realities facing classroom teachers are identified as factors contributing to discipline problems: compulsory education means that some students are in school against their will, and in addition, there is the ever-present distraction of the crowd. The classroom puts friends together in a small, crowded room, and then requires them to pay attention to the teacher and ignore each other. Maintaining discipline and control under such conditions is a time-consuming and nerve-wracking part of the teacher's job. As much as 40 percent of the teacher's time is directed toward this end.[14]

Teachers see themselves as the essential catalysts in the learning process. Teachers may limit their teaching strategies partly due to the need for classroom control, but they also base their actions on the belief that most students must be subjected to direct teacher instruction in order to learn. This may also help to explain why teachers make limited use of small groups, self-instructional non-print materials and other types of learning experiences outside the teacher-dominated, whole class teaching method. It may also help to explain why teachers do most of the talking in the classroom. Goodlad observed that teachers outtalked students by a ratio of three to one. He concluded "If teachers in the talking mode and students in the listening mode is what we want, rest assured that we have it."[11:229] Even when teachers ask students questions, they will seldom give them time to respond. Eisner[9] noted that the response time for students to answer was an average of three seconds! This point of view may also help to explain why teachers pay so little attention to independent study during school hours. The teachers observed in these studies wanted to teach, and anything which distracted students or teachers from classroom instruction was viewed as counterproductive.

Teachers prefer to teach in self-contained classrooms. Uninterrupted teaching can best occur when the classroom is self-contained and teachers can shut their doors. Teachers wanted clearly defined boundaries, a self-contained classroom, and no interference from other adults. This desire for what Lortie refers to as "boundedness,"[14:171] is undoubtedly linked to the teacher's notion of how learning occurs (the teacher as essential catalyst), the autonomy of the classroom, and the teacher's need for maintaining control. It influences the relationship teachers have with others. With parents, teachers want to determine the time and the conditions. Their relationship with the principal is more delicate. On the one hand, they recognize their need for support from the principal and yet they want to protect their own boundaries. In many schools, the practice seems to be allowing the principal hegemony over all areas of the school other than the classroom. As far as colleagues are concerned, teachers respect each other's boundaries, and tend to stay out of each other's affairs unless invited to participate.

TEACHING, CHANGE AND THE SCHOOL LIBRARY MEDIA PROGRAM

The concept of the school library media program has developed as a response to what schools are being expected to do. Documents such as *Partners in Action*,[15] and *Resource Services for Canadian Schools*,[3] developed as a response to

the needs of the curriculum. According to curriculum guides, instruction is individualized, geared to meet the learning needs and learning styles of individual students. Teachers select from many resources, in different formats, as they develop learning experiences which will help students master clearly defined objectives. Students are actively involved in the learning process. They read, write, discuss, and listen, and also view, record, photograph or videotape. One aim is to produce graduates who can cope with the information needs of the modern world, independent learners equipped with the skills required for life-long learning.

However, most schools are not meeting these expectations. There has been a change in *expectations* rather than a change in actual *practice*. Whether or not a school library resource center is seen as important and essential will depend upon what is actually happening in classrooms. Teachers who rely on textbook teaching, workbooks, and worksheets will have little need for a resource center. Students will not use it because it will be perceived (correctly) as not important in their overall evaluation. Another important factor to consider is teachers' sense of autonomy in their own classrooms. Teachers who jealously guard their classrooms will resist any attempt that appears to threaten that autonomy. Only in schools where teachers are seriously attempting to implement current expectations as expressed in curriculum guides will the school library resource center be seen as essential.

The perceived need for a school library media program, then, depends upon how serious we are about implementing current curriculum. Are classroom teachers really expected to follow current curriculum guidelines? If so, they will need considerable support. Teacher-librarians are familiar with the support needed for resource-based learning (as most of the curriculum is currently), and know that classroom teachers using that approach will require a centralized, organized collection of carefully selected resources and the specialized services provided by a fully qualified teacher-librarian. However, there is another area in which classroom teachers will need support that is perhaps not as familiar to teacher-librarians, and that is support in making a major change in teaching practice.

Major differences exist between what classroom teachers are actually *doing*, and what they are *expected* to be doing, as reflected in guidelines such as *Partners in Action*.[15]

For teachers accustomed to textbook teaching with its accompanying workbooks and practice sheets, this recommended approach will require learning how to use many resources effectively, in different formats, as part of the instructional process. If teachers are to feel comfortable with resources in different formats, and if they are to learn how and when to use them effectively, then they will need assistance.

However, to meet current expectations will also mean that teaching will no longer be an isolated activity (see table 1). If the classroom teacher is to participate as a partner with the teacher-librarian, then the whole notion of a self-contained classroom in which the teacher has full autonomy is challenged. For many teachers, it will be a major change to accept another teacher as a partner in the instructional process. And for some it will be a major change to carefully plan learning experiences based on precisely stated objectives formulated to meet the learning needs and learning styles of individual students. If teachers are to be expected to work cooperatively and incorporate resource-based teaching and learning strategies into classroom instruction, then they will need support.

Table 1
The Nature of Teaching and Expectations for Teaching as Exemplified in School Library Media Programs

Nature of Teaching	Expectations for Teaching
Isolated activity	Cooperative planning
Teacher autonomy	Team teaching
Vague goals	Precisely defined goals and objectives
Group instruction	Individualized instruction
Reliance on textbook	Variety of resources, different formats
Teacher control	Maximum freedom for the learner
Teacher as essential in the learning process	Teacher as creator of learning experiences leading to students becoming independent learners
Self-contained classrooms	Different locations

To ask teachers to change the materials they use for teaching, and the teaching approaches they use, is to require a change in their basic beliefs about how students learn. Teachers who believe that students must receive direct instruction in order to learn will find it very difficult to give students the freedom to learn independently, within carefully planned learning experiences. Many teachers will have to be shown that students can learn in situations where the teacher is more of a guide and a creator of learning experiences than a transmitter of information.

In recent years there has been a considerable body of knowledge accumulated on how best to achieve change in the school system.[1,10,16] This research has important implications for all those wishing to implement school library media programs, for it recognizes how complex such a change is, and how best to go about successful implementation.

Goodlad has been forceful in presenting the view that "the individual school is the key on which to focus for affecting improvement within the formal education system."[11,36] He, and others, recognize the classroom teacher as the central figure in implementing the curriculum, and point out that school staffs must work together for school improvement.

The consensus in the literature is that change will not occur through isolated and occasional inservice sessions. Teachers need time for guided reflection and integration; they need personal support and challenges, and they need to try out new ways of teaching in a non-threatening environment. The best place to provide this is in the school itself, with inservice involving the whole staff, including the principal, working together to improve instruction within the school.

Certain strategies were more effective than others in implementing change in the school system. Generally, the best practices are "essentially learning-by-doing."[1:28] Although "these strategies were not a panacea,"[1:28] and they may not work at all if applied separately, the following strategies did work together in an overall implementation strategy:

- concrete, teacher-specific, and ongoing training;

- classroom assistance when needed;

- opportunities for teachers to observe in classrooms where the change had already been successfully implemented;

- regular staff meetings which focus on practical problems arising from the change;

- involvement of the teachers in the development of any materials required for the change; and,

- the active involvement of the school principal (this last strategy is seen as vital for "it signaled the staff that their efforts were supported and valued."[1:30])

The teacher-librarian has an important role to play in providing the school level support that classroom teachers need if they are to live up to current expectations. The qualified teacher-librarian is in a unique position to work as a partner with the classroom teacher, so that the expert in the content to be taught (the classroom teacher) can be assisted by the expert in learning resources (the teacher-librarian). It is an impossible task, based on a naive notion of change, for the teacher-librarian within a particular school to attempt to single-handedly change teaching practice in the school. This is a complex change, and will require the active support of the principal and the involvement of the school staff. The literature on change in education reveals that change will only occur if administrators and teachers feel a definite need for it and if there is a broad base of support.

The impetus for improvement at the school level will not come from the teacher-librarian. The position has neither the authority nor the prestige to create such a demand. The impetus must arise from the recognition that good teaching requires such an approach. At the school level, the drive for change and improvement must be spearheaded by the principal. But in the long term, it is the classroom teachers who will either accept or reject the notion of teaching exemplified by the school library media program.

This does not mean that teacher-librarians have no role to play in the change process. Indeed, they have very important roles to play. Their first, and probably most important role, is that they interpret and communicate to teachers, students, administrators, and parents what a quality school library media program should be. This demands that they fully understand it themselves. They must also be mindful that they will be judged by the tasks they perform. Teachers who only see the teacher-librarian performing clerical or technical duties will perceive the role as only clerical or technical. If teacher-librarians want to be taken seriously as professional "partners in action," then the literature on change is clear that they must act like professionals.

Those who presently work as teacher-librarians must be enthusiastic optimists, willing to prove to colleagues that different teaching approaches can work. They need to understand the curriculum and the teacher's world, so that they can work with the classroom teacher to help implement the school's program. They need to understand the nature of educational change, so that they can function as change agents at the school level. Such people need extroverted personalities, allowing them to work well with others and to have the confidence to try out innovations. Being on the forefront of expectations in the curriculum, teacher-librarians have a responsibility to understand what is expected, to communicate this to their colleagues, and to show how a school library media program is necessary to provide the essential resources and services that teachers need to teach and students need to learn.

REFERENCES

1. Berman, P. and M. W. McLaughlin. *Federal Programs Supporting Educational Change, Vol. VIII: Implementing and Sustaining Innovations.* The Rand Corporation, 1978. (ERIC Document Reproduction Service No. ED 159289)

2. Block, R. "We Already Know Our Problems Out Here in the Field." *Phi Delta Kappan*, volume 65, number 3 (1983), page 183.

3. Branscombe, F. and H. Newson, editors. *Resource Services for Canadian Schools.* McGraw-Hill Ryerson, 1977.

4. Brown, W. "Education Spending Cuts: Pulling Up the Ladder on Young Canadians." *ATA Magazine*, volume 65, number 2 (1985), pages 4-7.

5. Burke, R. J. and C. Bolf. "Economic Recession and the Quality of Education." *ATA Magazine*, volume 65, number 2 (1985), pages 7-11.

6. Crocker, R. K. *The Use of Classroom Time: A Descriptive Analysis.* Memorial University of Newfoundland, 1983.

7. Crocker, R. K. "Determinants of Implementation of an Elementary Science Program." *Journal of Research in Science Teaching*, volume 21, number 2 (1983), pages 211-20.

8. Eisner, E. *The Educable Imagination.* Macmillan, 1979.

9. Eisner, E. "The Kind of Schools We Need." *Educational Leadership*, volume 41, number 2 (1983), pages 48-55.

10. Fullan, M. *The Meaning of Educational Change.* OISE Press, 1982.

11. Goodlad, J. *A Place Called School.* McGraw-Hill, 1984.

12. Jackson, R. W. *Life in Classrooms.* Holt, Rinehart and Winston, 1968.

13. Lieberman, A. and D. A. Shiman. "The Stages of Change in Elementary School Settings" in *The Power to Change: Issues for the Innovative Educator*, edited by C. M. Culver and G. J. Hoban. McGraw-Hill, 1973.

14. Lortie, D. *Schoolteacher: A Sociological Study.* University of Chicago Press, 1975.

15. *Partners in Action: The Library Resource Centre in the School Curriculum.* Ontario Ministry of Education, 1982.

16. Sarason, S. *The Culture of the School and the Problem of Change.* 2d edition. Allyn & Bacon, 1982.

The Integrated Approach to School Library Programming

James Henri

There is little doubt that Canada is at the very forefront in the development of an effective role for teacher-librarians in schools. In recent years two outstanding documents have been written in two quite different Canadian provinces, both supplying a partnership and integrated approach to the role of teacher-librarian and the use of learning resources in schools.

It is sometimes argued that one cannot successfully transplant developments and innovations in education from one country to another. However, in the case of Canada and Australia there are clear similarities in the philosophy of education and in the goals of education and much of the thrust of the Canadian publications *Partners in Action* and *Focus on Learning* can (and should) be applied to Australia.

The 1981 policy document *Our Schools and Their Purposes* presented the aims for South Australian schools as helping students develop:

- lively inquiring minds, a love of learning, and a willingness to apply effort to worthwhile tasks

- the ability to think rationally

- the use of the imagination

- powers of creative self-expression

- powers of judgment

- physical and mental health

- self-confidence, a sense of worth, and respect and consideration for others

- a coherent set of personal and social values and a commitment to them

- decision making and problem solving skills

- an understanding of themselves and their world

- competence in intellectual, social and physical skills

- knowledge of skills relevant to adult life and employment.

These goals are not only quite similar to the goals of education as articulated in other Australian states but are also surprisingly similar to those of the Canadian provinces. The Ontario goals of education, for example, are designed to help each student develop:

- a responsiveness to the dynamic process of learning

- resourcefulness, adaptability, and creativity in learning and living

- the basic knowledge and skills needed to comprehend and express ideas through words, numbers, and other symbols

- physical fitness and good health

- satisfaction from participating and from sharing the participation of others in various forms of artistic expression

- a feeling of self-worth

- an understanding of the role of the individual within the family and the role of the family within the society

- skills that contribute to self-reliance in solving practical problems in everyday life

- an acceptance of personal responsibility in society at the local, national, and international levels

- esteem for the customs, cultures, and beliefs of a wide variety of societal groups

- skills and attitudes that will lead to satisfaction and productivity in the world of work

- respect for the environment and a commitment to the wise use of resources

- values related to personal, ethical, or religious beliefs and to the common welfare of society.

If we accept the view that the goals of education in Australia and Canada are very similar, does this sameness in goals imply that successful attainment of those goals could be reached through the use of similar approaches to education? Certainly the writers of *Partners in Action* and *Our Schools and Their Purposes* have very similar ideas about learning.

> Formal classroom learning is not the only kind that occurs in schools. Much learning occurs outside the classroom, and young people are a powerful influence on their fellow students.

Likewise

> All learners should be guided towards the situation where they assume much responsibility for their own learning. Asking questions, raising problems, and being encouraged to think critically and positively, while increasingly accepting responsibility for one's own learning, are important steps towards a person's maturity.

The trend in education is towards the view that teaching and learning are quite distinct activities and that either can occur without the other. Now there is nothing much new in this, but what is relatively new is a concurrent belief that the student not only needs to develop certain chunks of information/knowledge, but also needs to learn appropriate ways to learn effectively. There is therefore an increasing emphasis on and value attached to the process of learning and the ways of knowing. These processes have a value perhaps as great, perhaps greater than the student's achievement of learning outcomes and knowledge. The question is "is it more important to know who holds the world record for the 100 metres dash or to know how to locate that information?" If this trend is pushed towards the limit it would be easy to distinguish between the 'one time' teachers who had a set of facts to impart to each student each day to the 'now time' teacher who establishes an environment in which children are encouraged to discover the world. In line with this thinking the Ontario Ministry of Education views the learner as:

> an active participant in education who gains satisfaction from the dynamics of learning. The concept of the learner as a mere processor of information has been replaced by the image of a self-motivated, self-directed problem-solver,

aware of both the processes and uses of learning and deriving a sense of self-worth and confidence from a variety of accomplishments.

Although the goals of education and the predominant view of learning held in Canada and Australia are very similar one thing is quite different. The writers of *Our Schools and Their Purposes* make no reference to the school library program or to the teacher-librarian and make only passing comment on the role of school-based learning resources in the promotion and achievement of goals in education. The connection may be quite obvious to a teacher-librarian but not quite so obvious to many educators and classroom teachers. Not only do the writers of both *Partners in Action* and *Focus on Learning* talk about the role of the teacher-librarian but they also provide a bridge between the goals of education for their particular province and the expected learning outcomes that a school curriculum is designed to achieve.

> Resource-based learning is a concept that provides the teacher with a holistic approach for designing curriculum and acts as a bridge between Ontario's goals for education and the classroom program. Teachers may select from a wide range of *learning activities, locations* or *facilities*, and *resources* to create curriculum plans that actively involve the participants. Choices from these three components are made by the teacher in response to the learning needs and styles of individual students.

The resource based approach to teaching and learning is ideal because it provides the players in the education game with a wide range of choices. Educational programs which involve the use of a wide variety of resources to satisfy curriculum objectives can:

- Provide for individual differences in rate and style of learning.

- Maximize opportunities for exceptional students.

- Provide opportunities for creativity.

- Communicate factual content and enhance the learning of facts and concepts through oral, pictorial, and written clues.

- Motivate students to acquire the skills required for independent and lifelong learning.

- Familiarize students with the use of modern technology as a learning tool.

- Provide a link between the classroom and the outside world.

- Develop the learner's self-confidence, independence, and feelings of self-worth.

- Help students appreciate and enjoy various forms of artistic expression such as music, literature, and film.

Through the linking of resource-based learning to the effective achievement of education objectives, a door is opened for the teacher-librarian who is the prime manager of school-based learning resources. Even within this environment, the impact that the teacher-librarian has on the curriculum is not guaranteed to be large but certainly in a situation where teacher-directed learning is preferred to resource-based learning the role of the teacher-librarian is likely to be minimal.

Does it matter how much effect the teacher-librarian has on the curriculum? Does it matter whether or not departments of education articulate and formalize policy in support of resource based learning? John Caldwell has argued that it does matter. His view is that if we do not support resource-based learning, we are, in effect, not meeting the individual needs and learning styles of all our students. He stated further:

> One thing is for certain: all children do not learn equally well with the same learning materials or activities. We cannot expect those students who do well on a written research assignment to do equally well on a practical or hands-on activity. In most of our library resource centers, certain students are at an advantage because we organize our library resource centers and our cooperatively planned units around what is most accessible to us. Since the largest percentages of our collections by far are composed of print material, activities are based on print and thus the learning styles of particular students are nurtured. Unfortunately, we have other students who do not perform as effectively with print-based activities. Their needs are not being met.

Caldwell's argument is that resource-based learning is essential but on its own it is not enough. It is also essential to give due consideration to learning styles. Every person has a preferred learning style which reveals the way s/he perceives and orders the world.

There are also strong indications that educators tend to teach according to a preferred style. Adopting a resource-based approach in conjunction with an attention to learning styles is likely to overcome some of the bias that is shown by teachers towards certain types of learning materials and activities.

Figure 1 illustrates the idea of the library program (in terms of inputs, processes and outputs) responding to the goals of education (formulated in terms of student needs) in order to create learning outcomes both directly from the library program itself as well as indirectly through the school's instructional program. The greater the effect that the library program has on student outcomes, the more valuable the library program in terms of education dollars.

The problem here is that it does not provide any clues in terms of how the library program should link in with the school program. Such a model can be greatly affected by other factors. For example resource-based learning will be greatly inhibited in a school which time-tables the library. Flexible scheduling and resource-based learning go together hand in glove. Likewise the model does not help us decide the best arrangements in terms of the role of the teacher-librarian or on

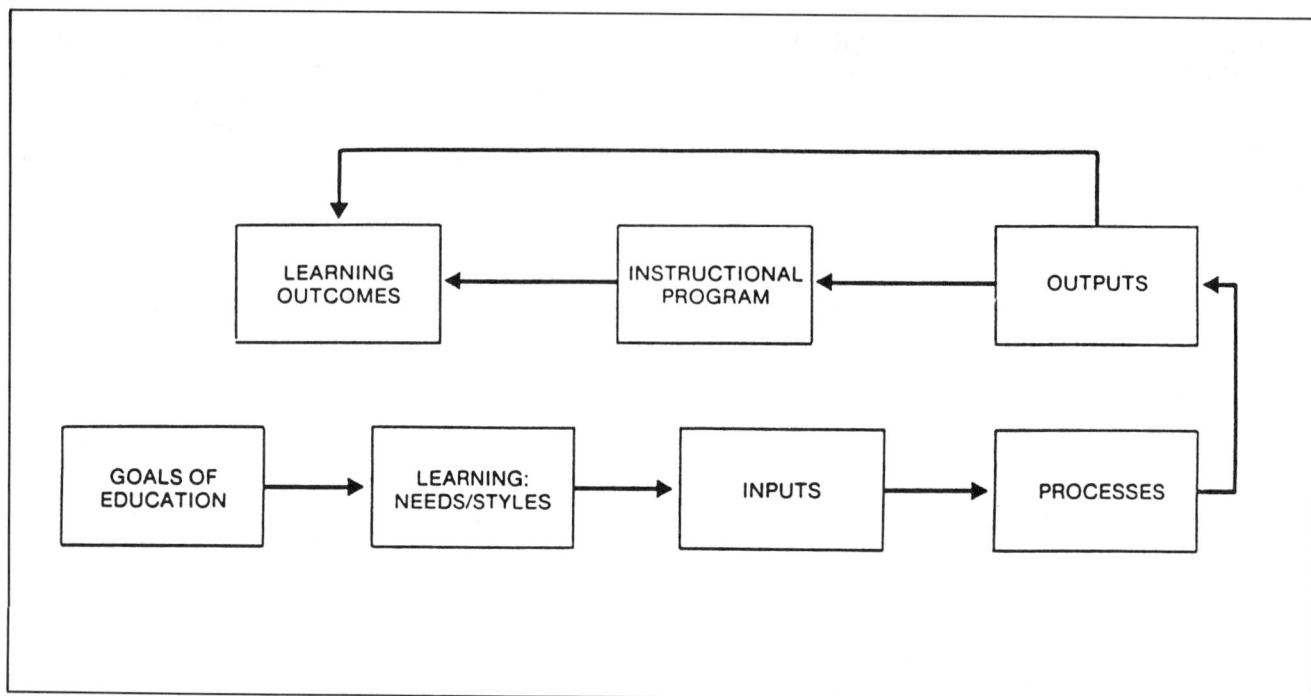

Fig. 1. The School Library Program and Learning

the appropriate interaction between teachers and teacher-librarian. Let us then attempt to rebuild Figure 1 into a more useful model.

The teacher-librarian is likely to be the school expert on learning resources: what learning resources exist, how to acquire them, how to organize them, how to use them effectively. So the teacher-librarian must be actively involved in the process of deciding what resources are likely to support certain curriculum objectives and also be used to help frame curriculum objectives in light of his/her knowledge of learning resources. That is, the teacher-librarian should be an active participant in school decisions about learning content. Likewise, since the teacher-librarian is an information specialist, it is essential that the teacher-librarian be involved in decisions about appropriate learning skills. What 'information' skills will children need before they will be able to do unit x, y, z? If a school has one teacher-librarian it would not be feasible for that person to spend every working hour on curriculum matters but certainly this role must be fundamental. Other time spent by the teacher-librarian should support this role rather than detract from it.

Ken Haycock has argued that the teacher-librarian's major task is to work with classroom teachers to plan, develop and implement units of study which integrate research and study skills (information skills):

Teaching involves three professional functions—the ability to diagnose learning needs, to design programs to meet those needs, and to assess the degree to which the programs have been successful. For the teacher-librarian to be successful, these are done in conjunction and consultation with the classroom teacher.

Ken Haycock has provided the clue which is needed to link the philosophy and practice of resource-based learning to an effective use of the teacher-librarian and the library program. He is in essence advocating a cooperative programming model for the teacher-librarian. It is this cooperative model which has largely revolutionized the perceived and actual role of the teacher-librarian in many Canadian schools. (Ken Haycock is, in my opinion, the world leader in the school librarianship debate today.) Yet because the concept of cooperative planning is relatively new it is still somewhat loose and unrefined. The Calgary (Alberta) Board of Education for example stated that there is really a continuum of shades or types of cooperative planning. This is illustrated by figure 2.

The Calgary Board agrees that each type of cooperative planning has a place in a school library program. However, they believe that if the library program is integral to the achievement of expected student learning outcomes, then

	TYPE 1	TYPE 2	TYPE 3	TYPE 4
DEFINITION	Consultation leading to provision of resources.	Consultation leading to enhancement of classroom program.	Consultation leading to enhancement of classroom program through team planning/teaching.	Consultation leading to equally enhanced resource center and classroom programs through co-operative planning, teaching and evaluating.
TEACHER-LIBRARIANS ROLE	Provides resources upon request. or Suggests resources.	Provides resources and related 'utilization ideas'. Informally contributes to classroom program.	Slots into planning/teaching situations as requested, needed or appropriate.	Full partner with teacher in planning, teaching and evaluating
TEACHERS ROLE	Asks for resources which are often taken to the classroom. or Responds to suggestions re suitable resources.	Talks with librarian about classroom needs/program	Teacher develops unit/program and consults with teacher-librarian in regard to specific activities that will be planned/implemented cooperatively.	Cooperatively plans, teaches and evaluates unit with teacher-librarian.
RESOURCE CENTER PROGRAM PROFILE	Can range from "skills in isolation" to "parallel" to no program at all. Skill development through 'literature' appreciation is one recommended approach.	Can range from "skills in isolation" to "parallel" to no program at all. Skill development through 'literature' appreciation is one recommended approach.	Library program and classroom program are inter-related - more conscious integration of library-related strategies.	Complete integration of resource center and classroom program.

Fig. 2. Types of Cooperative Planning

types three and four will be in evidence throughout the school year across the school curriculum. There is in essence nothing mysterious about cooperative program planning. But as a concept it provides an excellent measure of the level of activity and influence the teacher-librarian, through the library program, has across the school curriculum.

We often talk about an effective school library program. But what is an *effective* program? Many writers seem to believe that an effective school library program is measured by the personality of the teacher-librarian. Others would say that the circulation rate is a measure of an effective library program. Many other suggestions could be offered. In 1984, Alberta Education laid down the following policy directive:

> Students in Alberta schools should have access to an effective school library program integrated with instructional programs to provide improved opportunities for student achievement of the Goals of Basic Education for Alberta.

In 1985, Alberta Education published *Focus on Learning* which outlines a recommended model for developing an effective, integrated school library program. Figure 3 is a slightly modified version of this model.

The integrated model consists of three components—instruction, development and management—with instruction and student outcomes being the primary focal points. Excellence in the instruction component is impossible, however, without the groundwork of developmental planning and the day to day fulfilment of management tasks:

Direct interaction between the teacher-librarian and the learner in a formal or informal instructional setting forms the instruction component. The purpose of this interaction is to develop student competency in the retrieval, processing and sharing of information and to encourage student appreciation of knowledge and culture.

Included in the development area are program building activities initiated and carried out by teachers and teacher-librarians. These activities include a needs assessment based on the current situation and an ongoing consultative process of instructional program planning. Careful evaluation and selection of resources and professional in-servicing serve to develop further the integrated program. Strength in this component lays the foundation for instructional excellence for students.

The management component completes the triad. Qualified personnel must manage and administer the day-to-day operation of an integrated school library program. Their managerial efficiency ensures that the instruction and development components mesh smoothly. Support for instructional programs is provided in the form of finances, personnel and facilities. On-site resources are ordered, processed, cataloged and circulated to teachers and students. Sharing agreements with other libraries and community agencies provide sources for additional materials and services to meet instructional needs.

At the heart of the model and integrating each of the component parts lies the concept of cooperative planning and implementation. Cooperation between administrators,

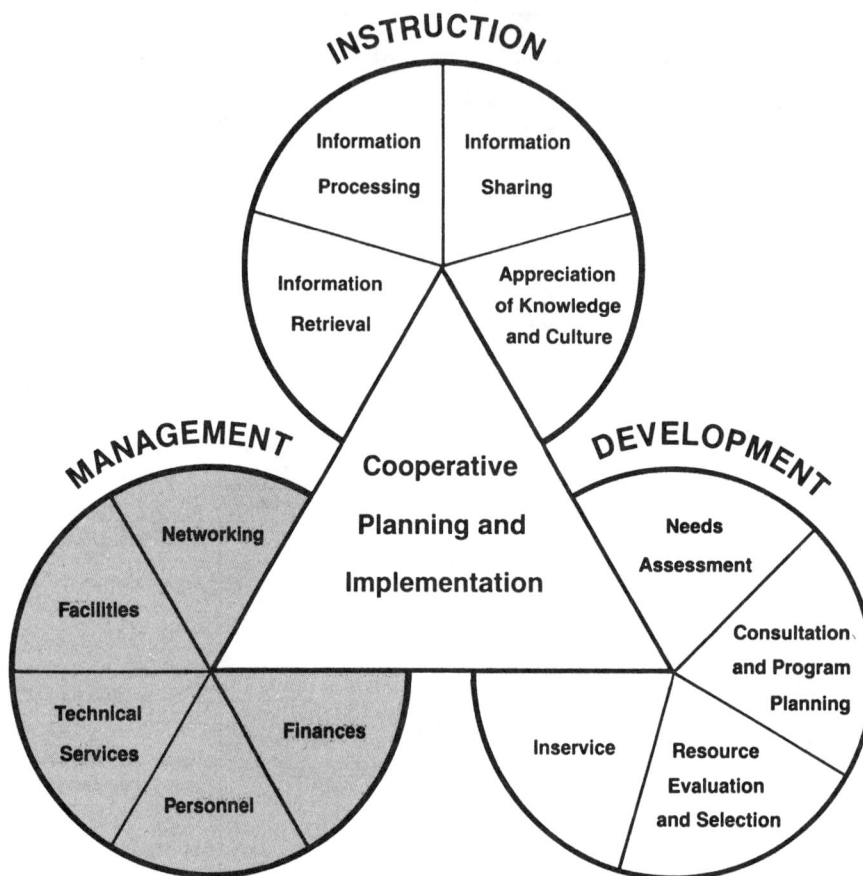

Fig. 3. An Integrated Program Model for School Libraries

teachers and teacher-librarians is the nucleus of commitment and creates energy that cohesively binds the components of instruction, development and management. The more dynamic and pervasive the form of cooperative planning the more integrated the library program will be in the overall school program and philosophy.

The point is that cooperative planning and teaching is not yet another role for the teacher-librarian. It is rather what has been shown in Canada to be the most effective way of integrating the players—administrators, teachers, teacher-librarian, students—in a resource-based approach to education in order to maximize the actual achievement of student learning outcomes. The teacher-librarian's rationale continues to be the maximization of student learning outcomes. Cooperative planning provides the means to that end.

Is it possible to achieve the goals of education without the implementation of an integrated school library program? Given the information explosion and the range of preferred learning styles, it is doubtful. Is is possible to have a fully integrated school library program without a commitment to cooperative program planning and teaching? Given the lessons of the last two decades of school libraries, this too is doubtful. How does a school implement a policy and program of cooperative program planning and teaching? Certainly the intensive three-day program offered by Ken Haycock and Carol-Ann Haycock lays the groundwork. The two month

staff development program at six sites in Australia and New Zealand by this team provided specific strategies and plans for building a more solid foundation for school library development. Through a mutually supportive network and planned follow-up and coaching, the model should take hold, and augurs well for the future.

RESOURCES

Provincial/State Documents

Focus on Learning: An Integrated Program Model for School Libraries. Edmonton: Alberta Education, 1985.

Issues and Directions. Toronto: Ontario Ministry of Education and Ministry of Colleges and Universities, 1980.

Our Schools and Their Purposes: Into the 80s. Adelaide: Education Department of South Australia, 1981.

Partners in Action: The Library Resource Centre in the School Curriculum. Toronto: Ontario Ministry of Education, 1982.

Policy, Guidelines, Procedures and Standards for School Libraries in Australia. Edmonton: Alberta Education, 1984.

OTHER SOURCES

Beswick, Norman. *Resource-based Learning.* London: Heinemann, 1977.

Butler, Kathleen. *Learning and Teaching Style: In Theory and Practice.* Maynard, Mass.: Gabriel Systems, 1984.

Caldwell, John. "Learning." *Reviewing Librarian.* Volume 10, Number 4 (Summer, 1985), pages 122-24.

Haycock, Carol-Ann. "Developing the School Resource Center Program: A Systematic Approach." *Emergency Librarian.* Volume 12, Number 1 (September-October, 1984), pages 9-16.

Haycock, Carol-Ann. "Information Skills in the Curriculum: Developing a School-based Continuum." *Emergency Librarian.* Volume 13, Number 1 (September-October, 1985), pages 11-17.

Haycock, Ken. "Strengthening the Foundations for Teacher-Librarianship." *School Library Media Quarterly.* Volume 13, Number 2 (Spring, 1985), pages 102-109.

Henri, James. "Teacher and Teacher-Librarian: Kinship in Curriculum Development." *Orana.* Volume 21, Number 4 (November, 1985), pages 165-69.

Irving, Ann. *Study and Information Skills Across the Curriculum.* London: Heinemann, 1985.

Knight, Ron and Alan Knight. "Input—Joint Planning: Output—Super Science Projects." *The Bookmark,* Journal of the British Columbia Teacher-librarians' Association. Volume 26. Number 3 (March, 1985), pages 40-45.

McCarthy, Bernice. *The 4mat System: Teaching to Learning Styles with Right/Left Mode Techniques.* Oak Brook, Ill.: Excel, 1980.

Soon, Gerald. "Cooperative Program Planning and Teaching: The Implementation of a Program for Effective Instruction." *The Bookmark,* Journal of the British Columbia Teacher-librarians' Association, Volume 26, Numbers 4 & 5 (May, 1985), pages 153-75.

Teaching Students How to Learn: Ideas for Teaching Information Skills. Hobart: Education Department of Tasmania, 1984.

Developing the School Resource Centre Program: A Systematic Approach

Carol-Ann Haycock

INTRODUCTION

The need for clearly defined approaches to developing a resource-based program is expressed frequently, but university classes and articles are too often of the "glad tidings" or "how I run my library good" nature. The three- to five-year plan outlined here refers to a resource centre program based on cooperative program planning with colleagues to develop, teach, and evaluate units of study in a flexibly scheduled resource centre.

This approach necessitates that the teacher-librarian clearly understand and be able to articulate this role, and have a strong commitment to it. The major function of the role is to plan, develop, and teach programs cooperatively with classroom teachers as equal teaching partners. To suggest that this is but one facet of the role, or one that takes place after the resource centre is made technically perfect, or one that takes place at a different level—once teachers have been "won over"—is to move it from a central focus to a peripheral position.

Two common attitudes tend to characterize teacher-librarians who do not have a clearly defined role that is internalized. First, there are those who, because they presume rejection, continue to function as reactors rather than initiators. Second, there are those who hold the view that they must start "where the teachers are at."

Each of these types operate from positions of servitude or relative powerlessness because they lack not only a clear understanding of this specialized role, but also of the process of change itself.

The very nature of the role of the teacher-librarian is that of initiator and change agent. This includes not only encouraging teacher and student use of the resource centre, but also involvement as an equal partner in planning for research and study skill development and language improvement. A jointly planned and taught program such as this often involves a change in the teaching strategies and learning activities commonly used in the school. The collaborative input and involvement of teachers becomes essential for a successful resource centre program.

It is important for teacher-librarians to be aware of both the formal and informal structure of the school and to be prepared to work at both levels, particularly since the fate of most programs is decided at the informal level. The "informal covenant" or agreement that exists between administrators and teachers regarding the day-to-day operations of the school supports the administrator as spokesperson for the school and grants some decision-making power regarding school policies and programs; the teacher, however, maintains final authority in the classroom and expects (and gets) administrative support for instructional decisions. Any school program then needs a two-level implementation plan—administrators are critical in the adoption phase of a program while teachers are critical in the implementation phase.

THREE PHASES OF DEVELOPMENT

The developmental approach is described in three phases. Throughout these phases, strategies for change and a multi-level plan for implementation are interwoven.

Phase I

1. *Assess The Current Situation*

Knowledge of the present status, behaviour, and expectations for people and programs in the school is important. Analyze the strengths and weaknesses of the facility, collection, and budget. Also analyze the administration, teaching staff, support staff, student population, and community. Identify key people on staff. On any given staff, ten percent "set the tone" and "run the school." They have a lot of power, whether they recognize it or not. Support from people in these positions is essential for successful change. Identify key programs or subject areas in the school and look for entry points into them. The focus might be on the effective use of existing materials for a new social studies program or an emphasis on inquiry skills in the science program, or the need for a sustained silent reading program. Based on this assessment, identify the discrepancies between the current and the desired resource centre program.

2. *Define the Role*

One of the major tasks in the development and implementation of any new program is to define the program itself and the roles and responsibilities of those to be involved. This is also an important step when the teacher-librarian is new to the school. Never presume that the role of the resource centre and the teacher-librarian is understood. Similarly, never confuse support for the teacher-librarian as an individual with understanding of, and commitment to, the *role* of the teacher-librarian.

Roles and responsibilities need to be defined formally, through discussion with the principal, through in-service sessions, and through staff meeting presentations. In all cases,

the purpose is to provide information and seek support. (Seeking permission is a dangerous approach! What if the answer is "no"?) Adopting a collaborative approach, assuming a partnership and a trial period, asking for a chance to try out a role or an approach with teacher and administrator support is a much more successful way to gain acceptance and bring about program adoption. For example, you might conclude an orientation for teachers by saying, "My major goal for this term is to plan just one unit with each of you. I hope you will support me in this. I'll get in touch with each of you tomorrow to schedule some planning time."

Definition of the role of the resource centre and the teacher-librarian should also take place informally, through the school's daily bulletin, a corner in the monthly newsletter, displays of new materials, and over coffee or lunch in the staffroom.

3. *Establish Guidelines*

Two sets of guidelines can serve the teacher-librarian well: guidelines for flexible scheduling and guidelines for cooperative planning and resource sharing.

Guidelines for flexible scheduling should specify that:

(1) Cooperatively developed programs take precedence for teacher-librarian time and available space.

(2) Classes are not booked on a regular (every Tuesday at 9:30) basis.

(3) Total class bookings presume cooperative planning between the teacher-librarian and teacher and that the two are functioning as partners in the teaching and supervision of the class.

(4) Small group bookings may involve cooperative planning followed by either the teacher-librarian and students working together, or independent work on the part of the students for which space and materials have been made available.

(5) Individual students are welcome at any time with a library tag; in this instance, the classroom teacher assumes responsibility and is reasonably confident that the student understands and can carry out the specified task, whether it is to select a book for recreational reading or to find information. The teacher also establishes a specific time limit with the student.

Guidelines for cooperative program planning and resource sharing can be provided through the use of a monthly topics sheet. The topics sheet should be a "two-minute item" for teachers—filling in the topics to be covered in each subject area for the upcoming month and checking off whether or not resources are required and planning time needed. (See Appendix A for example.) Resources are pulled or secured and shared among teachers on the basis of the topics sheets submitted each month. Through this approach, one teacher doesn't end up with all the dinosaur books or all the resources on insects while others go without. The topics sheets are compiled into a monthly program chart which is distributed to the entire staff. The administrator's copy is asterisked to indicate the teacher-librarian's involvement in programs at each grade level. This monthly program chart indicates the

TOPICS

For the month of _____

Teacher _____

Please return by _____

Language Arts	
Social Studies	
Science	
Math	
Other	
Support Materials Needed	Library
	School
Planning Time	Do you wish to arrange **PLANNING TIME** for cooperative teaching? Yes _____ No _____

Appendix A

curriculum that is being taught throughout the school at a glance. It facilitates the communication and sharing of ideas among staff as well as the sharing of resources.

The rationale for, and benefits of, the topics sheet should be discussed first with the administrator and then outlined, with examples, in a presentation to the staff. Most teachers are very receptive to this approach, and even a partial return of forms means that the teacher-librarian has more information than would have otherwise been the case.

The topics sheet facilitates cooperative planning in both a formal and an informal sense. There is a place provided on the sheet for teachers to indicate whether or not they would like planning time. Entry points into other programs can often be identified and informal approaches to teachers made on this basis. One of the advantages of this system is that it provides specific information for the teacher-librarian and points of discussion with teachers, thus eliminating the "how can I help you?" shopkeeper approach to teacher-librarianship.

4. *Communicate Often and Well*

Regular communication with the administrator, as well as with staff members, is of paramount importance. Effective communication can create an awareness of, and support for, the adoption of the program. Possible strategies for implementing changes, based on assessment of the current situation, should also be discussed. Through such discussion, priorities can be established and both teacher-librarian and administrator can concentrate efforts in specific areas.

Focus on program strengths and weaknesses, not individuals and personalities. Keep in mind that the most successful approach is to emphasize the positive aspects of the program and the progress being made *before* introducing the problem or issue to be discussed. Remember—all of the problems in the school end up at the principal's door! Seek advice, but don't presume the administrator is going to take action. Be prepared to act on suggested approaches or solutions if they will indeed enhance the program.

5. *Start with One Teacher (Start Small ... Think Big)*

Based on the initial assessment, identify the teachers who appear to be most receptive to new ideas and programs or with whom you succeed in establishing rapport quickly. Start with them to ensure that you and they meet with success! Never underestimate the "ripple effect"—accept small increments of change and avoid large-scale disappointment. Keep the developmental approach clearly in focus!

Be sure to write up units of study which are developed with teachers and keep these on file as a basis for sharing with others and to ensure availability for use in subsequent years. This is well worth the extra time and effort in the long run; it provides a foundation for continued development and saves time when redesigning and revising units and programs to use again. The importance of this component cannot be over-emphasized.

6. *Establish a School-Based Skills Continuum*

It is essential that a continuum of research and study skills be developed and agreed to by staff to ensure that some skills are not being omitted, that a developmental approach is being taken to skills coverage, and that skills instruction is being integrated with, and embedded in, the curriculum. This provides a framework for cooperative planning and a needed structure for resource-based programs.

Teacher involvement in this process is crucial. If teachers work as partners in developing a continuum that is relevant to the teaching and learning situation in a specific school, they will assume some responsibility for skill development. (The term "library skills" is both too narrow in scope and inappropriate to this process; it suggests a regular dose of skills given by the librarian, in the library, in total isolation. The terms "research and study skills" or "information skills" help to overcome this problem.) Appropriate aspects of cultural and literary appreciation might also be included in this type of continuum.

The following five-step process has been initiated and successfully worked through with several staffs in order to develop a school-based, research and study skills continuum:

Step 1: Select or devise a research and study skills list as a starting point for staff to react to. Provincial or state curriculum guides, school district guidelines, or any one of a variety of standard sources of resource and study skills lists might be used. The simpler the list, the easier the task.

Step 2: Don't ask each staff member to react to a long skills list initially. Provide the appropriate sections to groups of staff. For example, ask primary teachers to react to a list of primary skills and intermediate teachers to react to a list of intermediate skills. Work with grade levels or primary/intermediate groups, or subject groups, depending on the size and nature of the staff. Meet with each group, in sequential grade level order, to come to a group/grade level consensus.

Have each grade level provide input/feedback both a grade level below and above the level at which they are presently teaching.

Step 3: Seek ratification from the primary and intermediate/junior sections of staff. Meet with each group and look at the continuum for each grade level within that group.

Step 4: Submit the rough draft to the total staff for reaction. Discuss the "transition" years, such as grades 3-4, 6-7, and 9-10, in particular.

Step 5: Seek final staff ratification of the document as a statement of expectations for which they accept some responsibility.

The teacher-librarian has several important roles to play in this process—initiator, partner, and liaison, among them. Regardless of the particular expertise which the teacher-librarian may bring to this task, it is important to keep these roles in mind, or teachers may be inclined to view the final product as the teacher-librarian's list and, therefore, not a shared responsibility.

7. *Be Accountable*

Establish credibility and support through regular reporting procedures. A monthly written report to the administrator might consist of a listing of planning meetings, cooperative programs, and other professional undertakings, such as committee involvement and in-service presented or attended. Technical or support services which have involved a considerable amount of teacher-librarian time or energy might also be listed in this category; examples might include the preparation of major book and media orders, or reorganization of the audio-visual collection. Written reporting can also provide the basis for oral reporting to both staff and administration.

An annual report is mandatory for teacher-librarians who are operating a flexibly scheduled resource centre based on cooperative program planning, whether or not it is required by the district or administrator. The annual report serves several purposes. It provides an overview of the year, highlights the progress made in program development, and assists the teacher-librarian in feeling some sense of closure at year end. The annual report also serves as the basis for establishing program priorities for the following year.

If cooperative program planning and teaching is the framework for the resource centre program, then the emphasis in the annual report should be placed here. A chart of cooperatively developed programs can be drawn as a major part of the annual reporting procedure. The chart provides an overview of the year and highlights the strengths and weaknesses of the program. It serves as a useful discussion paper with the administrator. It can also be used to facilitate sharing of program ideas among staff. (See Appendix B for example.)

The various strategies described for Phase I can be accomplished over a period of a year to eighteen months, provided there is effective, continuing communication with the administrator and no "waffling" on the part of the teacher-librarian. Strategies for Phase II extend and build on those outlined in Phase I.

Phase II

1. *Be High Profile*

The teacher-librarian must be as visible, accessible and involved as possible in order to be viewed as a professional *teaching* colleague. Continue to initiate and/or provide in-service for staff. Provide an in-service session for new teachers at the beginning of the year and invite all teachers—and be sure that the administrator attends. Provide in-service for student teachers. There are double dividends here. Student teachers provide one more avenue to working with staff. And who knows—one of those student teachers may be a colleague one day!

Where teacher-librarians are part-time, work in two different schools, or in a situation where there are multiple buildings on site, post and distribute a timetable, indicating "locations" for morning coffee and lunch breaks. Times and locations for planning with teachers should also be established.

Become a member of the professional development committee, or other key committees in the school. Is there a school budget committee? How are budget decisions made? Is there a school interviewing committee? There is a sound rationale for the teacher-librarian being a member of this committee. If in fact the teacher-librarian is expected to plan and work with all teachers on staff, then it seems only reasonable to have some involvement in the decisions made regarding the hiring of new staff members. This involvement may be in a variety of forms. If a staff interviewing committee exists, the

teacher-librarian should be a member. If it is a committee of one—the administrator—then the process of interviewing for new staff members and the criteria by which decisions are made are still worth discussing. Perhaps the administrator would include a question about resource centre use in his or her interview format! (Examples: "Can you tell me how you've made use of the resource centre in your teaching?" "How have you worked with the teacher-librarian?" "How have you ensured coverage of the necessary research and study skills?") Through questions such as these, the administrator will have an idea of the candidate's experience with, and attitude towards, resource centre use. The administrator is essentially saying, "I feel the resource centre is important in this school."

Establish a profile with the community. Set an objective to attend all parent meetings, or every second one, or select those you feel are important and be there. Arrange to make at least one presentation to the parent group each year. Make every effort to find out what their questions, concerns, and perceived needs are. Communicate through interpreters if necessary in a multi-ethnic community and provide pamphlets and written messages in translation. One of the most effective means of addressing parent groups is through a brief slide presentation. Let parents see their children at work in the resource centre.

Seek out adult volunteers in the community. Be sure to talk to them about the role of the teacher-librarian and resource-based programs in the school. Adults who give their time are often the community members who have a wide sphere of influence.

Establish liaison with the local public library branch. Invite the children's librarian to tell stories, give booktalks, collaborate on a puppet show, and explain the services of the public library. Encourage student and class visits to the public library.

Maintain visibility through report card inserts—a bookmark will do! Send notes home with student library monitors. When assessing student work in cooperatively planned and taught programs, always comment on the work and sign your name. That always gets home!

2. *Change the Approach/Not the Tune*

Continue to meet with the administrator on a *regular* basis. Be careful not to stop at the "awareness level" and silent support! Place the emphasis in Phase II on the administrator's role regarding expectations of and for teachers. It is unreasonable to expect that the teacher-librarian will succeed in working well with all teachers on a staff without administrative support. If the resource centre program is viewed as a partnership, there will be some expectation that classroom teachers will work with the teacher-librarian to ensure adequate development of research and study skills, and effective resource centre use, on the part of the students for whom they are primarily responsible. The only place this expectation is going to come from is the administration.

Active, positive, administrative support can increase teacher commitment to a successful resource centre program. Suggest subtle ways that the administrator might commend a staff member for a program that has been planned. Visiting the resource centre while the program is in operation, a note in the teacher's mail box, a word in passing in the hallway, or, better still, in the staffroom where other staff members will

COOPERATIVE PROGRAM PLANNING AND TEACHING - THE YEAR IN REVIEW										
GRADE	SEPT	OCT	NOV	DEC	JAN	FEB	MAR	APR	MAY	JUNE
K	Orientation (Ba,Bu) 3 sessions			Bears theme stories & listening centre (Bu) 4 sessions	Chinese New Year stories (Ba,Bu) 3 sessions	Dragon stories (Ba,Bu) 3 sessions		Farm Animals stories and (4 sessions)	theme collage	
1	Orientation (J,H,R) 3 sessions					Gr. 1,2,3 Dennis Lee program at V.P.L. 3 sessions			Research project/Pets (J) 4 groups/5 sessions each	
2	Orientation (Pi,M,Pa) 3 sessions			Jacob Two-Two Day (M,Pa)	Mammals Research (H) 3 groups/4 sessions each	Space Research(E) 3 groups/5 sessions each				
3	Orientation (PI) 3 sessions Dictionary (Pi) 6 sessions		Dictionary Skills (PI) 3 groups/8 sessions each			Reptiles research group (F) 7 sessions	Chocolate Day (Pi)		Dinosaurs Research (Pi) 4 groups/5 sessions each	
4	Orientation (S,R,P) 2-3 sessions		Gr. 4/5 Enr. groups Xmas research (S) 2 sessions		O.A. Jacob- Two-Two Day (R,P)	O.A. Research/Human Body (F,N) 2 total group lessons 3 groups/3 sessions each				
5	Orientation (P,G,W,M) 3 sessions		S.S. unit/Pioneers (W) 20 sessions Novel Study Group (M) 15 sessions			Research on Beavers (M) 4 groups/ 5 sessions		Fur Trade Project (W) 15 sessions Ancestry Unit (G) 3 sessions	Novel Study Group (M) 10 sessions	
6	Orientation (W,B,G) 2-3 sessions Culture Realms Picture Study (G) 12 sessions		Human Body Research (B) 4 sessions notetaking	B.C. Study (G) 2 groups 6 sessions each	Japan research (G) 10 sessions Novel Study Group (G) 9 sessions				Pre-Camp program (G,B) 3 groups/4 sessions each	
7	Orientation (M,C,Mc) 3 sessions S.S. Research/ Pre-historic Man (C,S) (S) 7 sessions each			Gr. 6/7 Enr. Groups f(s. project 4 groups/2 sessions		Research Project/Greece (P,P,P) 3 classes/10 sessions each	Pre-Camp Program 8 groups/ 1 session			
OTHER	New Teacher Orientation Student Teacher 4 sessions	Sci. Space Research (D) 5 sessions In-Service	Mothers Program Canadian Lit. Program	Primary Stories I.R.P. Xmas Party & Puppet Show		E.S.L. group Alphabet Book	Preschool Program Activities			Class visits re. Public Library Summer Programs

Appendix B

3. *Take Bigger Steps/Grade Level Planning*

Once you have succeeded in planning at least one unit with the majority of teachers, there is another approach to be taken in Phase II. Approach teachers at one grade level and attempt to plan a program together as a team. Base the approach and planning on the research and study skills continuum developed in Phase I. Emphasize the importance of those skills outlined in the continuum that require resource centre use. Again, start at the grade level where there is the greater likelihood of success, and persuade other grade levels by effective example.

Highlight the benefits of grade level planning. Sharing ideas, materials, and the preparation workload can be stimulating, challenging, and time-saving. When a group plans, develops, and implements a program together, everyone tends to put forth their best effort. The benefits for students lie in what are often better programs. The prerequisite should be that at least one cooperative program exists for each grade level.

Hold grade level meetings to discuss the progress being made with research and study skills commitments. Are all areas being taught? If some are being missed, or need greater emphasis, how can this best be done? Is revision of the continuum necessary? At the same time, review the cooperatively developed programs which are on file for that grade level and attempt to agree on a program, or choice of programs, that will provide for development of a specific skill and a common experience for all students at that grade level. This helps strengthen the developmental aspect of the resource centre program by providing a link from year-to-year, yet it remains a strong, curriculum-integrated approach.

There are other benefits to this type of approach as well. Most importantly, it allows some teachers to become involved at the cooperative teaching or implementation stage, rather than at the planning stage. If it is a positive, successful experience in which educational benefits and student enjoyment are demonstrated, those more reluctant or hard-to-convince teachers may be inclined to get involved at the cooperative planning stage in future programs.

Phase III

By the beginning of Phase III, there is a solid foundation and strong framework for the resource centre program, firmly establishing it as an integral part of the school's curriculum.

The teacher-librarian's initiative and leadership to this point creates a position to take the development of the resource centre program to its logical conclusion.

Take a Giant Step/Total School Programming

In its simplest form, total school programming is often undertaken in preparation for a theme day, week, or month. (See Appendix C.) The type of total school program referred to here, however, is one which, regardless of the curriculum area(s) included, involves extensive cooperative planning and teaching with all staff members and working with all students in the school. It is one in which the resource centre is truly the central focus, or such an integral part that the total school program could not function without it. It is developmental and it is one which staff have a long-term commitment to.

The key to total school programming is often a staff member with expertise and interest in an area, whether it be environmental education or computer literacy. The "seed" for a total school program can be most successfully planted by first working through a program with that teacher and subsequently developing a proposal to take to the entire staff.

Planning for a school-wide program includes:

(1) the identification of a subject-related scope and sequence continuum of content and skills, to ensure a developmental approach across the grades,

(2) the integration of research and study skills from the school-based continuum at each grade level,

(3) a specific approach to program planning, development, and implementation to determine and facilitate the process staff will work through,

(4) a realistic timeline,

(5) opportunity for evaluation and revision of the program by all teachers, and finally,

(6) provision for the maintenance of grade-wide units developed in Phase II.

Essentially, throughout Phase III, this means there will be a minimum of two grade-wide programs in existence, providing a strong basis for further program development of this nature.

CONCLUSION

The introduction of any change involves a number of steps. For teacher-librarians, one might identify five stages in the change process:

Awareness—
An understanding of the roles and responsibilities of teachers, teacher-librarians, and administrators in developing an effective resource centre program is not going to happen by osmosis. While district leadership is important, effective program implementation requires someone at the school level to take responsibility for explaining the program. If not the teacher-librarian, then who?

TOPICS FOR THE MONTH OF _____November_____

GRADE/TEACHER(S)	LANGUAGE ARTS	MATH	SCIENCE	SOCIAL STUDIES	OTHER
Kindergarten					
Gr. 1 (Smith) (Petersen)	Dolch primer, blending consonants, creative writ.	Joining; sets	The Sky (Planetarium Visit)	All About Me! Nutrition	Cooking
	Blending, Alphabet review	Addition to 10, Greater-Less, Shape	Planets/Space/Weather/ Seasons	All About Me! Community Helpers/Nutrition	
Gr. 2 (Johnson) (Taylor)	Dinosaurs Poetry Journals	Sums and Differences to 20 Missing addends	Weather, cont.	Communities - cont.	
Gr. 3 (Scott) (Neeland)	Journals Double Vowels	Math Stations Multiplication	Nutrition	Trains	Hansel & Gretel (Musical)
Gr. 4 (Wesley) (Meyers)	Fairy Tales & Unlikely Comparisons, Flights Backpacks/Nature	Complete Measurement Numbers & Numerals Review Add'n & Subt'n			
Gr. 5 (Anderson)	Basal reader, Cr. Writ. Cinquains & Haiku, News Spelling, Novel,Notetaking	Geometry, Number drills logic, games re place value, & multiplication	Human Skeleton/ Nutrition	Routes to East/Shipbuilding Explorers	
Gr. 5/6 (Bragg)	Novels	Problems, Patterns, Area Volume	Human Skeleton/ Nutrition	Middle East	
Gr. 6/7 (Howell)					
Gr. 7 (Rankin)	Punctuation/History of writing & writing styles	Complete Geometry/ Start Percentage and Average	Tree Study/Mapping Small Places/Completion of Rock Study	Continue Local Area Mapping Study - public service in the area	Pacific Press Visit (Nov. 25th)
ESL (Ferrier) (Diggings)					
LEC (Twaits)	Communication/Time Inventors/Inventions		Dinosaurs		
LAC (Poon)					

Appendix C

Understanding—
A well-articulated rationale and full information can assist administrators and teachers to understand the conceptual framework of a resource centre program. Understanding can streamline communication and planning.

Acceptance—
Demonstration and practice lead to acceptance. Interaction among the teacher-librarian, administrator, and teachers promotes cooperation.

Commitment—
Professionalism is determined not only by level of academic achievement, but also by degree of commitment. The professional teacher-librarian will have a strong commitment to a clearly defined role in resource-based learning. Administrative support is critical and is also the most effective means of gaining and/or solidifying teacher commitment to the implementation of a program.

Renewal—
Review and Revision should be an ongoing part of the change process. If teachers remain active partners in implementation, the continuation of a program is much more assured. And the measure of successful implementation is in program continuation.

New areas of expertise take time to develop. Implementation should be viewed as a process. As a process, it should involve a well thought-out plan covering a three-to-five year period. If this three phase approach cannot be accomplished in a period of five years, it is probably time to decide that it is just not going to happen in this school, or that someone new might be able to do it in this particular situation ... and, in either case, transfer!

The key criteria to success with this approach are a strong commitment to a well-defined role, administrative support, a high profile, and accountability.

The result should be a resource centre program that is embedded in, and essential to, the school curriculum and, as a consequence, is both educationally viable and politically justifiable.

The School Librarian and the Classroom Teacher: Partners in Curriculum Planning

Antoinette Oberg

The role of the teacher-librarian has expanded to include cooperation with classroom teachers in planning the instructional program. This cooperation takes many forms, depending on the skills and inclinations of both teacher-librarians and teachers. When a full planning partnership develops the teacher-librarian can provide not only a welcome support to the classroom teacher, who usually faces the complex and demanding task of curriculum planning alone, but also an occasion for expanding and improving the curriculum planning process. The extent to which this occurs depends largely on the teacher-librarian's knowledge of curriculum planning.

Curriculum planning is something every teacher does daily. Regardless of how detailed the provincial or state curriculum guides may be, teachers have a great deal of planning to do to tailor guide suggestions or prescriptions to their own and their students' knowledge and interests. Although most teachers plan their programs with apparent ease and efficiency, curriculum planning is actually a very complex process. Proper planning requires not only a thorough grasp of the subject matter of a lesson or unit, but also a sensitive understanding of the learners for whom it is intended, and awareness of the many contextual factors which define and influence the situation, as well as knowledge of the planning process itself.

Ideally, in order to marshall the knowledge and resources necessary, curriculum planning is carried out in groups rather than individually, by people who all have first-hand knowledge of the situation for which they are planning. School department or grade level groups are best suited for this task. However, regardless of how well experienced and proficient their members may be in individual curriculum planning, such groups typically lack knowledge of the subtleties and complexities of joint curriculum planning.

It is in this area that the teacher-librarian can make an important contribution. When department and grade level groups are not active in joint planning projects, the teacher-librarian's role becomes even more important. It is the teacher-librarian who can change the teacher's solitary curriculum planning into a more broadly based and cooperative venture.

The teacher-librarian is ideally positioned for this role as a member of a large or small curriculum planning team. First, as a regular member of the school staff, the teacher-librarian has first-hand, intimate knowledge of the school setting—school curriculum policies; principal expectations; teacher predilections, interests and non-interests; parent sentiments; available facilities and materials. Second, the teacher-librarian has expert knowledge of prescribed curriculum and of available print and non-print resource materials. When knowledge of the curriculum planning process is added to this already substantial body of expertise, the teacher-librarian is in a position not only to respond to teacher requests for help in curriculum planning, but also to go beyond teacher requests and make suggestions that can improve the curriculum planning process.

A TRADITIONAL VIEW OF THE CURRICULUM PLANNING PROCESS

For the better part of this century, teachers and curriculum developers have been taught that the ideal curriculum planning process is a rational series of steps beginning with the definition of goals and objectives (sometimes preceded by identification of student or societal "needs") and ending with a check on the accomplishment of those objectives and subsequent revision of instructional plans.

A typical version of this Tyler planning model, named after the man who first laid out its rationale[21] can be summarized in eight steps:

1. Specify goals and objectives.

2. Assess student status.

3. Determine needs.

4. Rank needs.

5. Plan a program.

6. Implement program.

7. Evaluate program.

8. Continue, modify or abort program based on the evaluation.[19]

This view of curriculum planning has a number of things to commend it as a prescription for the planning process. For one thing, curriculum planners should certainly consider what educational ends they are aiming for, although these need not and often should not be stated in terms of precise student behaviors, as later interpreters of the Tyler rationale (most notably Mager and Popham[6,12]) have insisted.

Another commendable feature of the Tyler model is its emphasis on what happens with students as an important ingredient in subsequent planning. The teacher's sensitive judgment of the nature of the students' experiences in relation to educational aims should be the primary determinant of what is subsequently planned.

Unfortunately, these emphases have tended to be overshadowed by a view of curriculum planning as a technical process initiated and controlled by the precise specification of behavioral objectives. Not only does this view mistake important features of education, as Stenhouse[18] argues, but it fails

to capture what little is known about how teachers go about the planning process either individually or in groups.

CURRICULUM PLANNING AND DELIBERATION

A better representation of the curriculum planning process as it actually occurs in groups of experts is the model developed by Walker.[22] The three key elements in this model are the curriculum's platform, its design, and the deliberation associated with it. (See Figure 1.) The platform consists of the curriculum planner's assumptions, and it is the source of educational aims and goals. The platform includes conceptions or beliefs about what exists and about what is possible. For example, "We believe there is a learnable strategy for interpreting historical events," states a conception of what is learnable. The platform also includes theories, or beliefs about what relations hold between existing entities. An example

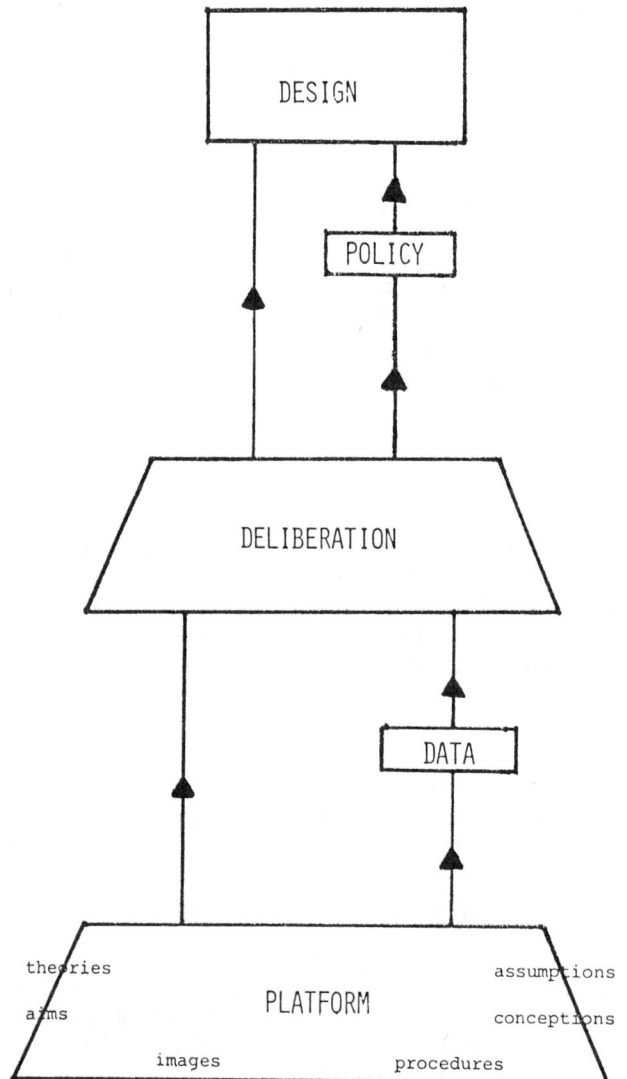

Fig. 1. Walker's Naturalistic Curriculum Planning Model

given by Walker, "The teacher imparts attitudes toward a subject, and, indeed, attitudes towards learning itself," states a theory about how attitudes toward learning develop.

Beliefs about what is educationally desirable are also part of the platform. Another of Walker's examples, "We teach a subject not to produce little living libraries on that subject, but rather to get a student to think mathematically, to consider matters as a historian does, to take part in the process of knowledge getting," states a general aim of education. Two other less explicit but nevertheless important platform components are images and procedures. Images are another form in which some educationally desirable condition or state of affairs is thought of, without specifying why or in what way it is desirable. Heroes are cultural images. So are outstanding works of art or admired scientific theories. The image of a home may be a very important source of aims and goals for an elementary teacher.[1]

Images are realized through procedures, which specify courses of action or decisions that are desirable without specifying who or in what way they are desirable. Some people would also call these principles.[4,10,11] Examples include, "Be honest," and "Minimize the time necessary to learn," and "Create situations in which learners can share with each other."

The significance of the platform is two-fold. First, every curriculum planner has a platform whether it is made explicit or not. When teacher-librarians plan with a teacher, they work from a platform. When curriculum planners appear to speak at cross purposes or do not see eye to eye, it is often because they are working from different curriculum platforms. Making platforms explicit is a useful way to get beyond misunderstandings and even disagreements about curriculum and curriculum planning. Secondly, the curriculum planning platform is the source of justification of all the decisions made during planning. A teacher decides to have students generate their own questions about air pollution rather than answer the ones on the worksheet because he or she believes the development of inquiring citizens is an important educational aim. In order to defend a curriculum or a curriculum decision, one refers to the platform on which it is built.

The key element in Walker's model with which teacher-librarians are likely to be most concerned is the process of deliberation. This is a way of describing the planning process teacher-librarians and their teacher colleagues undertake. According to Walker,

> The main operations in curriculum deliberations are (1) formulating decision points, (2) devising alternative choices at these decision points, (3) considering arguments for and against suggested decision points and decision alternatives, and, finally, choosing the most defensible alternatives subject to acknowledged constraints.[22:54]

The process is actually more circular than it sounds in this description, with each decision influencing every other one, so that early decisions must always be considered in light of later ones. There are five important bodies of experience which must be considered during deliberation. These are (1) the subject matter, (2) the learners for whom the plan is intended, their abilities, aspirations, anxieties, (3) the milieu in which the

learning is to take place; that is the classroom, the school community, biases, expectations, beliefs and values, power relationships, social norms, and so on, (4) the teacher, her approach to learners, to the subject matter, to planning, to teaching, and to colleagues, and (5) curriculum planning.[14] All of these must be considered equally, without overdue emphasis on any one, especially subject matter and the materials which embody it.

As Walker points out, deliberation is a horribly complicated process.

> We should not be surprised to find out that curriculum deliberations are chaotic and confused. But we must not be misled into believing either that such confusion is worthless or that it is the inevitable consequence of deliberation. Deliberation is defined by biological, not sociological, criteria, and it may take many forms. The most common form in current practice is argumentation and debate by a group of people. But it could be done by one person, and no logical barrier stands in the way of its being performed by a computer.[22:55]

Schwab makes the same point and adds another. He argues that "the process of deliberation is not only difficult and time consuming; it is also often unsatisfying because there is no point at which it is clear that the course has been completed and completed well."[15:292]

The final component of Walker's model is the design of the curriculum. His conception of design is different from the traditional definition of design as the arrangement of the parts of the curriculum; that is, the relationship among objectives, activities, content, materials, and evaluation. Instead, Walker sees design as the set of relationships embodied in the materials-in-use which can affect students. He explains,

> We are accustomed to speaking of curricula as if they were objects produced by curriculum projects. The trouble with this view is that the curriculum's effects must be ascribed to events, not materials. The materials are important because their features condition the events that affect those using the materials. The curriculum design—the set of relationships embodied in the materials-in-use which are capable of affecting students—rather than the materials themselves are the important concerns of the curriculum specialist. The trouble with the concept of design is that the curriculum's design is difficult to specify explicitly and precisely—one way to specify a curriculum's design is by the series of decisions that produce it. A curriculum's design would then be represented by the choices that enter into its creation.[22:53]

This concept of design reminds us that students may demonstrate accomplishment of objectives in ways not anticipated, depending on how the lesson proceeds. When teachers are oriented to learners and what they are experiencing rather than to subject matter or prescribed outcomes or discipline or the clock, what happens in the classroom is and ought to be unpredictable except in very general terms. The teacher works with the potential inherent in the curriculum materials, in students, and introspectively to create the best possible opportunities for learning.

Let us return to the core of the curriculum planning model, deliberation. This conception of curriculum planning as deliberation is quite different from the objectives-first, subject matter dominated model on which we have all been brought up. It portrays curriculum planning as circular, indeed circuitous, uncertain, complex, and time consuming rather than as a unidirectional, ends-driven deductive process. Perhaps the most important difference between the deliberative and the Tylerian models is that while the Tylerian model was developed to guide curriculum developers through a tidy planning procedure, the deliberative model was developed to describe what groups of teacher-experts actually did in planning a curriculum. Understanding that it is the inherent nature of the curriculum planning process-in-action to be unstraightforward might alleviate some of the frustration of finding it so.

The aim of this planning process is to clarify what kinds of learning (not behaviors) are desired and why, and what materials, arrangements, and activities are likely to contribute to them. If realizing that planning is as complex as teaching is little comfort for the teacher-librarian attempting to facilitate it, perhaps some general knowledge of how teachers tend to approach curriculum planning will help. Interestingly, this description of deliberative curriculum planning as it occurs in groups is compatible with an entirely different body of literature which describes what we know about individual teachers' planning predilections. Although teacher planning may not always exhibit the ideal characteristics of deliberation as described by Walker and Schwab, it is closer to the deliberative model than to the objectives-first model, into which curricularists so often try to force teachers.

HOW INDIVIDUAL TEACHERS PLAN

One group of teacher planning studies groups teachers into two sorts of planners: comprehensive and incremental. Comprehensive planners build detailed plans of how the lesson content and activities will be worked out, based on expectations of how students will react. Incremental planners, on the other hand, plan only an initial activity and then try it out with students before planning further.[3] Most teachers do not begin their planning with statements of objectives.[23] Some consider objectives later in the planning process, and some do not consider them explicitly at all, though they are implicit in every planning decision, buried subconsciously in the teacher's platform.

There are also some differences depending on subject matter and grade level. Teachers of English and social studies tend to consider broad goals more and more often than do teachers of mathematics, science, and geography, who tend to focus instead on content.[20] It seems that many teachers rely on the teacher's manual or the curriculum guide statement of objectives and see planning as the generation of a set of reminders about how they intend to go about accomplishing what is prescribed in the guide.[7] The emphasis in plans of secondary teachers is typically on content, while the emphasis in plans of elementary teachers is typically on activities.

The biggest influences on the selection of content and activities are the teacher's perception of student interests and anticipated student responses. Teachers plan what they think will grab student interest and keep the lesson flowing smoothly. The second strongest influence on planning decisions is the teacher's own preference, knowledge, and skills. Teachers will select activities and content which they themselves like and feel comfortable handling. The third most important influence on teacher planning decisions is curriculum materials.[5] Here is a particularly potent point of influence for the teacher-librarian. Teachers tend to plan around materials they have at hand. They avoid topics for which they lack materials.

Some teachers do not write down many plans at all. For them, planning is primarily a mental activity during which they rehearse the lesson privately.[7] The actual plan comes alive only in interaction with students. Most teachers plan, as they teach, in isolation. They typically do not refer to professional publications, colleagues, consultants, or the principal.[8] Given all these things that teachers tend to consider during planning, one might ask in what order teachers typically make these considerations. The answer is that there is no typical order of consideration. Moreover, there is no correlation between order of consideration and quality of the plan which results. Planning procedures are variable among expert planners as well as regular classroom teachers.[9] The circularity and circuitousness characteristic of deliberation seem to be the order of the day.

IMPLICATIONS FOR TEACHER-LIBRARIANS AS CO-PLANNERS

If we adopt deliberation as our view of the planning process, then successful planning sessions are those in which all five commonplaces (subject matter, learners, milieux, teachers, planning) are thoroughly considered, alternatives have been considered before choices were made, and planners can justify their decisions in terms of their curriculum platform. Achieving success in these terms is a tall order even for expert planners. A group of experienced teacher-librarians with whom these ideas were shared listed some key points for those who undertake curriculum deliberation to keep in mind:

1. Objectives need not be considered first.

2. The platforms of both teacher-librarian and teacher should be clarified.

3. Planning involves risk taking.

4. Some platforms may not mesh.

5. Knowing student interests helps teachers plan.

6. Find out what student responses the teacher expects.

7. Make teachers aware of resources appropriate for their particular students.

8. Be aware of the content of curriculum guides.

9. Focus on process as well as content learning.

10. Build good relationships with teachers and supervisors.

11. Teacher-librarians need many different approaches to curriculum planning.

12. Flexibility in planning approach is essential.

13. Planning is different in each situation.

SOME CONCEPTS IN CURRICULUM PLANNING

Other points useful in curriculum planning can be gleaned from some distinctions among key curriculum concepts: curriculum materials, curriculum content, and learning activities.

Curriculum materials. Materials are an embodiment of subject matter and although they loom large as an influence on the teacher's planning, Schwab advises that they should not overshadow the importance of the other commonplaces, namely learners, milieux, the teacher, and the curriculum planning process itself. Schwab's admonition is easily taken into account if curriculum materials are used not, as teachers typically use them, to define de facto the curriculum, but in the way teacher-librarians are more likely to see them, as resources which can be used in a variety of ways. Decisions about how to use any given set of curriculum materials are made in light of students' needs, community and school expectations, and teacher preferences. For example, students who are knowledgeable about a particular historical event may be given by a teacher who values critical thinking two sets of source materials from that era, not to learn more about the historical event, which they could do with those materials, but to compare the opposing points of view presented in the materials. Schwab[14] says that any given materials may be used by students in three different ways: (1) to learn what the materials convey, for example, a story, a scientific explanation, an historical event; or (2) to learn how a story, scientific explanation or historical account is constructed; or (3) to learn how to interpret the story, scientific explanation, or historical account. Helping teachers see the potential in curriculum materials in varied ways is a valuable function of the teacher-librarian. It is easier to see the varied potential uses of curriculum materials if one is clear on the distinctions between curriculum content and curriculum goals.

Curriculum content. Conceptions of curriculum content are often fuzzy. Teacher-librarians who can clarify what is meant by curriculum content in their own minds will be of greater help to teachers than those who cannot. Content is the facts, ideas, concepts, skills, attitudes, and so on which make up the curriculum. Sometimes the content is defined entirely by the goal or objective statement. "Students should know the causes of the revolution" is a goal statement which also defines the curriculum content. The content is the concepts and generalizations which define the causes of the revolution.

Sometimes the content is only instrumental to the goal. If the goal is that students should learn skills of critical thinking, any of a wide variety of content areas, likely one from the social sciences or humanities, may be used for this purpose. Typically, content plays an instrumental role when the goal is a cognitive skill. Clarifying the kind of learning intended puts curriculum content and materials in perspective.

In order to determine the appropriate relationship between content and materials then, it is important to know which type of goal is intended. Curriculum goals are of four types: cognitive knowledge, cognitive skills, affect, and psychomotor skills. Teacher-librarians are most often working with teachers concerned with one or more of the first three types. If teachers are not explicit about the goals they intend, then teacher-librarians must uncover these goals in their conversations with them. Note that goals are statements of intentions about what students will learn; that is, what they will know about (cognitive concept knowledge), what they will know how to do (cognitive skill knowledge), what they will be able to do (cognitive skills), what traits they will exhibit (affect). Note also that goals or objectives need not be stated behaviorally, except for psychomotor skills goals. There is usually a variety of observable indicators of what a student has learned, and to restrict the demonstration to one behavior is unnecessarily and harmfully limiting. So, for example, "to build a cedar box" is not a goal because it does not reveal what students are intended to learn. As soon as the teacher explains what she wants the students to understand about West Coast native culture through the activity of building the box, the teacher-librarian as well as the teacher will be in a much better position to suggest appropriate learning materials.

Activities. Knowing what kind of goal is intended is also important for determining appropriate activities. The crucial feature of learning activities (presuming we are intending some kind of cognitive or affective learning) is what kind of mental activity they occasion. Building a cedar box is an appropriate activity if students are to calculate and measure, to attend to the physical and/or aesthetic qualities of the wood, to demonstrate artistic prowess in the decoration of the box, to show care, diligence, and attention to detail in their work, to reflect on the life-style and values of the native people who produced such boxes, or any of a number of other worthwhile goals. Notice that goals, along with other elements of the planner's platform, provide the justification for the learning activities.

CONCLUSION

This article has touched only briefly on a number of complicated curriculum matters. The aim here has been not to present recipes and formulae, but to share some theoretical and practical distinctions and some empirical findings which might be helpful to teacher-librarians in thinking about their role as a help to teachers in their curriculum planning. Because the planning process is inherently complex, unpredictable, and contingent, it cannot be accomplished well with straightforward technical procedures. What is required for successful curriculum planning is broad and deep knowledge of subject matter, learners, teachers, and milieux; sensitivity to the way these elements combine in any given case; and a capacity to revel in the many intricacies and multiple possibilities in any given instance of planning.

REFERENCES

1. Clandinin, J. *A Conceptualization of Image as a Component of Teacher Personal Practical Knowledge in Primary School Teachers' Reading and Language Program.* Unpublished doctoral dissertation, University of Toronto, 1983.

2. Clark, C. and P. Peterson. *Teachers' Thought Processes* (Occasional Paper No. 72). Institute for Research on Teaching, Michigan State University, 1984.

3. Clark, C. and R. Yinger. *Three Studies of Teacher Planning* (Research Series No. 55). Institute for Research on Teaching, Michigan State University, 1979.

4. Elbaz, F. *Teacher Thinking: A Study of Practical Knowledge.* Croom Helm, 1983.

5. Leithwood, K., S. Ross and D. Montgomery. *An Empirical Investigation of Teachers' Curriculum Decision Making Processes.* Paper presented at the 1978 Annual Meeting of Canadian Society for the Study of Education, Fredericton, New Brunswick.

6. Mager, R. *Preparing Instructional Objectives.* Fearon, 1962.

7. McCutcheon, G. *How Elementary School Teachers Plan Their Curriculum: Findings and Research Issues.* Paper presented to the 1979 Annual Meeting of the American Educational Research Association, San Francisco, Calif.

8. Oberg, A. *Information Referents and Patterns in Curriculum Planning of Classroom Teachers.* Unpublished doctoral dissertation, University of Alberta, 1975.

9. Oberg, A. *Characteristics of Classroom Teachers' Curriculum Planning Decisions.* Paper presented at the 1978 Annual Meeting of the Canadian Society for the Study of Education, Fredericton, New Brunswick.

10. Oberg, A. "Using Construct Theory as a Basis for Research and Professional Development." *Journal of Curriculum Studies.* (In press)

11. Peters, R. S. *Authority, Responsibility and Education.* Allen and Unwin, 1959.

12. Popham, W. and E. Baker. *Systematic Instruction.* Prentice Hall, 1970.

13. Schwab, J. "The Practical: A Language for Curriculum." *School Review*, Volume 78, Number 1 (1969), pp. 1-23.

14. Schwab, J. "The Practical 3: Translation into Curriculum." *School Review*, Volume 81, Number 4 (1973), pp. 501-22.

15. Schwab, J. "The Practical: Arts of Eclectic." *Science, Curriculum and Liberal Education: Selected Essays of Joseph J. Schwab*, edited by I. Westbury and J. Wilkoff. University of Chicago Press, 1978.

16. Schwab, J. "The Practical 4: Something for Curriculum Professors to Do." *Curriculum Inquiry*, Volume 13, Number 3 (1983), pp. 239-365.

17. Shavelson, R. and P. Stern. "Research on Teachers' Pedagogical Thoughts, Judgments, Decisions and Behavior." *Review of Educational Research*, Volume 51 (1983), pp. 455-98.

18. Stenhouse, L. *An Introduction to Curriculum Research and Development.* Heineman, 1975.

19. Tankard, G. *Curriculum Improvement: An Administrator's Guide.* Parker, 1974.

20. Taylor, P. *How Teachers Plan Their Courses.* National (UK) Foundation for Educational Research, 1970.

21. Tyler, R. *Principles of Curriculum and Instruction.* University of Chicago Press, 1949.

22. Walker, D. "A Naturalistic Model for Curriculum Development." *School Review*, Volume 80, Number 1 (1971), pp. 56-65.

23. Zahorik, J. "Teachers' Planning Models." *Educational Leadership*, Volume 33 (1975), pp. 134-39.

Cooperative Program Planning— A Model That Works

Carol-Ann Haycock

"Separating learning experience into blocks of time or into subjects taught in isolation is contrary to what is known about how children learn...."

Cooperative program planning and teaching is a concept ... a strategy or approach to teaching and learning. The term does *not* constitute a "set" program of instruction, but rather a philosophical framework for the development and implementation of resource-based programs which reflect what we know about how students learn. For the classroom teacher it is one more strategy or approach to be added to their teaching repertoire.

We know that people learn best when they can relate present learning to past knowledge and experience or create connections to the knowledge and experience of other areas of their lives. We know that it is only through such connections or meaning that the transfer of learning is facilitated. The purpose of cooperative program planning, then, is to develop learning experiences or units of study that effectively *integrate* the student's resource center activities (whether literature- or research-based) with other learning experiences.

There are some cornerstones that lay the foundation for effective cooperative planning. First, the role of the teacher-librarian as a professional colleague and equal teaching partner must be clearly defined and understood in order to develop the partnership necessary for cooperative planning. Such a partnership does not place the teacher-librarian in a subservient, service role, nor in a superior, consultant role. Rather, each partner brings specific expertise to the planning process. Second, a school-based information skills continuum, developed by the staff, and for which each staff member acknowledges some ownership and accepts some responsibility, provides a necessary framework for the planning process. Finally, a planning model, or checklist, greatly facilitates the efficiency and effectiveness of the planning process.

There are also some conditions that are conducive to effective planning sessions. First, the teacher-librarian must be prepared to initiate planning with teachers, rather than waiting for teachers to come to them. If teachers don't know about, or understand, the service they can't be expected to seek it out. Second, the teacher-librarian must be prepared to present suggestions in such a way that the teacher can respond. Responses to "May I help you?" or "How may I help you?" may vary from silence, to "No thanks," to "I'm not sure." Determining a teacher's needs and preferred teaching strategies, and offering specific suggestions about the options that might be pursued, affords the teacher a greater, more positive opportunity to respond as a full partner in the planning process.

There are many paradigms of the planning process. If one holds the view that the teacher is a professional decision-maker, there are several decisions teachers make before, during, and following instruction. Such decision-making is an ongoing, cyclical process, and may be represented as follows:

PROGRAM PLANNING PROCESS

Objectives
Teachers determine what the students they are responsible for are going to learn. Direction, in many subject areas, is provided by curriculum guides and similar documents. But the teacher, based on a knowledge of student backgrounds, abilities, interests, and needs, makes the final decision about specific learning objectives.

Content
Teachers decide the content of student learning, including what that content will be and how much, or how little, will be taught.

Organization
Teachers make decisions about how the content will be organized to best facilitate student learning. Topical, thematic, chronological, and a variety of other organizational approaches are possible.

Methodology
Teachers make decisions about the instructional methods to be employed to best facilitate student learning. A variety of approaches such as direct teacher instruction, audio-visual presentation, discovery learning, resource-based learning (to name but a few) are possible.

Activities
Teachers make decisions about the learning activities to be developed to best facilitate student learning. Again, a variety of learning activities are possible and both instructional strategies and learning activities should be varied enough to appeal to each of the learning modalities.

Evaluation
Teachers make decisions about how student growth and learning will be evaluated, as well as how the effectiveness of a unit of study will be judged.

Traditionally, resource center use and teacher-librarian involvement have "plugged in" to the teachers' program at the learning activities stage. At this stage, the emphasis is on what students are to do and on what adjunct services, if any, are required. Typically, a teacher may contact the teacher-librarian with requests for resources to support a unit of study, "starting tomorrow," or to schedule their class in to undertake a research activity. In many instances, it may be only after the third or fourth student request for information that the teacher-librarian is able to determine that an assignment has been given somewhere, by someone. Frustrating? Certainly. It is professionally difficult, if not impossible, to be placed in a service role that purports to help teachers meet their teaching/learning objectives, if in fact these objectives are not known but, instead, must be deduced ... either from written research assignments carried by students, or from the oral interpretation of students.

The cooperative planning process moves the involvement of the teacher-librarian back to the objectives stage, where the focus is on what students are to learn. Graphically the cooperative partnership looks like this:

Objectives ... what students are to learn
　　Content
　　Organization
　　Methodology
Activities ... what students are to do
　　Evaluation

Teacher-librarians in successful programs move from the activities phase to the objective setting phase, cooperatively established by the teacher and teacher-librarian.

When teachers and teacher-librarians are planning for resource-based learning programs, the learning objectives established involve both content or knowledge objectives as well as information skill objectives. This is an important point to emphasize, since both teacher-librarians (who are not, and can't be expected to be, subject specialists in every area), and teachers (who are classroom generalists or subject specialists) often express some confusion with, and even lack of confidence in, the planning partnership until this is understood. What each partner contributes to the cooperative planning process can best be represented as follows:

What the Teacher brings to the Planning Process
　　—knowledge of the students
　　—knowledge of the content area

What the Teacher-Librarian brings to the Planning Process
　　—knowledge of resources
　　—knowledge of information skills

The teacher-librarian's contribution is considerably more complex than a superficial glance at this graphic representation might suggest. Rather than a "simple" knowledge of the availability of resources to support a given topic of study (and that, in itself, is not a "simple" task), more importantly, and at a much more sophisticated level, the teacher-librarian requires the skills necessary to determine the suitability of those resources to support the learning objectives and to meet student ability levels and learning styles. And, rather than a "simple" knowledge of information skills, and again at a much more sophisticated level, the teacher-librarian requires a

knowledge of suitable strategies for integrating information skills instruction, and/or application into units of study.

Cooperative program planning is a process of communicating ... of creating something. In planning sessions, communication will not proceed in a rigid way, not will it necessarily proceed in the order outlined in the planning checklist. Often, many of the points in the checklist will be addressed simultaneously, and almost always, there will be a back and forth flow between the points or stages in the process.

All of the information suggested by the checklist is crucial for successful and effective teaching/learning experience and programs. The teacher-librarian needs to be skilled at employing effective questioning techniques to get at this information as expeditiously as possible.

- Initiate contact and schedule planning time

- Establish subject/topic/grade and ability level(s)

- Review previous skills and activities

- Establish general goal

- Establish specific objectives
  - knowledge/concept objectives
  - information skill objectives

- Select and locate resources

- Determine teaching strategies and learning activities
  - minimum expectations
  - responsibility for preparation and teaching of each component
  - scheduling of learning activities

- Evaluation

- Record and retain unit (note strengths/weaknesses on completion).

THE PLANNING CHECKLIST AND THE PLANNING PROCESS

Initiate Contact and Schedule Planning Time

Planning operationalizes the cooperative partnership. Planning must therefore be seen as a priority, and time must be set aside for it. Scheduling planning time to follow an initial contact allows each partner valuable "think time" in preparation for a planning session. The teacher might be asked to think about proposed learning objectives, preferred instructional strategies, and a timeline for a unit of study. The teacher-librarian might be thinking about the availability and suitability of resources to support a proposed topic of study and proposed techniques for grouping students and integrating information skills, given the number and nature of the resources available.

Establish Subject/Topic/Grade/ Ability Levels

The discussion of student ability levels will most often include the following areas of consideration:

- conceptual level ... What concepts are involved in the area of study? Which of these do students understand? Which will need to be taught?

- knowledge base ... How much information or knowledge do students already have about the area of study? How can this be determined?

- skill level ... What skills will students need to access and/or process the information required? What skills do students possess?

- reading ability ... What is the range of reading ability among a given group of students?

- learning styles ... What is the range of learning styles among a given group of students?

Review Previous Skills and Activities

An information skills continuum greatly facilitates this stage. Reference to a school- or subject department-based continuum assists the planning process in determining what has been mastered and, developmentally, what the next steps in skill development should be.

Establish General Goal

A goal may be defined as a statement of the purpose of a unit of study, in terms of the individual learner. A goal statement should answer the question "Why are we studying this? (i.e. what are students to learn?)" It is most effective to approach establishing the purpose (general goal) for a unit of study by talking in terms of the learner(s) rather than in terms of the teacher(s).

Establish Specific Objectives

An objective may be defined as a statement of the behavior a student will be able to demonstrate at the end of a lesson or unit of study. Objectives break the goal into specific components. This stage of the planning process is one of refining and more specifically structuring a topic of study, since objectives provide the basis for selecting instructional strategies, learning activities, and evaluation procedures. Both knowledge and skill objectives need to be addressed.

Selection of Resources

The selection of suitable resources involves matching available resources to each of those considerations identified under "Student Ability Levels" ... concepts to be included, the knowledge base of students, their skill levels, reading abilities, and learning styles. Once this has been done, the next stage is to determine what information resources still need to be sought out or prepared (i.e. rewritten, taped, presented in picture or graph form).

Determine Teaching Strategies and Learning Activities

As stated, the learning objectives will provide the basis for selecting both teaching strategies and learning activities. At this stage in the planning process it is perhaps most effective for the teacher-librarian to be prepared to present things in such a way that the teacher can respond ... to specific questions, suggestions or examples of specific approaches.

- **Minimum Expectations.** Minimum expectations should be designed to assure success for all students but should not act as a "ceiling" for more capable students. Minimum expectations should be established for the processes of gathering, recording and presenting information. This may involve structuring assignments to guarantee success, through such techniques as built-in checkpoints, or it may involve differentiating assignments to allow for varying ability levels.

- **Responsibility for Preparation and Teaching.** Specific responsibility for the preparation and teaching of various components of a unit of study should be determined during the planning process. Teachers who are new to the cooperative planning process sometimes presume their responsibility ends with planning and sometimes teacher-librarians who are new to the process corroborate this by assuming sole responsibility for the preparation and teaching of resource center learning experiences. This approach reduces cooperative program planning and teaching to "parallel" planning and teaching, which differs considerably from effecting the full integration of information skills and resource center experiences into the curriculum. The important point to emphasize here is that while responsibility may not be shared 50-50, it needs to be shared.

- **Scheduling of Learning Activities.** The scheduling of learning activities depends on the overall time frame for a unit of study and on student grouping. These factors will determine the time and sequence of scheduled activities, as well as the location of students and resources.

Evaluation

Discussion of evaluation procedures should include some focus on each of the following aspects:

- **Evaluation of Process** (i.e. information skills). This type of evaluation, obviously, is on-going throughout a unit of study, and involves both teacher and teacher-librarian in the observation of students and in record keeping to track individual student progress. These evaluation procedures are largely tied to minimum expectations set for students.

- **Evaluation of Product:** Criteria for evaluation of student products should be determined and made clear to students at the outset of a unit of study.

- **Student Involvement:** Students may be involved in evaluating their progress in process skills and/or the quality of their final product.

- **Evaluation of Unit:** Criteria for evaluating the effectiveness of a unit of study should be discussed during the planning process and time for this procedure established at the end of the unit of study.

Record and Retain Unit

Strengths and weaknesses and suggested revisions should be recorded at the end of the unit of study. This facilitates revision and adaptation for future use—the unit can be used again the following year, again stressing with appropriate revision and adaptation, and introduced and used by other teachers working at the same grade level, or serve as an example for teachers you are just beginning to plan with, or can be shared with other teacher-librarians and teachers in the district. A copy can also be taken by the teacher or teacher-librarian leaving the school. Retaining units of study is important for total program strength and growth over time.

CONCLUSION

The results of the cooperative program planning process are resource-based learning programs and experiences for students which (a) maximize the use of all school resources to the best possible effect for the student population; (b) ensure the integration of information skills instruction and application, developmentally, across the curriculum; (c) guarantee successful learning experiences for all students. The impact of this approach on the rate and degree of student learning can and should be measured.

The successful implementation of this approach has been documented in the Vancouver (British Columbia) school district, as well as in the majority of school systems across Canada. In 1986 both Australia and New Zealand launched a concerted national training program to assist teacher-librarians in the implementation of the approach. The philosophy is reflected in the new American guidelines for school library media center programs and is currently being successfully implemented in some school districts in the United States.

THE COOPERATIVE PROGRAM PLANNING GUIDE AND RECORD OF UNIT OF STUDY

The term "cooperative program planning and teaching" was coined by Ken Haycock in 1978 based on several years of research and professional experience in teacher-librarianship. It refers to the essential role of the teacher-librarian in planning units of study with classroom teachers to integrate those skills and processes necessary to develop students committed to informed decision-making, cultural and literary appreciation and lifelong learning. Cooperative program planning and teaching provides the philosophical framework for the work of the teacher-librarian; it is not just another service function. The approach differs from team teaching, which, in many instances, became "turn teaching." It also differs from parallel planning and teaching where, following a brief "planning session," the teacher plans and executes classroom instruction and learning experiences and the teacher-librarian plans and executes library instruction and learning experiences to parallel those of the classroom. This approach to the effective use of collaborative personnel in the school is now being used with similar success in learning assistance programs and gifted and talented programs.

Almost a decade ago, when planning a half day workshop for all teacher-librarians in the Vancouver (British Columbia) school district on cooperative program planning, a group of teacher-librarians identified the need for a formal planning guide to provide structure for the in-service program and support for follow-up work in schools.

Working with Ken Haycock, then coordinator of library services, Ruth Lindgaard provided the original impetus for a district approach, and Carol-Ann Haycock brought a structure and process for cooperative planning which she had developed and used successfully in her school for individual, grade-wide and school-wide cooperative planning; this resulted in the planning checklist on page 63.

The committee consolidated this structure and process with other planning guides and developed a draft guide for district use. The resulting "model" was field-tested in a number of schools prior to district workshops and revised accordingly.

Following the six half day in-service programs, led for groups of 25 teacher-librarians, additional field testing took place in more than 75 schools. The original guide of four pages was expanded to six (reduced back to four in this issue); objectives and evaluation were placed side by side to ensure that it was in fact the evaluation of learning activities; the format was revised to allow inclusion in three ring binders; and a number of smaller changes were made as well.

The resulting planning guide and record of unit of study is used extensively throughout the Vancouver school district. In most schools it is used to refer to the planning checklist and record units so they can be revised and adapted rather than begun again each year; many schools, however, do use the form while planning with teachers. It is perhaps interesting to note that the initial response was more favorable from classroom teachers and curriculum and program consultants than from teacher-librarians themselves but this changed with use. Everyone is looking for more efficient and effective ways to plan and this guide has provided considerable direction and support to that end. It also facilitates the development of the district's guide or index to cooperatively planned and taught units of study throughout the system, arranged by subject, topic, skill area and grade level.

Additional information is available from Liz Austrom, District Principal—Curriculum Resources, Vancouver School Board, 1595 West 10th Avenue, Vancouver, British Columbia V6J 1Z8.

PLANNING GUIDE
AND
RECORD OF UNIT OF STUDY

SUBJECT _____ TOPIC _____

GRADE AND ABILITY LEVELS _____

TEACHER(S) _____

DATES/TIMES FOR PLANNING (1) _____ (2) _____ (3) _____

CHECKLIST

In planning sessions, communication will not proceed in a rigid way nor this order necessarily and occasionally some steps will be undertaken simultaneously. Nevertheless this information is crucial for successful programs.

☐ Initiate Contact and Schedule Planning Time

☐ Establish Subject/Topic/Grade and Ability Level(s)

☐ Review Previous Skills and Activities

☐ Establish General Goal

☐ Establish Specific Objectives - knowledge/concept objectives

☐ Select and Locate Resources

☐ Determine Teaching Strategies and Learning Activities

☐ Minimum Expectations

☐ Responsibility for Preparation and Teaching of Each Component

☐ Scheduling of Learning Activities

☐ Evaluation

☐ Record and Retain Unit (note strengths/weaknesses on completion)

GENERAL GOAL	PRIOR INFORMATION SKILLS
	KNOWLEDGE CONTENT
	LEARNING ACTIVITIES

TIME ALLOTMENT	DATES/TIMES

INTRODUCTORY LESSON(S)/MOTIVATION

How will students be prepared for purposeful research (e.g. know essential vocabulary, have written directions, beassured of success)?

CONCLUDING LESSON(S)

OBJECTIVES -

What is the student to learn?
(1) Specific content/concepts
(2) Specific Information Skills from School Information Skills Continued.

Content/Concept Objective

Information Skill(s) Objective

Content/Concept Objective

Information Skill(s)

Content/Concept Objective

Information Skill(s) Objective

INFORMATION SKILLS - GENERAL CLUSTERS

Resource Centre Orientation / Research Strategies / Locating Information - General Sources / Locating Information - Subject Sources / Acquiring and Analyzing Information / Organizing and Recording Information / Communicating and Presenting Information

BE VERY CLEAR - SPECIFY AND ARTICULATE SKILLS

SPECIFIC EXAMPLES OF EACH CLUSTER WILL BE IN THE SCHOOL'S CONTINUUM OF INFORMATION SKILLS

EVALUATION ·	TEACHING STRATEGIES AND LEARNING ACTIVITIES ·
How will student competence be assessed? This relates directly to each objective in the left column.	What is the student to do in order to accomplish the objectives? Any written directions or materials should be appended or noted.

Learning Activity:

No. of students:

Location:

Resources:

Minimum Expectations:

Who will prepare?

Learning Activity

No. of students:

Location:

Resources:

Minimum Expectations:

Who will prepare?

Learning Activity:

No. of students

Location:

Resources:

Minimum Expectations:

Who will prepare?

RESOURCES

ARE ADEQUATE RESOURCES AVAILABLE? CHECKED COLLECTION SPECIALIZATIONS LIST, DISTRICT COLLECTIONS, INDEXES TO PERIODICALS, UNION LIST OF PERIODICALS, ETC.

EASIER	MORE DIFFICULT

PARTICULARLY GOOD RESOURCES

EVALUATION OF UNIT

STRENGTHS	WEAKNESSES

RECOMMENDATIONS FOR REVISION

ACKNOWLEDGMENT

Prepared by Carol-Ann Haycock, Ruth Lindgaard, Patricia Shields and Ken Walters with Ken Haycock, Coordinator of Library Services, and with considerable field testing and input from teachers and teacher-librarians of the Vancouver School Board, British Columbia. (1981)

Teacher-Librarian Collegiality: Strategies for Effective Influence

Ronald Jobe

Establishing relationships in today's world is increasingly challenging whether it is between two people or amongst staff members. A societal barrage of slogans such as, 'Don't get involved,' or 'Do your own thing' makes this even more difficult. People appear to be constantly too busy to set aside time for others. Relationships work only when people take the time to care about one another. It is as true for a teacher-librarian and staff, or a teacher and students.

It is important to be realistic in developing relations with a staff. Not every teacher will be enamored with the teacher-librarian. This fact should not cause undue distress because there can be many reasons for this apparent lack of enthusiasm: poor past experiences, pressures resulting from challenging class situations, or lack of awareness of the potential for school libraries. It should also be noted that service cannot possibly be given on an equal basis in a large school. Those teachers who are interested and demand attention receive service. Other teachers become included in this expanding sphere of influence through patient encouragement.

It is of the utmost importance for teacher-librarians to have established their personal resource centre philosophy, to be confident in themselves as people, to be self-reliant as teachers, and to be innovative, enthusiastic members of the staff. This is the first premise of successfully relating to colleagues. Be secure in yourself and be assertive about your professional privileges and responsibilities.

Collegiality involves being one of the teachers. It demands a sense of presence. The resource centre should be the focal point of activity for teacher-librarians. However, to increase their visibility and availability they should be using the entire school as a resource facility. This includes undertaking such activities as teaching in a classroom, having coffee in the staff room, visiting a teacher to see a new project, or talking to the children on the playground.

Acceptance of the teacher-librarian as a teacher is crucial to cooperative teaching. Muttered lamentations reflecting moans of rejection often do more harm than good. Such complaining does not usually achieve the desired results. However, honest reactions to events often bring staff understanding. Mutual exhaustion at the end of a hectic day, the need for coffee on certain mornings, and the innate pleasure of success will give credence to the evidence that teacher-librarians are colleagues too!

More things are achieved over a cup of coffee than are ever achieved at staff meetings! Insignificant as this statement may appear, it harbours a simple truth: teacher-librarians have to be where the action is. Inevitably the relief centre of the school is the staff room. A place for the whole staff to relax, blow off steam, express irritations, as well as to laugh at themselves. Physical presence makes one part of the mood of the moment and contributes to being looked upon by the staff as 'one of us.' What better place to become aware of what is really happening in the school than the staff room? An alert observer will make note of the expressed problems, frustrations, and desires of the staff for future action.

Whose resource centre is it? Each person in the school should feel free to state that this is 'our' resource centre. One small word can make an enormous difference in the teachers' perception of school resources. A sense of belonging develops when the teacher-librarian openly encourages the mutual selection and utilization of materials. This sense of unity evolves into a commitment to the success of the school resource program. However, the advancement of this program is determined by the positive image which the teacher-librarian projects. This image must reflect a focus of the teacher-librarian as an active participant in the educational program of the school.

What is your image? Only you can change it. What do the teachers on staff really see you doing? Do they actually see you or are you merely a part of the wall decor? Now is the time to consider some strategies which might elicit new spheres of influence for you.

STRATEGIES FOR EFFECTIVE INFLUENCE

Active Listener

You must *make time* for the important things! An observation of the time spent on your activities will be a fairly accurate indicator of your current priorities. Make time to listen. A sympathetic listener is needed in every school. Teachers as well as students have to have someone to talk with, to share their joys, frustrations, problems and defeats.

Complimentor

What every school needs too is a person who cares enough to offer genuine praise where it is deserved. People blossom with compliments. Tension is relieved and they think of themselves in more positive terms. Often teachers will continue to pass such compliments on to their peers and to their students. Such action, although worthy in its own respect, also brings rewards because of the fact that you appear to be more open and approachable.

Written compliments are also most appreciated. When was the last time you wrote a colleague a thank you note for a favour done, or for sharing materials? Don't forget to write to a class of students, the principal, or a parent, too. The effect of such thoughtfulness can be quite overwhelming. Who should you write to today?

Environmental Designer

You can control the school's environment. Simply look around you—do you like to work in such an atmosphere? If not, change it! No you don't have to do all the work, merely provide the opportunity for others to help.

Three swift suggestions for immediate changes include the following:

A. Use colour boldly, plentifully, and freely. Students and teachers are very aware of colours and a duo-colour (red-yellow, blue-brown) is most tantalizing.

B. A little from many creates a lot! If each class contributes only two or three drawings or book characters, you'll have a multitude of sharings.

C. Plan ahead. Teachers like to have two to three weeks notice so that they can plan too! Surprises are just not appreciated.

Start with the resource centre and then gradually flow along the halls. Take over the bulletin boards immediately for visual vitality, then use display cabinets to share hobbies, collections, or travel souvenirs. Always include books and AV materials in these displays to stimulate resource centre use.

Curiosity Coordinator

What's this? Who's eye? Can you see it? How small is small? You are able to enrich the lives of the students who come to the resource centre by asking stimulating questions, creating high interest displays and evolving thought-provoking activities. If the children are from rather uncreative, non risk-oriented classrooms, stimulating curiosity about the exciting facts in books, making literature live, and sharing an enthusiasm for reading will all contribute to opening up new vistas. Success is achieving a glint in the eyes! Special attention should be given to making sessions both interesting and enjoyable for teachers, too! If the teacher wants to return the children will certainly be there as well.

Free Agent

Giving unrequested service proves to be a surprisingly effective means to arouse reluctant resource centre users. It proves that you are with it, know what's happening, and are concerned with each teacher individually. You must keep alert to current classroom projects, types of materials the teachers and students are borrowing, as well as current news events. In essence a major strategy to develop is that of being a professional eavesdropper! Overhearing comments made during informal conversations allows you to become aware of colleagues' needs without their realizing it. You then appear to be a mind reader!

Sustained Ideator

Teachers frequently need a shot in the arm. New ideas in small doses are always welcome. If you don't think up ideas readily, you might devise a collection of ideas which you keep for just this purpose. Quick one period art activities, language arts game ideas, crossword puzzles, mysterious science activities, or geography clues are most applicable. You must also maximize your use of periodicals. Quickly skim new issues for articles and ideas which might appeal to individual teachers. The time spent writing quick notes to colleagues will prove to be most beneficial, especially if you let two or more teachers know about the same article!

Library Promoter

Teachers are paid to read! You should take it as a challenge to motivate your colleagues to open a book! If they already read try to expand their reading tastes and interests. The only way to get staff members interested in books is to talk about them, preferably in a crowded staff room. Borrow books from colleagues and then quickly return them along with your comments. These informal book discussions often spur others to read too! Make books visible for the teachers by casually leaving them lying around on the staff room tables. Did you ever think to put some in the washrooms? Explosive results are assured—at least they'll be noticed!!

Avid Articulator

One of your most effective strategies is to be able to exhibit a high degree of oral competency within the staff. Always insist on a regular time during each staff meeting for a resource centre report. This must be an enthusiastic sharing of the program including new skill sessions to be offered, possible followup activities to storytelling, as well as recently arrived materials. Be sufficiently courageous to give book talks. Relate good books for children as well as those books in the collection which are of interest to adults.

Corner the consultants or visiting specialists in your school. These people are usually full of ideas and suggestions. Sharing this information with the staff sharpens your curricular awareness and gives you a point of departure for discussing school programs.

How are you at answering children's questions? We always need to improve this skill. Do you actually answer the question? Do you give sufficient specific information? Do you overtalk? Listen to yourself!

Colourful verbal barrages against much of the required 'donkey' work of a resource centre even serves to educate teachers into the 'secret' activities of teacher-librarians. Mutual respect evolves when teachers realize that you have a heavy work load too!

Skills Exemplar

Don't forget that your image must include an expertise in research skills. Show it! Take every opportunity to get involved with the teachers and students in their practical assignments.

Volunteer your services to teach a specific skill such as the use of the thesaurus or note taking from an encyclopedia. Remember that you are often instructing teachers too!

Individual research projects with either eager or reluctant youngsters are a grand opportunity to exhibit what can really be achieved when individual needs are recognized. These youngsters, who have themselves experienced success, can consequently serve as tutors for their peers. You become a successful skills promoter only when you can show the purposeful integration of research skills into subject areas. Teachers must see the direct value of taking time to focus on skill ability, before they will integrate such practices into their teaching styles.

Theme Planner

That's a great idea!
And you could also include...
Did you think about...
Why don't we try it?

You start simply with sincere interest and your eager enthusiasm continues to captivate your colleagues into becoming involved. It's crucial that you include yourself in the planning and participation of such themes.

The duration of thematic units can be one class period, one day, a week, or even a month. Success will often extend the time interval. Single focus sessions could highlight on the students' interests in crazy hats, underground war movements, great disasters, explosive moments in history, or indeed musicians alive today. Special days can be a "Salute to Edith Cavell, Helen Keller, or Florence Nightingale." 'I'm Blue!' might motivate a colour day with everybody wearing blue clothing and acting blue! A week of mystery, mice, or outerspace creatures can be followed by glimpses of aardvarks, King Tut, or magnetic attractiveness!

Each theme can include a selection of book talks, slides, pictures, poetry, excerpts from novels, related eye witness accounts, art prints, music, realia, or sharings of personal experiences. The secret is for you to start out conservatively with small units and build on each successful happening. It won't be long before you are literally exploding with special events!

Curriculum Architect

The most complex, time consuming, intellectually demanding yet rewarding strategy that you can undertake is to design an aspect of curriculum. This is usually done with a team of teachers sufficiently in advance so as to allow time for establishing objectives, searching for resources, detailed planning, and integrating subject areas. A good starting point is to challenge your co-workers to try to make a routine topic more stimulating and enriching not only for the students but also for themselves. The Middle Ages, astronomy, urban redevelopment, pollution, sports psychology, nutrition, China, and survival of the oceans all offer imaginative possibilities for fresh approaches. This strategy is our ultimate goal, but it is only possible after you have successfully established a resource program and have achieved the confidence of your fellow teachers.

Collegiality? It's up to you! Only you can establish mutual bonds of respect, admiration, and influence between the teachers and yourself. No one can do it for you. Determine which strategies are successful for you now and try to adopt new ones. Frankly, you can't start any sooner in life than today!

Communication Skills and Strategies for Teacher-Librarians

Barbara Howlett

Cooperative planning and teaching techniques between the classroom teacher and the teacher-librarian constitute an effective method for the teacher-librarian to be more directly involved in the instructional process. However, the professional literature reveals that teacher-librarians must overcome a variety of negative perceptions about their role, before they can become completely accepted as professional teachers in their own right. Alixe Hambleton found, for example, that "the school library seems to play only a marginal role in the total educational program, and that the low regard for the school librarian militates against a direct involvement in the instructional program of the school"[7:5] and participants in a survey conducted by C. Jennie Casciano-Savignano[4:30] identified several common impediments to cooperative relationships between teachers and teacher-librarians. These include lack of awareness of teacher-librarians of the school program, defensiveness by teacher-librarians regarding the use of the library, lack of understanding of the role of the teacher-librarian, and lack of frequent contact with the teacher-librarian. Suggestions made to remedy these problems almost all involved increased contact and improved communication between teachers and teacher-librarians.

It is evident that teacher-librarians must improve their image and the perception of their role within the school community. One way to accomplish this is to study different models of successful communication and to apply basic principles to develop better intra-school relations. There are several ways to facilitate communication between teachers and teacher-librarians which, in turn, should aid in developing more favourable relations and increased cooperation. These areas include those personality traits that lead to positive and effective communication, the development of improved interpersonal skills, and the cultivation of certain "selling skills" that help to promote services offered by the teacher-librarian.

Of primary importance to the teacher-librarian's success in promoting the resource centre is a sense of confidence. It is essential that the teacher-librarian in fact believe in the role of the teacher-librarian. Having confidence in the worth of the service will inspire the confidence of others; commitment will help sell it to the rest of the school. The confident teacher-librarian will make overtures, and not be discouraged by rebuffs. It takes strength and a solid self-concept to survive the rejections that are experienced in approaching other teachers.

The teacher-librarian might also be less cautious in interaction with other staff members. Risks must be taken in introducing new ideas and concepts; the teacher-librarian must not be inhibited by any reticence or hesitation to "force" him or herself on others. Both Alixe Hambleton and Shirley Blair comment on the effects of cautiousness in teacher-librarians. Hambleton states that "cautiousness may be partially responsible for the lack of cohesiveness within the librarian group ... and the tendency to perform most often those tasks that relate to library expertise rather than those which involve the librarian in the teaching program."[7:7] In her study she also found low cautiousness scores to be associated with high effectiveness scores. Blair notes that one of the best predictors of high circulation of materials is extroversion.[2:97] One of the prime characteristics of extroversion is less cautiousness.

A third personality trait that makes for successful cooperative interaction is communicativeness. The effective communicator is vocal, willing to speak up to convey ideas and attitudes, to support them, to see that they are carried out, and to advertise their eventual success. The teacher-librarian must also be proficient in organizing written communication, preparing briefs, articles, and reports. Providing in-service is another important aspect of a teacher-librarian's communicativeness. Workshops and in-service sessions are essential in "getting the message across." As well, informed conversations over coffee provide a valuable means of communicating with teachers. Blair notes the great influence that such informal conversations have on teacher use of the library.[2:97] Above all, effective communication necessitates being visible and getting involved!

The successful promotion of the resource centre will also involve innovative programs and novel approaches which tend to capture the imagination of others, and often may succeed where other concerted, though perhaps less creative, efforts have failed. In seeking access to a teaching partnership, it is important to have fresh ideas and a diversity of interests to explore. Of interest here is Hambleton's observation that "school librarians rated high on both original thinking and cautiousness."[7:7] Her hypothesis was that although teacher-librarians had original ideas, they were prevented from implementing them because of their extreme cautiousness. Clearly this is not the route to improved teacher/teacher-librarian cooperation.

A further characteristic which enhances the effectiveness of teacher-librarian interaction is determination or drive. A teacher-librarian may possess desirable personality traits, but unless he/she is persistent in practicing them, they will be of little benefit. It is difficult to overstate the importance of such assertiveness in the teacher-librarian's role. Although one must not, of course, become too aggressive and hence offensive, to be determined in pursuing the goals of the program is both worthwhile and admirable.

In order to counteract low sociability, teacher-librarians must increase their efforts to be cheerful and friendly, to establish a pleasant and inviting atmosphere in their libraries, and to encourage teacher input in connection with both programs and facilities. Teacher-librarians should concentrate on being a part of the social aspect of school life and avoid sealing themselves off in isolation as too many are prone to do.

INTERPERSONAL SKILLS

Teacher-librarians tend to achieve low scores in measures of personal relations as compared to scores on other traits. A need, then, seems to exist for improved interpersonal relations between teacher-librarians and those with whom they interact. The very nature of the phrase "cooperative planning and teaching" implies the use of interpersonal skills in the achievement of cooperation, as the essence of an interpersonal relationship involves "working cooperatively with others in trying to achieve ... goals."[6:26] Gerard Egan goes on to say that "successful interaction requires the development of effective interpersonal skills."[6:17] These skills are important in helping the individual "develop feelings of interpersonal competence" and in enabling him/her to "establish effective working relationships."

Interpersonal skills may be roughly grouped into two areas—the skills of letting yourself be known, and the skills of responding. The former group involves the specific skills of self-disclosure, concreteness, and the expression of feeling; the latter encompasses listening and responding techniques, empathy, acceptance, warmth, and trust. Openness, spontaneity, and authenticity characterize both skills of expression and skills of response.

Self-disclosure involves revealing thoughts, attitudes, beliefs, and feelings so that others may come to know us as we really are. The key to effective self-disclosure lies in not over-disclosing (talking too much about oneself, or talking too intimately in a casual situation), or underdisclosing (speaking little or not at all about oneself, even when the situation calls for it). The person who wishes to communicate effectively in a casual social situation with co-workers would be moderately self-disclosing, revealing enough to establish social relationships, but not enough to be threatening or offensive. Concreteness involves speaking about specific experiences and feelings rather than speaking vaguely or in abstractions. The latter creates distance between the speaker and the person with whom he/she is communicating. If self-disclosure is to be effective and immediate it must be concrete. Feelings and emotions arise in any interpersonal interaction and their proper expression must be considered. Interpersonal skills emphasize an open expression of honest feelings; they should not be disguised or repressed, but neither should they be manufactured for effect. Whether emotions are positive or negative, they can be expressed constructively, and although they are often difficult to verbalize (since their expression involves a degree of risk), emotional assertiveness "allows for emotional ventilation, (while leaving) the doors of communication open."[6:75]

The skills of responding have a great effect on the success of interpersonal relationships. These involve practicing effective listening and responding techniques, and communicating empathy, acceptance, warmth, and trust. The teacher-librarian who is skilled in these techniques will find it much easier to involve another teacher in an instructional partnership.

The aim of communicative interaction is to demonstrate understanding of the other. However, before this can occur, effective listening must have taken place. Effective listening involves attending to what is being said and not engaging in any peripheral activities. In demonstrating this attention, one adopts a posture of involvement, facing the speaker squarely, leaning toward him/her, maintaining eye contact, and above all being relaxed. Such careful attention is far more likely to make an impact on the other person than a half-hearted attempt to listen. In effective listening, it is important to attend to both verbal and nonverbal behaviour, for response must be to the words. Larry Samovar states that "what a receiver sees guides his understanding of what he hears."[5:287] and conversely, from the sender's viewpoint, "visual feedback clues sent by the receiver provide an invaluable index to the effect of the message."[5:287]

Once effective listening has taken place, and understanding achieved, proper response techniques come into play. According to Alton Barbour, responses may be confirming or disconfirming. It is important, of course, to endeavour to provide confirming responses to someone who is communicating with you. Techniques of confirming include "direct acknowledgement, agreement about content, supportive responses, clarifying responses (those that elaborate on what has been said by asking for more information), and expressions of positive feeling."[1:23-33] To be avoided are such disconfirming reactions as impervious, irrelevant, impersonal, incoherent, or incongruous responses.

The communication of a listener's empathy, acceptance, warmth, and eventual trust are all closely related responding skills. Empathy involves the listener's ability to understand another individual—to interpret correctly his/her feelings, beliefs, and attitudes. It gets at not only what another person states, but also what is implied or left unstated. To communicate empathy, one must create a climate of support, not feigning understanding, answering with a question or a cliché, restating what the other person has said, or jumping in too quickly.

Leading from empathy, and essential to it, is acceptance. In addition to being understood, it is necessary for the speaker to feel accepted. If the speaker feels warmly regarded, he/she is much more likely to communicate with the listener in a genuine and relaxed manner. Acceptance and warmth gradually develop and eventually lead to trust, an essential ingredient

in all interpersonal relationships. According to Kim Griffin, a listener develops trust in a speaker according to his/her perception of the speaker's expertness, character, good will, dynamism, and personal attraction.[1:29] Kaul and Schmidt found that "a person is trusted if he respects the needs and feeling of others, offers information and opinions for the benefit of others, generates feelings of comfort and willingness to confide, and is open and honest about his motives."[6:139] Trust is such an essential ingredient in interpersonal relationships because in its absence very little communication will occur; no one is willing to take the risks involved. Clearly, if a teacher-librarian can communicate such empathy, acceptance, warmth, and finally trust to another teacher, he/she is well on the way to achieving that elusive cooperative relationship.

Despite the best of intentions, and the most accomplished interpersonal communicative skills, occasions will arise where conflict and opposition will occur. The teacher-librarian must be aware of such problems, and be prepared to deal with them effectively. According to Robinson,[14:137] interpersonal conflict among co-workers often stems from jealousy, rivalry, or a personality conflict. He recommends approaching the problem positively, with the first step being to identify the source of the conflict. Try to operate from the other person's frame of reference to attempt to understand and resolve the problem. The most important thing to remember is not to feed the negative aspects of the situation. Try to be constructive and positive, realizing that often it is not necessarily a "bad" characteristic of the other person that is the source of the conflict, but how that person makes one feel—inadequate, awkward, etc.

Opposition to cooperative planning and teaching is encountered by every teacher-librarian upon some occasion. A teacher may be reluctant to give up total control of students in order to create a team teaching relationship. Seyfarth found that "teachers moving from a self-contained into a team teaching situation ... are attracted by the chance to take part in a new type of program ... but at the same time they are reluctant to surrender the freedom of action inherent in the self-contained classroom."[16:297] The teacher-librarian should try to anticipate problems with this type of attitude and endeavour to deal with them before attempting to implement a cooperative program. Teachers must be reassured that the teacher-librarian is sincerely interested in helping the classroom teacher to attain mutually agreed upon objectives, and not in taking control. Since the success of the entire cooperative teaching process depends upon the classroom teacher's favourable attitude, the importance of overcoming this kind of opposition cannot be overemphasized.

No one technique is likely to solve all conflicts, or counteract all the types of opposition that a teacher-librarian will come up against, but sensitivity combined with a knowledge of problem-solving techniques, and a competence in basic interpersonal communication skills will go a long way toward their resolution.

SELLING THE SERVICE

A field much concerned with the presentation and promotion of products, ideas, and services is that of marketing. The teacher-librarian would do well to study sales techniques and incorporate them into efforts to "sell" a program of cooperative planning and teaching to the classroom teacher. These include having a thorough knowledge of the product or service to be sold, using the tools of effective communication, being persuasive, and knowing how to cope with resistance and objections.

In any sales presentation, good "product" knowledge is an indispensable asset. Only by being well prepared in advance, and having developed some expertise in the knowledge of the product or service to be sold, can a sales person expect to communicate its advantages. As well, the product must be explained in terms meaningful to potential customers. Most products and services have both features and benefits. A feature is a "desirable characteristic that is inherent in the products or in its performance."[15:23] However, people don't buy a product for its features. Rather they buy what the features of the product will do for them or its *benefits*. A benefit is a "definable advantage, improvement, or satisfaction customers acquire or experience that derives from a feature of the product they buy."[15:24] So it is the benefits to the customer that must be concentrated on in the acquisition of product knowledge. The teacher-librarian, in selling programs to the staff, must prepare a case well, and make sure that it is the advantages that accrue from cooperative planning and teaching that are being emphasized.

Effective communication is as important a skill in salesmanship as it is in interpersonal interaction. Sales communication, however, tends to emphasize the effective presentation of an idea, the communication of a message rather than concern itself primarily with the interpersonal aspects of a given situation. Of course interpersonal skills such as showing empathy, interest, and listening attentively will come into play, but a sales person is chiefly concerned with other aspects of communication such as presenting him or herself and the product or service clearly, and using varied and effective selling tools — visual presentations — to reinforce the appeal of the product or service being offered. Certain principles of communication common in the establishment of good public sales relations are useful to anyone who is attempting to communicate the benefits of a service.

The audience should be preconditioned to receive favourably the service that is being promoted. As in the case of reassuring the classroom teacher who is reluctant to share control of the class, considerable advance groundwork promoting the benefits of the service will increase its chances of a favourable reception upon presentation. Once the audience has been prepared for the presentation, it is then important to tailor the message and the means of its communication to the predisposition of the intended audience. (The term "audience" as used here denotes any number of listeners from one to a large group.) The message should not be a one way outpouring of facts and information, but a two way communication with opportunities for audience interaction and participation. It should also stress positive benefits for the "customer," recognizing and dealing with the self-interest motive, the "What's in it for me?" attitude that is an essential and constructive component in selling a service. The presenter of the message must take care to speak the receivers' language, and to keep the presentation within the context of the interests and experience of those toward which it is directed.

Having devised an appropriate message and means of delivering it, the next concern involves the audience to whom it should be first presented. It has been found effective in sales and public relations to approach first those who are sympathetic to your views and who may be in a position to influence others.[10:340] The satisfied customer is the greatest selling tool there is. The teacher-librarian who can reach and convince one or two key staff members probably won't have to sell others on the value of the programs — they will do it. A final principle important in sales communication is that of repetition. It takes a long time for a message to get through to busy people who are involved with many different concerns. The message must be repeated often (in a variety of ways so as to avoid boredom or irritation) until it makes an impression on its intended audience. Sometimes the very repetition of a message creates a tendency toward belief — it gradually becomes accepted as true.[10:341]

The art of being persuasive is inseparable from the art of selling. The whole sales "pitch" — the approach, the presentation, the close — is an act of persuading the prospect that a need exists and then motivating him/her to take action to fulfill that need. Learning certain principles of the persuasion technique will better equip teacher-librarians to convince other staff members of the value of their programs. It is important to first present the problem, then its solution. If this is done in the reverse order, it is not always easy to understand the solution's relevance because a need has not yet been established.

Studies in the art of persuasion have found that an audience is more receptive to the persuasive appeal if points that all agree upon are discussed first, before moving to any items of disagreement.[3:59] Similarly, positive arguments can be discussed and refuted. "When people hear supporting arguments first, they become persuaded by those arguments and are, therefore, closer to the position of the source."[3:57] One other variable that has been found to affect the persuasiveness of a message is the intensity of language used in its communication. For example, a program that will "drastically reduce" a teacher's marking load for an assignment sounds more appealing than one that will "decrease" or "cut down on" the marking load. Other ways of intensifying language are by inserting qualifiers such as "certainly," and by using metaphors to dramatize a description or comparison.[3:62]

Like the salesperson who regularly comes up against resistance and objections, the teacher-librarian will also need to use good interpersonal skills and conflict management techniques to overcome opposition to innovations. There are also effective sales techniques that can overcome objections. First of all, however, it is worth noting that objections do not necessarily constitute a refusal to accept the proposal being offered. Often objections are to be welcomed, as they at least indicate that the proposal is being thought about, and provide feedback as to where, in the eyes of others, its potential problems lie.

In handling resistance, it is important to safeguard the other's pride, and exonerate him/her from any blame for expressing an objection. Often it is a good idea to accept part of the objection, to make a concession before trying to overcome it.[9:148] Most sources that deal with sales methods for overcoming resistance agree on some basic techniques. One tactic is to give validity to the objection, but detract attention from it by pointing out other features or benefits of the proposal that offset or compensate for it. Or, a variation of this technique is to agree, then convert the objection into a reason for accepting the proposal. Another suggestions is to treat the objection as a question, agreeing that it is a good question which should be dealt with. Sometimes it is possible to postpone answering an objection, or to avoid it entirely, especially if it is somewhat frivolous. Finally, it is even possible upon occasion to make a direct denial of an objection. This technique should be used with caution and usually only when the objection voiced is completely untrue, or is personally derogatory in some way.

In an effort to engage the classroom teacher in a teaching partnership and/or to maintain that partnership, the teacher-librarian can (if self-confident, creative, determined, and skilled at communication and less cautious!) make use of an almost unlimited number of strategies. Some of these strategies reflect the acquisition of interpersonal communication skills, others, a mastery of sales techniques. Some are designed to advertise the library and improve public relations, others are specifically intended to demonstrate to the teacher that the teacher-librarian is willing and able to share in teaching. Some involve personal interaction; others are visual, oral and written. All will be useful in developing effective cooperative planning and teaching programs with the classroom teacher.

SPECIFIC SUGGESTIONS

Blair found that at least three techniques, if practiced by the teacher-librarian, had a positive effect on the degree of resource centre use. One of these strategies involves working with the teacher in cooperative curriculum planning (visiting classrooms, observing programs, assisting in curriculum development, providing consultative assistance for teachers, helping the teacher select materials, assisting in student evaluation). Another practice is to provide in-service by disseminating information from professional journals, conducting orientation for new staff members, utilizing and producing instructional materials, and demonstrating the services and equipment that are available in the resource centre. A third method was to involve teachers in the selection and evaluation of library resources.

Elizabeth Hoffman, like Blair, recommends "encourag(ing) the interest, support, and participation of others in the selection and use of materials."[8:32] Also important in her eyes is the need to relate to students, fellow teachers, administrators, and parents by soliciting their suggestions, keeping them informed, and thanking them for their cooperation. Various methods of publicizing the library in the community include inviting school board members and parents to visit on special occasions such as Book Week, or Library Week, displaying student-designed bookmarks in local bookstores, informing the owner of popular titles so that they may be stocked, and offering information on your activities to local newspapers.[8:33-34] Hoffman suggests that it is important in successful library program promotion to "build your relationships long before you need them."[8:35]

At a workshop on communications, members of the Ontario Library Association School Libraries Division made several recommendations.[12] Personal techniques of communication involve the teacher-librarian being visible, available, having an open door policy, inviting teachers and parents in to the library, holding staff meetings in the library, encouraging "non-library" happenings in the resource centre, knowing key personnel, and participating in in-service presentations for staff. Further suggestions indicate that the teacher-librarian who wants to interact effectively with the school staff should smile (!), visit the staff room frequently, encourage social contact, invite feedback from teachers, and be positive. In connection with the teacher-librarian's instructional role, recommended practices include attending other department meetings, keeping in touch with outside resources, visiting teachers in their classrooms, discussing new curricula, and offering one to one assistance to teachers.

The visual and aural strategies include displaying notices, poster or calendars of coming events, and graffiti boards; producing bulletin board or displays in show cases, film festivals and slide and/or tape presentations of activities; showing new materials to heads of departments; and advertising positive results attained in library programs.

Graphic techniques of communication again chiefly promote the service offered by the library, only this time in written or pictorial form. Such things as resource lists for staff and student library handbooks, reports on library service, letters to parents, surveys of student and teacher interest, and questionnaires to parents about library service demands are all suggested tactics for advertising some of the library's important functions.

Other miscellaneous methods of communication include having a coffee pot in the library to encourage informal visits and chats, installing a suggestion box in the library or staff room, getting involved with other programs in the school, planning wine and cheese or coffee and goodies meetings, displaying new acquisitions in equipment and materials, and holding September orientations for new staff and students.

Teacher-librarians are bound to occasionally encounter conflict, resistance, and objections in their efforts to establish or improve communications with teachers. Various skills for countering such opposition have been suggested, and likely these will prove of value in coping with difficult encounters. However, more specific strategies to follow in dealing with unapproachable teachers may further clarify the steps to be taken. When having problems communicating with a teacher, it might prove useful to offer assistance in a concrete way by making your own suggestions. Sometimes an invitation to come in for coffee might have profitable dividends, or promoting materials to the students of the class might cause a difficult teacher to seek your aid. Ideal occasions to try some of these approaches occur in the staff room—informally, at the beginning of a new project, or after the receipt of particularly useful materials. And remember at all times to be friendly, diplomatic, and complimentary!

Only by striving to develop assertive personality traits, by learning and practicing effective interpersonal and sales communication techniques, and by employing specific strategies designed to facilitate teacher/teacher-librarian interaction, can the teacher-librarian hope to be successful in efforts to establish a meaningful and productive program of cooperative planning and teaching in the school. To quote

Hambleton again: "Communication ... will not take place ... without a realization ... that both teaching and learning go on in a school library, that the school librarian makes an important contribution to the intellectual and social growth of the student, and that this contribution is possible because of an expertise which effectively blends librarianship and teaching skills. This will be realized only when that expertise is both practiced and effectively communicated in such a way that it becomes recognized as a necessary part of the educational enterprise."[7:7]

REFERENCES

1. Barbour, Alton. *Interpersonal Communication: Teaching Strategies and Resources*. Urbana, Illinois: Eric Clearinghouse on Reading and Communication Skills, 1974.

2. Blair, Shirley. "Teachers and the School Resource Centre." *Canadian Library Journal*, Volume 35, Number 2 (April, 1978), pp. 93-100.

3. Burgoon, Michael, Judee K. Heston and James McCroskey. *Small Group Communication: A Functional Approach*. New York: Holt, Rinehart, and Winston, 1974.

4. Casciano-Savignano, C. Jennie. "Interpersonal Relationships in Secondary Schools." *NASSP Bulletin*, Volume 60, Number 399 (April, 1976), pp. 26-30.

5. Cathcart, Robert S., and Larry A. Samovar, editors. *Small Group Communication: A Reader*. Dubuque, Iowa: Wm. C. Brown Company, 1970.

6. Egan, Gerard. *Interpersonal Living*. Monterey, Calif.: Brooks/Cole Publishing Company, 1976.

7. Hambleton, Alixe. "Static in the Educational Intercom: Conflict and the School Librarian." *Emergency Librarian*, Volume 6, Number 5-6 (May-August, 1979), pp. 5-7.

8. Hoffman, Elizabeth P. "The Art of Public Relations." *School Media Quarterly*, Volume 9, Number 1 (Fall, 1980), pp. 31-35.

9. Kinder, Jack, Jr., Garry D. Kinder and Roger Staubach. *Winning Strategies in Selling*. Englewood Cliffs, N.J.: Prentice-Hall, 1981.

10. Marston, John E. *Modern Public Relations*. New York: McGraw-Hill Book Company, 1979.

11. Nebgen, Mary K. "Coping with Conflict in Educational Circles." *Thrust for Educational Leadership*, Volume 9, Number 2 (November, 1979), pp. 25-27.

12. Ontario Library Association. School Libraries Division. "Communication with Administration, Teachers, Students, and Community." Toronto: The Division, Spring, 1973.

13. Reid, Allan L. *Modern Applied Salesmanship*. Pacific Palisades, Calif.: Goodyear Publishing Company, 1975.

14. Robinson, Louie. "How to Cope with People You Dislike." *Ebony*, Volume xxxiv, Number 5 (March, 1979), pp. 135-42.

15. Seng, Roger W. *The Skills of Selling*. New York: Amacom, a division of American Management Associations, 1977.

16. Seyfarth, John T. and Robert Lynn Canady. "Assessing Causes of Teacher Attitudes toward Team Teaching." *Education*, Volume 98, Number 3 (March-April, 1978), pp. 297-300.

17. Taylor, Donna. "Cooperation: Teacher-Librarian Style." *Elementary English*, Volume 46, Number 1 (January, 1969), pp. 66-68.

Maximizing Learning in Small Groups

Igor Kusyszyn

Do you want to increase learning, performance, and enjoyment in your group or class? You can do so by using these methods.

Take care of the means and the end will take care of itself. —M. Gandhi

If you give a man a fish, he will eat it and soon be hungry. If you teach a man to fish he will never be hungry. —Chinese Proverb

FUNDAMENTALS

Many people fail because they conclude that fundamentals simply do not apply in their case. —M. L. Cichon

1. Learn each student's name. Get the students to learn each others names. (Use name tags if you like.) Use first names when addressing each other.

A man's name is to him the sweetest and most important sound in any language. —Dale Carnegie

2. Arrange the seating in a circle so that each student can maintain eye contact with other students.

Pressed into service means pressed out of shape. — Robert Frost

3. Seat the more talkative students opposite the more quiet ones.

4. Learn the student's concerns about the work of the group, i.e., is attendance required? exactly what are we responsible for? exactly how will we be evaluated? are you a hard marker?

5. · Disturbances and excitements must take precedence. If they are ignored you will lose the student. He/she will turn off.

6. (i) Find out early what the students' interests are in relation to the subject matter. Ask them to write their interests down. Give them as much time as they require to do this, down to the slowest student. Collect the writings and systematically consider each student's interests in front of the group. Ask each student to elaborate on his/her specific interests. Invite the students to inquire about each other's interests.

(ii) Make the subject relevant to the students' interests. If you don't they will forget it all.

An effective leader establishes objectives that help individuals reach their personal goals. — L. Peter

7. Learn how knowledgeable the students are about the subject matter (no matter how many "prerequisites" they may have taken). Bring the less knowledgeable students up to the level of the more knowledgeable ones before proceeding further. Encourage peer teaching at this early stage.

8. Allow those students who are only interested in passing the course a way to do so which is fair to you, to them, and to the institution.

9. Be enthusiastic about the course material. Enthusiasm is contagious.

Nothing great was ever achieved without enthusiasm. — Emerson

10. You may initiate a discussion by setting a problem, by asking an open ended question, or by beginning with a controversy. Discussion is hindered when you ask questions that have "right" answers. Invite them to speculate. Allow them to play with ideas.

Learning depends on the process of discovery. — Ruth C. Cohn

11. To increase participation talk less and listen more. Encourage the students to talk directly to one another instead of going through you each time. Try not to be the centre of attention most of the time.

Tis wisdom sometimes to seem a fool. — English Proverb

12. Do not make decisions for the group. Decisions should be made cooperatively through discussion. This increases interest and involvement.

13. Assign readings periodically as they become relevant to the topic under discussion. Do not hand out a long reading list.

14. Allow the group freedom to progress at a pace comfortable to them and not to you.

He who treads softly goes far. — Chinese Proverb

15. When the meeting is to span more than 75 minutes allow time for a short break.

16. Inform the students well in advance how they may prepare for a specific meeting. Make it easy for them to prepare by making the necessary materials easily available.

17. Clarify the goals or objectives for each meeting. Is today's goal subject matter mastery? Or is the goal to solve a problem? Or is the goal to discuss an issue?

He flung himself from the room, flung himself upon his horse, and rode madly off in all directions. — Stephen Leacock

18. If the goal of the group is subject matter mastery, the material should be pre-read and the following format adopted: clarification of terms, the author's message, major and minor themes, integration of the material with other knowledge, application of the material, and evaluation of the author's presentation.

19. If the goal of the group is to solve problems the best results are obtained by first asking each individual to write down as many solutions in front of the whole group for discussion. Research has shown that this method produces the highest quality and the greatest number of solutions.

When we think alike, no one thinks very much. — W. Lippmann

20. Break up larger groups (8 to 30) into smaller units (1 to 5) from time to time.

21. Do not set yourself up as an authority (even though you may be one). This produces anxiety, discourages participation, and invites resentment.

The fish has no right in the Cormorant's beak. — Hindu Proverb

22. Listen carefully to each student in order to learn his/her unique frame of reference. Half the time what you hear is not exactly what the student means. Ask the speaker to elaborate.

There is something that is much more scarce, something finer far, something rarer than ability. It is the ability to recognize ability. — E. Hubbarb

23. Don't rush in order to cover all of the course content. If you do they will quickly forget it. Don't be concerned if all of the content isn't covered. It is more important to be effective than efficient.

That carpenter is not the Best who makes more chips than all the Rest. — A. Gutterman

24. (i) Use praise often. Praise builds confidence and enhances desirable behaviours.

(ii) Rarely criticize. Criticism damages a person's ego but does not stamp out the undesirable behaviour.

A pat on the back is only a few vertebrae removed from a kick in the pants, but is miles ahead in results. — V. Wilcox

25. Regard your students as mature, as individuals, and as experts in areas in which you are not.

Every man I meet is in some way my superior; and in that I can learn of him. — Emerson

26. Recognize minority opinions. You can use them to upgrade the quality of discussion and increase cohesiveness.

27. Allow periods of silence to occur. The students may be thinking!

Deliberating is not delaying. — Ecclesiasticus

FOUNDATIONS AND OTHER CONSIDERATIONS

a) Existence
Humans have a need to confirm their existence. We confirm our existence when we become mentally and emotionally excited. You may help a student confirm his/her existence by getting him/her aroused through the methods recommended in this guide.

I think therefore I am. — Descartes

b) Worth (Esteem)
Humans have a need to confirm their worth. You can confirm a student's worth with rewards such as praise, grades, recognition (listening attentively, using his/her name) and by validating his/her thinking by agreeing with the student.

The deepest principle in human nature is the craving to be appreciated. — William James

Learning will be more enjoyable and more permanent the more often the existence and worth needed are given satisfaction in the group.

We both exist and know that we exist, and rejoice in this existence and this knowledge. — S. Butler

c) Effectance
Humans have a need to have an effect on their environment. You can help satisfy the students' needs for effectance by reacting to what they say and do. You can also allow them the freedom to affect the other students. Allow them to be productive, creative, critical, provocative, etc. The more that you allow students to affect you and the others in the group the more meaningful, lasting, and satisfying will their learning be. (The need for effectance is similar to the need for power.)

The bigger they are the harder they fall. — Anonymous

d) Reward and Punishment
Social rewards such as praise and recognition lower anxiety, raise self-esteem, promote more active participation, and produce a comfortable climate in which more creative work emerges. Social punishment such as criticism produces anxiety, frustration, and silence.

He that has been shipwrecked shudders at still waters. — Publius Ovidius Naso

e) Activate
At all times try to get the students to be active (thinking, feeling, speaking) rather than passive (listening only). If they are not active they will not learn.

Learning is an active process. We learn by doing. — Dale Carnegie

f) Feedback
Give the students many chances to improve. Set many mini-tasks. Give feedback constantly. The more feedback the faster the learning. The less feedback the greater the confusion.

g) Allow them to fail
Establish a comfortable, non-threatening atmosphere in which the students can risk saying "stupid" things (can risk failing). Students need many opportunities to fail safely. Safe failing is conducive to learning and creativity. Thomas Edison failed more than 2,000 times before he perfected the light bulb.

The world ceases to be a pleasure when it ceases to be a speculation. — Balzac

h) Leadership
Groups with leaders function better than groups without leaders. However, do not monopolize the role. Allow students to occupy the role of leader often. Several leaders may emerge during the course of a single meeting.

I've got to follow them, I am their leader. — Ledru-Rollin

i) Resources
For maximal performance the group should exploit the resources (skills, natural abilities, unique experiences, knowledge) of its members.

The variety of individual personalities is the world's highest richness. — J. Huxley

j) Self-Disclose
Be open about your background, your training, your knowledge, and lack of it, and about your professional and personal biases. All of these will influence the functioning of the group. Self-disclosure promotes trust and produces disclosure in others.

He who persists in genuineness will increase in adequacy. — T. Lynch

k) Use Spontaneous Humour
Laugh at your subject and yourself when appropriate occasions present themselves.

l) Don't Lecture for More than a Few Minutes
How much do you remember of what your professors told you? How much are you trying to tell your students? (It may be telling.)

The only thing to do with good advice is to pass it on, it is never of any use to oneself. — Oscar Wilde

m) Amount of Structure in Group Work
Some is better than none. Less better than more.

n) Do Not Stress Grades
Dr. Donald Hoyt's (1965) review of 4 research studies concludes, "Present evidence strongly suggests that college grades bear little or no relationship to any measures of adult accomplishment." This was found to be true in any area studied: business, teaching, engineering, medicine, scientific research, studies of eminence, miscellaneous occupations, and in non-vocational accomplishments. Do not stress grades. Foster involvement.

It is unfortunate that young people must go to school and interrupt their education. — George Bernard Shaw

Networking — Essential to Survival

Ken Haycock

We continue to witness a peculiar paradox in our profession: a strong trend to networking for the sharing of resources (thus linking us and our collections to others) while at the same time a renewed attention to the isolation of the teacher-librarian in the school and the children's/YA librarian in the public library. While we continue to develop partnerships with colleagues in teaching situations and system-wide library programs perhaps we should also focus on the potential of networking us as individuals for the sharing of program ideas and expertise. There is no place for false modesty here — we all have things to share just as we all have things to learn.

When you're selecting new materials for a special unit or theme, who do you call? When you're starting a new teaching program in an unknown subject area who do you contact for ideas? When you're faced with your first puppet show for kindergarten age youngsters where do you look for support and assistance? If you're the only librarian serving the mentally handicapped in your area where do you find a soul-mate who faces the same problems, hopes and frustrations?

For a group connected with the information and communication industries we seem decidedly remiss in informing each other about what we do and hope to do and in communicating with each other so that we might be contacted for support. Even within our own systems we rarely know the strengths of our colleagues and the specifics of the programs they have in place.

If we do have that willingness to share and to be contacted, it becomes essential to establish the mechanisms and processes for fostering this support for growth. Our coordinators and consultants, dwindling in numbers, should be putting us in touch with each other rather than bringing greetings from "downtown" or having another kaffee klatsch with publishers' representatives. The concepts of teachers teaching teachers and planned peer observation are powerful motivators and supporters for program development which should be fostered by those in positions to do so.

On a broader scale our association can connect districts and systems through newsletters and programs which build in continued support after the sessions have ended. With computer technology of even the most basic type we can develop much more sophisticated mailing lists and sorting devices to connect librarians with common goals with each other in the joint pursuit of excellence.

We know so much — and we have so much to learn and to share. Why don't we take that risk and join an active people network dedicated to the best possible programs for young people?

People networks can provide encouragement, support and motivation for professional renewal and improved performance. All we need to get started is your organizational talent and commitment to sharing program ideas and a willingness to risk disclosure of your trials, tribulations and successes.

We need each other — let's commit ourselves, our district staffs and our associations to supporting and extending our collective talent.

Part 4
INFORMATION SKILLS ACROSS THE CURRICULUM

The flood of information is unmanageable; people do not value information-based decision-making or libraries as a source of information; teaching library skills in a vacuum is not fruitful. What is to be done? Roy Lundin provides sound advice for the teacher-librarian to take an across the curriculum approach to information skills teaching. Carol-Ann Haycock develops six skills clusters for teachers and teacher-librarians and provides the necessary steps to developing a school-based continuum as a reference point for cooperative program planning and teaching. The teacher-librarian must take the initiative and be prepared to provide leadership and expertise in the articulation and specification of information skills. And if the teacher-librarian can't do this, who can?

Sharon Walisser extends this foundation through the school-based research strategy. The overall goal of a research strategy in the elementary school is to enable students to select and narrow a topic, plan the scope and direction of the research, locate sources, identify and record significant information and prepare and make a presentation based on standard formats appropriate to the level. Sharon extends the school-based research strategy by linking process writing to the approach. Iris Spurrell then applies similar methods to her developmental approach for a student strategy for research.

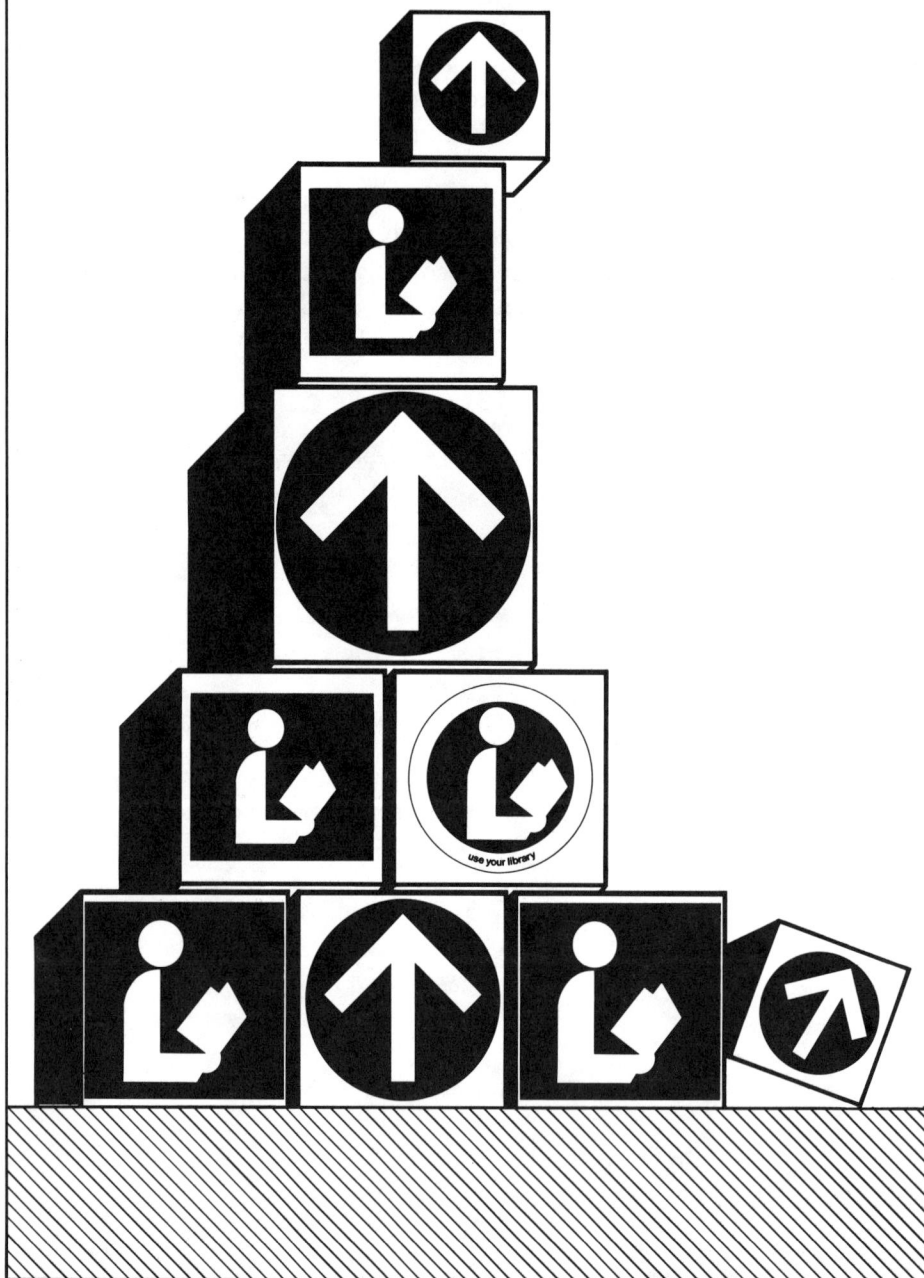

LIBRARIES...
For the Building Blocks to Learning

The Teacher-Librarian and Information Skills— An Across the Curriculum Approach

Roy Lundin

THE RATIONALE

Four conclusions I have arrived at over the past fifteen years should be kept in mind throughout this paper. They provide a kind of rationale for an integrated approach to skills development across the curriculum.

Conclusion 1: The flood of information is now unmanageable.

There is little doubt that the flood of information, which is in fact accelerating, is completely unmanageable by any person. For most students—and principals, teachers, and teacher-librarians, for that matter—the enormous bank of information is relatively unknown; they are simply not aware of the magnitude of the universal data base.

Those who have a glimmer of the amount of information available, even in areas of specialization, are absolutely exasperated and even terrified. Libraries and librarians are also finding it impossible to cope; all the skills possessed by reference librarians still seem not enough to manage the growing amount of information, even with the aid of automated storage and retrieval systems.

How much, then, can we expect of school students in their attempts to survive in this deluge?

Conclusion 2: People do not value information-based decision-making, nor libraries as a source of information.

Perhaps a personal example may be acceptable here. While visiting a brother in Canada some time ago, I was caught up in the idea of mixing up that Hawaiian drink called a "mai-tai." My brother's solution was to search a bookshop for a book of drink recipes which he could buy. I suggested, to his surprise, the public library where we did find a book with the appropriate recipe and obtained a photocopy of it for ten cents.

Information is everywhere but libraries do not have a monopoly on it. Many people are motivated to use information to meet various needs from time to time, but they obviously tend to go to sources other than the library to get answers. Why?

It may be true that the *need* for selected information will increase with increased competition for *survival*. Perhaps our main hope here is that schools at all levels will continue to work on the development and reinforcement of "information skills" so that new generations will increasingly value information-based decision-making. The importance of this cannot be underestimated. Information is of value to all forms of decision-making from voting and furthering one's education to purchasing a car or hi-fi equipment and getting a job.

Conclusion 3: The formal teaching of "library skills" in a vacuum to users is not a fruitful exercise.

Much more will be stated about this shortly, but skills are developed through experience and regular practice in constant settings. There are, of course, certain identifiable skills necessary in the location of information, but these skills do not necessarily apply to every search, nor is there automatic transfer of skills from one setting to another, nor has every user a perfect memory.

Autonomy in the *search* for information may be a good objective, but considering conclusions 1 and 2, it is unlikely that many users will ever become completely autonomous in running the maze.

"Resourcefulness" may be a better objective. It is the knowledge and ability to use alternative support systems. Above all, however, users need the skills of analysis, synthesis, and evaluation so that they can make effective use of the information obtained.

Conclusion 4: The role of the teacher-librarian is to coordinate and facilitate the organization and use of educational resources.

After fifteen years of significant development in school librarianship in Australia, we are now reaching the point where the role of the teacher-librarian is becoming clear.

The main aim of the teacher-librarian is working towards the improvement of the quality of the experiences which children and teachers have in schools. To achieve this, the teacher-librarian must fulfill the role of coordinating and facilitating the organization and use of educational resources.

The role, then, falls into two main parts: *I Resource Management* which involves the aspects of administration, selection, acquisition, and organization of the resources collections and systems of use in the school. *II Cooperative Planning and Teaching* which may well be a plain way of saying "involvement in curriculum planning and implementation."

These two aspects of the teacher-librarian's role are put very well into priority order by Ken Haycock:[9:5]

> In times of declining financial support for public institutions and services of all kinds, it is perhaps useful to remind ourselves of the basic principles on which school library services thrive and prosper and the major issues confronting the profession. Too often we deal well with the symptoms but ignore the causes, resulting in an inevitable rematch, as symptoms, like weeds, keep coming up.

The research and the experience of those developing support for teacher-librarians and school resource centres, is quite clear. The single most important role of the teacher-librarian is cooperative program planning and teaching with classroom teachers. This major shift for the teacher-librarian from determining what the student is to do, to cooperatively determining what the student is to learn, has resulted in the teacher becoming the primary focus. Cooperative planning and team teaching not only provide better opportunities for purposeful use of library resources and the integration of media, research, and study skills with classroom instruction but also provide better opportunities for classroom teachers and administrators to learn first hand the role of the teacher-librarian as a teaching partner, something quite different from a teaching adjunct.

* * *

It's time to stand up and be counted as a professional with integrity, confidence, and skill. The management of newer materials and technology, while important, will not save or even necessarily enhance the status of the teacher-librarian if undertaken outside this framework. The future lies in working closely with teachers within the context of a clearly defined role, understood and advocated by teacher-librarians and thus by administrators, teachers, and the community.

It is on the basis of these conclusions that the concept of integration of skills is proposed.

THE CONTEXT

The teacher carefully diagnoses the needs of the learners, then matches the strategies and resources which will meet those needs. There are a whole range of strategies from which the teacher can select, involving children in individual, small group, and large group activities. Unfortunately, the range of strategies used by teachers is often limited to lecturing, worksheets or projects with the odd film or excursion thrown in for good behaviour. Teachers still spend an average of about 70 percent of their time in the classroom talking.[14:77] With this amount of talk time there is little time left for children to learn and practice a range of information skills.

The "resources" element of the new curriculum paradigm helps to free up education—that is, to open up the educational options available to teachers and children in schools—and this is important to the quality of educational experiences. There is an intrinsic reward for children in the use of resources, and this use allows children choices of what to do and how—i.e., some control over their own learning.[1]

Most school syllabuses now contain outlines of content/knowledge, skills and attitudes, three basic areas. The importance of this is that skills are seen as a part of all curriculum

development so that integration of skills with content and attitudes can be ensured. It is the integration of skills which is the main focus here.

WHAT SKILLS?

There is no shortage of lists of skills, but there is some lack of sound organization of these skills.

MacColl[15:12] provides a clear definition of "skill":

"...the term 'skill' can be applied to the ability to do something with a degree of expertness in repeated performances."

"...implications for skill development which can be drawn out as follows: (i) a skill is an *ability*, which implies learning; (ii) it involves *'expertness'*, which implies mastery; and (iii) it involves *repetition*.

The skills domain includes four major areas:

Receptive: These involve the whole range of location, reading, looking, and listening skills:

- reading skills

- listening skills

- observation skills

- time and space skills

- data gathering (search or location) skills

- quantitative skills

Reflective: These internal, process skills bring the isolated bits of information into meaningful relationships:

- problem identification and solving skills

- critical thinking skills (especially inference, interpretation, association, assumption, analysis, synthesis, and evaluation)

- lateral thinking skills

Expressive: These skills enable the student to organize and pass on (communicate) knowledge gained through the receptive and reflective skills:

- writing skills

- speaking skills

- recording skills

- presentation (including production) skills

Personal/Social: These are forms of expressive skills which tend to have some influence, or tend to "colour" the other processes:

- manipulative skills

- interpersonal skills

- community participation skills

These categories could then be developed into an exhaustive listing of a myriad of skills and subskills and subsubskills.[15]

APPROACHES

Skills teaching has not only been a neglected area, both in research and in practice, but also has usually occurred in formal, unrelated isolation.

The most common approaches to the teaching of information skills are as follows:

The *structured, formal/unrelated* approach, sometimes referred to as the content approach, usually takes the form of class "library lessons," card kits, activity sheets or specially made up library assignments on such topics as: "How to Use the Encyclopaedia" or "Using the Dictionary Card Catalogue." A number of skill building kits are available commercially and tend to be fairly widely used. Quite frankly, such kits are not really needed. They encourage the skills to be taught in a fancy and expensive vacuum, and this leads to a *waste* of existing resources in a school's collection.

There are two types of *formal/related* approaches. The first is when the teacher-librarian, for one reason or another, runs a series of library lessons parallel to what teachers are doing in their classrooms in an effort to make relevant skills development happen as closely as possible to when they are needed. The hard-working teacher-librarian can make such a program fairly effective. The second type, also called the question approach, usually involves activities, in the library periods, built around needs or questions that students have or are likely to ask. Materials are developed or sessions conducted around questions such as: "How do I find a good book to read?" or "I want some materials on the topic—How do I get them?" Emphasis in this approach is on the learning of skills and processes that are transferable to other life situations.

The *unstructured, incidental* approach is effective as far as it goes in that the teacher and teacher-librarian seize on the teachable moment when a child expresses a need. The weakness is that many needs go either unexpressed or unnoticed.

By far the superior approach is the *integrated* approach. This is when the whole range of skills, knowledge, and attitudes are built into existing or cooperatively planned curriculum activities in the various areas such as science, social studies, language, mathematics, and so on. In this approach the teacher-librarian works with the teacher (a) at the planning stage, incorporating skills and resources into the unit, matching them to needs; (b) in the implementation of the unit, at times team teaching as appropriate; and (c) in the evaluation of the unit, to determine both student performance and the strengths and weaknesses of the program itself. This also allows for incidental, individual attention to ensure all students are able to master the skills.

This approach is based on the following principles of learning and teaching skills first published as an appendix to *Skill Development in Social Studies*, the 33rd Year Book of the National Council for the Social Studies[5]:

1. The skill should be taught functionally, in the context of a topic of study, rather than as a separate exercise.

2. The learner must understand the meaning and purpose of the skill, and have motivation for developing it.

3. The learner should be carefully supervised in his first attempts to apply the skill, so that he will form correct habits from the beginning.

4. The learner needs repeated opportunities to practice the skill, with immediate evaluation so that he knows where he has succeeded or failed in his performance.

5. The learner needs individual help, through diagnostic measures and follow-up exercises, since not all members of any group learn at exactly the same rate or retain equal amounts of what they have learned.

6. Skill instruction should be presented at increasing levels of difficulty, moving from the simple to the more complex; the resulting growth in skills should be cumulative as the learner moves through school, with each level of instruction building on and reinforcing what has been taught previously.

7. The student should be helped, at each stage, to generalize the skills, by applying them in many and varied situations; in this way maximum transfer of learning can be achieved.

The key processes are:

- cooperative planning which leads to

- an overall, coordinated program in which skills are

- integrated systematically, sequentially and accumulatively with all other aspects of the curriculum, and

- the teacher and teacher-librarian work cooperatively to ensure all students' needs are met.

There are a number of ways of approaching cooperative planning between teachers and teacher-librarian. Perhaps a simple but effective way is to plan topics or units of study on a form sheet with the following headings:

- Time

- Place

- Content

- Attitudes

- Strategy/ies

- Skills

- Resources

- Assessment

Such a form is easily copied and filed for future reference.

There is, some may say, an element of coercion involved in this process. That is, the students' motivation to learn and use skills come from the perceived need to meet the requirements set down by the teacher in league with the teacher-librarian. Caution is required here. Coercion as a form of extrinsic motivation can produce stress which, if not relaxed in a healthy way, can lead to fear, guilt, and neurosis rather than the development of positive values. This is well-documented in the literature which differentiates between motivation through the need to achieve and motivation from fear of failure. Such coercion, furthermore, will not necessarily lead students to the library or its services; they will go to each other for support. On the other hand, if there is a warm and supportive climate in the school where students are encouraged to take part in the planning as well, then the motivation comes through participation rather than coercion.

There is a great difference then between simply having a list of skills and having an effective integrated learning program. Sequencing and timing are important considerations here as well.

With regard to sequencing, consideration needs to be given to when a certain part of a skill should be introduced, how and when it should be repeated and added to, to result in skill building in an accumulative manner. Many schools have started with basic lists of research and study skills and then planned similar charts where the teachers and teacher-librarian have worked cooperatively to determine which skills should be where.

Timing is important in the introduction of skills, not only to match students' needs but also to take account of readiness. For example, it would be a mistake to introduce the complex use of subject headings in the card catalogue to primary students. A Canadian study showed that only around the ages of 11 to 15 years, in keeping with Piaget's stages of cognitive development, can children move from a specific to a general heading, e.g., cats to pets to animals.[12:36-37]

It is important that schools do not adopt, uncritically, charts, lists, or programs from other sources. To do this is not an easy way out; it simply reduces the relevance of the whole program. Again, cooperative planning by the school staff needs to be emphasized to ensure the development of an effective, relevant curriculum for the school.

SUMMARY GUIDELINES FOR PRINCIPALS, TEACHERS, AND TEACHER-LIBRARIANS

All members of the school staff should share the common goal of helping every student to become an autonomous learner. They should, therefore, share the responsibility of developing policies, setting up structures or systems, developing programs and teaching in such a way as to facilitate a well-rounded learning experience for every student.

Principals can facilitate the integration of skills by:

(a) providing opportunities for teachers and the teacher-librarian to plan cooperatively;

(b) involving teachers and teacher-librarians in the development of school goals and policies governing the curriculum;

(c) scheduling class and teacher times to facilitate resource-based/library-oriented programs;

(d) arranging in-service for teachers and teacher-librarians to help them update or upgrade their abilities;

(e) showing leadership through demonstration or pilot programs within the school, and supporting teacher/teacher-librarian initiatives;

(f) budgeting to allow for adequate provision of resources to support the programs;

(g) maintaining an open school climate where communication is free and where staff and students experience satisfaction;

(h) presenting a positive image of the school to the community.

Teachers can contribute to integrated programs by:

(a) participating in the planning and implementation of the school's total curriculum;

(b) involving the teacher-librarian in all stages of planning, teaching, and evaluating units of work;

(c) accepting prime responsibility for the learning experience of the students assigned to them;

(d) designing relevant activities for students to ensure the integration of content, attitudes, and skills in all subjects;

(e) actively selecting resources in cooperation with the teacher-librarian.

Teacher-librarians can contribute to an integrated program by:

(a) participating in the planning and implementation of the school's total curriculum, particularly by advising on the use of resources;

(b) selecting with the involvement of teachers, acquiring, organizing and operating a collection of resources and services appropriate to meet the needs of the school;

(c) cooperating with teachers in the planning, teaching, and evaluation of units of work;

(d) coordinating with teachers to determine what will be covered for particular groups of students, when and who will accept prime responsibility for the teaching and application of skills;

(e) teaching some of the skills as mutually agreed upon;

(f) giving incidental, follow-up support and reinforcement to individual library users;

(g) extending children's interests and skills beyond the traditional subject areas of the school's curriculum;

(h) assisting students to make transitions from one setting or stage to another — i.e., primary to secondary school, secondary to university, college or work;

(i) provide any service which will help improve the quality of the experience which teachers and children have in schools.

The all too common isolation of the teacher-librarian through the teaching of "library skills" lessons in separate library periods served only to provide a spare period for classroom teachers and to delay unnecessarily the integration of research and study skills and the teacher-librarian into the mainstream of the school's curricular concerns.

The integration of information skills across the curriculum on the other hand offers an exciting challenge for teacher-librarians not only to provide leadership in a critical educational area but also to forge new partnerships with administrators and teaching colleagues.

BIBLIOGRAPHY

1. Bahnisch, Brian. "Some Observations on the Role of the Teacher-Librarian." *Journal of the School Library Association of Queensland.* Volume 12, Number 2 (1980), pp. 15-16.

2. Berner, Elsa. *Integrating Library Instruction with Classroom Teaching at Plainview Junior High School.* Chicago: American Library Association, 1958.

3. *Beyond Reading Lists: Academics, Librarians, and Reader Education:* Proceedings of the Third Reader Education Seminar sponsored by the Association of Librarians in Colleges of Advanced Education, Queensland Division. Held in Brisbane from August 28-29, 1978 at the Library of the Queensland Institute of Technology.

4. Bowers, Norma. "Resource Based Skills Activities." *Journal of the School Library Association of Queensland,* Volume 12, Number 3/4 (1980), pp. 5-11.

5. Carpenter, Helen McCracken, ed. *Skill Development in Social Studies.* Thirty-Third Yearbook of the National Council for the Social Studies. Washington, D.C.: N.C.S.S., 1963.

6. Davies, Ruth Ann. *School Library Media Program: Instructional Force for Excellence.* 3rd edition. New York: Bowker, 1979.

7. Fraser, Barrie J. *Test of Enquiry Skills: Handbook.* Hawthorn, Victoria: Australian Council for Educational Research, 1979.

8. Guenther, Elsa. *How to Study Through Your Library.* Melbourne: Australian Library Promotion Council, 1972.

9. Haycock, Ken. "Editorial — Hard Times ... Hard Choices." *Emergency Librarian,* Volume 9, Number 5 (1982), p. 5.

10. Irving, Ann. "Teach Them to Learn: Educating Library Users in Schools." *Education Libraries Bulletin,* Volume 21, Number 3 (1978), pp. 29-39.

11. Johns, E. and D. M. Fraser. "Social Studies Skills: A Guide to Analysis and Grade Placement." Appendix in *Skill Development in Social Studies* edited by H. M. Carpenter. Thirty-Third Yearbook of the National Council for the Social Studies. Washington, D.C.: N.C.S.S., 1963, pp. 310-27.

12. Kogon, Marilyn. "Does Age Make a Difference in Ability to Use Subject Headings in a Catalogue?" *Moccasin Telegraph,* Volume 17, Number 2 (1974), pp. 36-37.

13. Lundin, Roy. "The Relevancy of the Library Skills Programme." In *Prospects,* edited by Peter J. Pegg. Brisbane: School Library Association of Queensland, 1973.

14. Marland, M. *Language across the Curriculum*. London: Heineman, 1977.

15. MacColl, P. "Skill Development." *Journal of the School Library Association of Queensland*, Volume 12, Number 3/4 (1980), pp. 12-16.

16. MacColl, P. "An Approach to Skill Development." Unpublished. Curriculum Branch, Queensland Department of Education, 1981.

17. Piper, K. "Evaluation in the Social Sciences for Secondary Schools." *Teachers' Handbook*. Canberra: A.C.E.R. and A.G.P.S., 1976, pp. 63-70.

18. Queensland, Department of Education. "Synopsis of Selected Seminar Papers, 1970. Library Research Skills— the Organizational Framework." Circular to schools, 1970.

19. Reed, Estella. "Building Library Skills at the Secondary School Level." *Education*, Volume 88 (1967), pp. 353-56.

20. *Resource Management for Secondary Schools*. 3rd edition. Library and Resource Services, Queensland Department of Education, 1981.

Information Skills in the Curriculum: Developing a School-Based Continuum

Carol-Ann Haycock

A few years ago educational and societal buzz words centered around the "knowledge explosion"; today we are constantly reminded that we live in an "information age." These are not fads ... they are here to stay and they require a substantial redefinition of the verb "to know." At one time it was reasonable to learn a body of information by rote memory and to call this knowledge; today there is a distinct need for a shift from passive absorption to interactive processing and use of information in a variety of contexts.

Just as teacher-librarians have moved from the term "library skills" (skills to use the library taught in the library by the librarian) to "research and study skills" (skills to locate and use materials taught either in the classroom and/or resource center by the teacher and teacher-librarian together) it is perhaps time to move to "information skills," denoting more clearly a total school commitment to assisting young people to develop the skills necessary for purposeful inquiry, informed decision-making and lifelong learning.

While the importance of information skills is receiving increasing acknowledgement, there tends to be decidedly little specificity and clear articulation in their development. Without a school-based continuum of information skills, classroom teachers and teacher-librarians face the difficulty and even professional danger of operating in a vacuum, without a framework or "curriculum" if you will. As a specifically trained professional in working with colleagues to teach young people to access and use information efficiently and effectively, the teacher-librarian should be able to specify and articulate information skills and guide their sequential development. Information skills are perhaps more easily understood if organized into smaller discrete parts. These component clusters of information skills suggest the broad categories of skills needed by students.

DEFINITIONS

Resource Center Orientation, e.g. location of the resource center, physical layout, basic procedures, etc.

Research Strategies, e.g. defining the problem and its scope and procedures to address it, knowing where/how to start, where to look next, steps to follow, etc.

Locating Information—General and Subject Sources, e.g. use of the card catalogue and indexes to encyclopedias, use of magazine indexes, use of specialized reference materials, maps and globes, etc.

Acquiring and Analyzing Information, e.g. using key words, skimming and scanning, listening, viewing, comparing and contrasting, recognizing bias, etc.

Organizing and Recording Information, e.g. taking notes, outlining, keeping a record of sources, crediting direct quotes, etc.

Communicating and Presenting Information, e.g. written and oral reports, slide-tape presentations, debating, etc.

While it is certainly not difficult to locate such a list of skills, and indeed many teacher-librarians have and use such a list, if it is not *integrated* with classroom instruction its short term value for the student, and the possibility of long term retention, are severely limited. Skills taught at each grade level are arbitrary and should differ from school to school, precisely the reason for a school-based continuum. The exact level at which skills are introduced is not important; what is important is that a school have a plan for the *sequential development* of information skills and that the plan reflect the goals and priorities of the school. This definitely leads to an improved basis for discussing objectives in planning with classroom teachers.

The National Council for the Social Studies offers a well-accepted and often quoted list of criteria or principles for effective skill development:

- The skill should be taught functionally, in the context of a topic of study, rather than as a separate exercise.

- The learner must understand the meaning and purpose of the skill, and have motivation for developing it.

- The learner should be carefully supervised in his first attempts to apply the skill, so that he will form correct habits from the beginning.

- The learner needs repeated opportunities to practice the skill, with immediate evaluation so that he knows where he has succeeded or failed in his performance.

- The learner needs individual help, through diagnostic measures and follow-up exercises, since not all members of any group learn at exactly the same rate or retain equal amounts of what they have learned.

- Skill instruction should be presented at increasing levels of difficulty, moving from the simple to the more complex; the resulting growth in skills should be cumulative as the learner moves through school, with each level of instruction building on and reinforcing what has been taught previously.

- Students should be helped, at each stage, to generalize the skills, by applying them in many and varied situations; in this way, maximum transfer of learning can be achieved.

- The program of instruction should be sufficiently flexible to allow skills to be taught as they are needed by the learner; many skills should be developed concurrently.

If we accept these basic principles, the need to provide for different learning styles, the need to provide for alternative means of reporting and presenting information, and a critical need to evaluate the processes of information use, as well as the final product of student research, then the planned sequential development of information skills and their integration with all aspects of the program become essential—to ensure that students are moving along a continuum towards independence and to ensure that some skills are not taught repeatedly to some students while not at all to others.

The question which arises is how to develop such a skills continuum for a school. The process outlined here is not sophisticated but it is systematic. The process does not require an extensive skills background but it does require initiative on the part of the teacher-librarian. The process does not intimidate or alienate teachers ... it does work and has been implemented in a large number of schools through in-service programs.

The teacher-librarian, as stated, must take the initiative and be prepared to provide leadership and expertise in the articulation and specification of information skills. It is essential to *involve* the entire staff, starting with the principal, who must understand the purpose for the process and the concrete benefits for the school. It is difficult to implement any change, particularly one involving staff participation, without the understanding and support of the school administration.

The process can take place over a series of short sessions, before and after school and/or at lunch hour.

Step 1—Locate a list of information skills for the staff to react to. This can be derived from district guidelines for information skill development, from state/provincial curriculum guides, or from other school examples. For ease of implementation, sample lists used for this process at a number of schools are included here. (*See Information Skills: Primary* and *Information Skills: Intermediate*.)

Step 2—Provide only the appropriate section(s) to groups of staff for reaction. Do not expect a grade 2 teacher or a grade 7 teacher to respond to a K-7 list. Work with specific grade levels or primary/intermediate groups depending on the size of school. *This is most effective if done sequentially.* Meet with each group to come to some consensus. Have each grade level provide input/feedback both a grade level below and above the level they are presently teaching. The role of the teacher-librarian as both a team partner at each grade level and as a liaison between grade levels is key to the development of the continuum.

Step 3—Seek ratification of the initial draft sections of the continuum from the primary and intermediate staff.

Step 4—Take the complete draft to the total staff for reaction. Pay particular attention to the transition years, Grades 4 and 7. Is too much expected at year four? Will students be sufficiently prepared for secondary school by the final year (in this case Grade 7)?

Step 5—Seek final ratification and perhaps adoption as school policy ... the emphasis must be on teachers accepting shared responsibility for information skills development.

The timeline for this process will vary according to the size of the school and the approach taken. If, for example, meetings are scheduled sequentially by grade level at Step 2 of the process, the timeline may be two to four weeks.

Meeting by primary and intermediate groups may be appropriate in small schools, but not as effective in large schools, though this approach takes less time. It is important to recognize that this stage of involvement in the process is where teachers develop a sense of ownership and commitment to the continuum of information skills which will serve as the future framework on which to build cooperatively planned and taught programs.

An information skills continuum for the intermediate grades is provided as an example of the developmental approach from year to year. Standardized formats for paragraphs, outlines, oral and written reports and bibliographies also ensure that teachers, teacher-librarians and students share expectations and a common approach to both processes and products of student research. Most importantly, standard formats contribute to success-oriented inquiry and learning. As students gain confidence in what to do and how to do it, they are freed to absorb information, process it and use it in a meaningful way.

The teacher-librarian and school resource center provide three levels of service:

Curriculum Implementation
Curriculum Planning and Development
Cooperative Program Planning and Team Teaching
Professional Development Services for Teachers

Curriculum Enrichment
Promotion of Material and Services
Guidance for Readers, Listeners, Viewers
Information Services
Design and Production of Materials
Cooperation with Outside Agencies

Curriculum Support
Administration of the Resource Center
Selection of Materials
Acquisition of Materials
Organization of Materials
Circulation of Materials

If the teacher-librarian endeavors to operate at the level of curriculum implementation, then he/she must have some knowledge and understanding of curriculum at all grade levels and in all subject areas. In other words, the teacher-librarian must know and appreciate the curriculum as interpreted through school-based programs. The teacher-librarian must also be able to analyze curriculum for entry points for the development of information skills through cooperative program planning and team teaching.

Most scope and sequence charts and much curricula have a materials orientation, stressing the location and selection of materials and content mastery. These skills are perhaps the most taught and least transferable. As with higher order thinking skills, more attention needs to be paid to comprehension, communication and production skills, to ensure that students have the ability to analyze and synthesize information.

With a strong commitment to a well-defined role emphasizing cooperative planning and teaching, and a school-based continuum of information skills, the teacher-librarian has a basis at each grade level on which to focus the planning and implementation of resource-based programs which build on prior process learning and lead to further independence for the student. It is only at this level that the resource center program has educational validity and a political chance of survival!

SAMPLE INFORMATION SKILLS PROGRAM INTERMEDIATE LEVEL

This Information Skills Program is organized into six categories or skills clusters:

1. **Orientation:** Finding the way to the library, feeling comfortable in the library, learning the proper handling and care of books, learning borrowing procedures, etc.

2. **Research Strategies:** Techniques for searching for information (i.e. knowing where/how to start, where to look next, steps to follow, how to narrow a topic, etc.)

3. **Locating Information:** Using the card catalogue and other indexes to locate specific, general or subject related information.

4. **Acquiring and Analyzing Information:** Using key words and the techniques of skimming and scanning to locate specific information, comparing and contrasting, classifying, recognizing bias and prejudice.

5. **Organizing and Recording Information:** Notetaking, outlining, interviewing, bibliography.

6. **Communicating and Presenting Information:** Written and oral reports, audio-visual and dramatic presentations, etc.

Grade 4

Locating Information:
1. Uses guide words as aids in locating specific words in dictionaries and encyclopedias.

2. Uses context clues in selecting the appropriate meaning of new words.

3. Can use a Junior Thesaurus as a source of synonyms.

4. Can use a variety of dictionaries appropriate for the Grade 4 level.

5. Can use a variety of encyclopedias appropriate for the Grade 4 level (e.g. Childcraft; Young People's Illustrated).

6. Has a beginning knowledge of the card catalogue (i.e. the card catalogue is divided into subject, author, title, or has three types of cards).

7. Can use the card catalogue to locate a specific book, either by title or by author.

8. Locates title, author, illustrator (a) on the book cover, (b) on the title page.

9. Locates the call number on the book spine.

10. Is aware of the atlas for information purposes (i.e. as a source of maps).

11. Is able to make use of resources available outside the school (public library, community resources and resource people.)

Acquiring and Analyzing Information:
1. Uses context clues in selecting the appropriate meaning of new words.

2. Uses titles, chapter headings, subheadings as a guide to contents.

3. Uses pictures for a specific purpose (i.e. to gain information on specific topics).

4. Identifies key words (phrases) in a question.

5. Uses key words (phrases) to locate information needed to answer questions.

6. Understands that different questions ask for different kinds of facts/information (e.g. Who? questions ask for facts/information about people).

Organizing and Recording Information:
1. Is able to paraphrase information or take point form notes on a given sub-topic(s) using one source.

2. Can state the source and authorship of information.

3. Uses a given report outline to organize information.

4. Makes point form notes on a given sub-topic(s).

5. Takes notes from (a) filmstrips (b) a tape.

Communicating and Presenting Information:
1. Can state a purpose for reading for information.

2. Understands (can state) a purpose for viewing for information (films and filmstrips).

3. Understands (can state) a purpose for listening for information.

4. Paraphrases information to answer questions (i.e. uses own words).

5. Can participate in group discussions for various purposes (e.g. sharing of information, ideas, opinions, and/or reaching consensus).

6. Can write an expository paragraph of five sentences (including indentation, topic sentence and appropriate punctuation).

Grade 5

Research Strategies:
1. Is able to use a simple search strategy for locating resources on a specific topic.

Locating Information:
1. Uses dictionary entry words.

2. Uses dictionary syllabication as a guide to pronunciation.

3. Can select the correct meaning from the dictionary.

4. Uses the index to an atlas to locate maps.

5. Can use the Children's Magazine Index to locate information in magazines.

6. Uses the card catalogue to locate a book on a given subject or topic.

7. Uses the pamphlet file as a source of information.

Acquiring and Analyzing Information:
1. Can interpret information presented in graph/chart/diagram form.

Organizing and Recording Information:
1. Uses point form notes to write a paragraph in his/her own words.

2. Can develop a simple report outline to organize information.

3. Can use a simple outline to write a short two or three paragraph report using his/her own words.

4. Is able to compile a simple list of resources available on a topic.

Communicating and Presenting Information:
1. Presents an oral report using point form notes as a guide and using concrete or visual aids.

2. Can present information in simple chart/diagram form.

Grade 6

Locating Information:
1. Uses dictionary aids such as accent marks and symbols for parts of speech (n, v, adj., adv.).

2. Knows the organization of the newspaper and the use of its index.

3. Can make use of 'see' and 'see also' reference in the card catalogue.

4. Uses latitude and longitude to locate specific places on a map.

Acquiring and Analyzing Information:
1. Is aware of the newspaper as a source of information.

2. Recognizes different types of maps (e.g. physical, political, population, contour).

3. Understands that the copyright date is a way of evaluating the currency of information in a given resource.

Organizing and Recording Information:

1. Takes notes on a given (sub) topic(s) using more than one source.

2. Lists resources used including author, title, date.

3. Can use basic interview techniques for gathering information.

Communicating and Presenting Information:

1. Demonstrates careful use of equipment (overhead projectors, opaque projectors, cameras.)

2. Writes a narrative paragraph of five sentences (including indentation, topic sentence, developing sentences, concluding sentence, proper punctuation).

Grade 7

Locating Information:

1. Can use indexes to encyclopedias to locate information.

2. Uses the newspaper as a source of information.

Acquiring and Analyzing Information:

1. Can compare information from different sources and identify agreement or contradiction (e.g. encyclopedia articles, newspaper articles, etc.).

2. Can use a given map scale to measure distance on a map.

3. Is able to proofread, using simple standard symbols, and identify omissions, insertions, spelling, punctuation, paragraph, indentation, tense.

Organizing and Recording Information:

1. Can write a simple bibliography, in proper format, for resources used.

Communicating and Presenting Information:

1. Writes an explanatory paragraph of five sentences (including indentation, topic sentence, developing sentences, concluding sentence, proper punctuation).

Information Skills: Primary (K-3)

Indicate the grade level at which you *introduce* each skill.

(Introduction means (a) students at that level *need* the skill and (b) the majority of students could master the skill appropriate to the grade level.)

The student ...

	Grade Level
1. demonstrates enjoyment in the resource center without supervision	
2. learns borrowing procedures of the resource center	
3. learns to recognize favorite authors, illustrators, characters	
4. learns the parts of a book's cover ... title, author, illustrator	
5. learns to recall information based on print or non-print materials	
6. alphabetizes to the first letter and locates words in a picture dictionary	
7. learns the location of easy books	
8. learns the location of nonfiction books	
9. locates story books and nonfiction books	
10. alphabetizes to the second letter and locates words in a picture dictionary	
11. alphabetizes to the third letter and locates words in a picture dictionary	
12. recognizes main idea and sequence in stories	
13. learns the location of nonprint materials	
14. is aware of the newspaper as a source of information	
15. learns a beginning knowledge of the card catalog	
16. demonstrates careful use of equipment (e.g. filmstrip viewer and tape recorder)	
17. knows how to take care of books	
18. learns how fiction books are arranged	
19. recognizes the difference between a dictionary and an encyclopedia and what each is used for	
20. learns to pick out the key words in a question	
21. learns to use the table of contents and index as guides to the contents of a book	
22. learns how nonfiction books are arranged	
23. is aware of magazines for recreational reading	
24. recognizes main idea, sequence and characters in stories	
25. understands and selects root words	
26. is able to convey information orally using complete sentences	
27. is aware of magazines for information purposes	
28. is selective in choosing a book for enjoyment or appropriate for a purpose	
29. conveys information orally, with confidence, using complete sentences	
30. uses books to lcoate specific information	
31. learns to use an encyclopedia of the appropriate reading level	
32. uses filmstrips to locate specific information	
33. recognizes main idea, sequence, characters, mood and setting in stories	
34. learns to take notes using key words and phrases	
35. is able to convey information in written sentences	
36. learns to present information in a variety of ways and can select from 2 or 3 given choices	
37. uses pictures to gain information and to present information	

Information Skills: Intermediate (Grades 4-7)

Indicate the grade level at which you would *introduce* each skill.

(Introduction means (a) students at that level *need* the skill and (b) the majority of students could master the skill appropriate to the grade level.)

The student . . .

	Grade Level
1. learns to use guide words as aids in locating specific words	
2. learns to use entry words	
3. learns to use context clues in selecting the appropriate meaning of new words	
4. learns to use a junior thesauras as a source of synonyms	
5. learns that the card catalog is divided into subject, author, title, or has three types of cards	
6. learns to use an atlas for information purposes	
7. understands (can state) a purpose for reading for information	
8. learns to paraphrase information or take point form notes on a given subtopic(s), using one source	
9. learns to understand and use an Atlas, index and map guide	
10. learns to use point form notes to write a paragraph in his/her own words	
11. learns to use dictionary aids such as pronunciation, symbols, syllabication and accent marks	
12. learns the arrangement of nonfiction materials on the shelf (i.e. a basic understanding of the Dewey Decimal System)	
13. learns to use the card catalog to locate a specific book, either by author or title	
14. learns to use the pamphlet file as a source of information	
15. is aware of and learns to make use of resources available outside the school (public library, community resource people, government agencies)	
16. learns to use see and see also references in the card catalog	
17. learns to write a simple bibliography	
18. learns to use a variety of reference books as sources of information	
19. learns to use a variety of indexes to locate information (i.e. Subject Index to Children's Magazines)	
20. learns that the copyright date is a way of evaluating the currency of information in a given resource	
21. learns to take notes on a given subtopic(s) using more than one source	
22. learns to present an oral report using point form notes as a guide	
23. learns to develop a report outline to organize information	
24. learns to interpret information in graphs/charts/diagrams	
25. learns to present information in graph/chart/diagram form	
26. learns a search strategy for locating resources on a specific topic	
27. learns to use dictionary aids (e.g. tenses, parts of speech, word origins)	
28. learns to use an outline to write a short report using his/her own words	
29. learns to use titles, chapter headings, subheadings as a guide to contents and to establishing a purpose for reading	
30. learns to compare information from different sources and identify agreement or contradiction	
31. understands (can state) a purpose for viewing for information	
32. demonstrates careful use of equipment (film projectors, overhead projectors, cameras, opaque projectors)	
33. learns basic interview techniques for gathering information	
34. learns to use different types of maps (e.g. physical, political, population, contour)	
35. understands (can state) a purpose for listening for information	
36. learns to participate in group discussions for various purposes (e.g. sharing of information, ideas, opinions, and/or reaching consensus)	

Developing a School-Based Research Strategy, K-7

Sharon Walisser

The teacher-librarian whose goal is to develop a school-wide, developmental, cooperatively planned and taught program is constantly in search of ways to involve staff and students in well-organized, systematic approaches to the development and application of information skills. The task of working with teachers to implement skills programs in the context of the curriculum is facilitated by an agreed upon approach to, and expectations for, skills development. A school-based research strategy, particularly when coupled with a continuum of information skills, provides a logical reference point on which to base unit and yearly planning and permits both teachers and the teacher-librarian to assess progress towards goals in the classroom and the resource centre.

The developmental nature of a research strategy ensures consistency in student approaches to information gathering, recording and reporting, while tailoring activities and expectations to individual needs and abilities. The strategy suggested here is divided into three developmental stages involving nine sequential steps (see Elementary Research Strategy: The Three Stages, on page 96).

THE THREE STAGES

At Stage I the nine steps in the process are introduced in their simplest forms. Much skills instruction and practice are necessary outside the context of a complete research project, but students should also be given frequent opportunities to work through the whole process. Stage I involves much instruction and direction as it is critical that students experience success in all aspects of the strategy.

At Stage II skills are developed and refined to greater levels of sophistication and greater independence is expected with instruction and guidance. Many opportunities are provided to apply the strategy and its component skills in a wide variety of subject areas.

At Stage III students apply the strategy with considerable independence. Frequent opportunities are again provided for the student to use the strategy in a variety of situations. Less direction is required at this stage as the process is monitored through a series of checkpoints (see glossary, page 99). Individual needs-based instruction is offered as problems are identified. Relatively sophisticated standard formats for outlining, presentation and bibliographies are used.

While the three stages may be viewed as roughly corresponding to early to primary (K-3), late primary to middle intermediate (Grades 3-5) and mid- to late intermediate (Grades 5-7), it is important to reiterate that the process is developmental. In addition, since this type of strategy should be modified to suit the unique needs of a school, specifics at each stage would vary. In the early years of implementing the strategy, elements of skills instruction may need to be compressed in situations where school-wide skills instruction has not been consistent. For example, intermediate students may need early webbing-related skills compressed and taught if they do not possess these skills.

The overall goal of a research strategy in the elementary school is to enable students to select and narrow a topic, plan the scope and direction of research, locate sources, identify and record significant information and prepare and make a presentation based on standard formats appropriate to the level. However, total independence is not expected and the process is monitored with guidance and instruction provided.

The implications of such a research strategy for secondary schools are several: students entering secondary school cannot be expected to be totally independent in research; clear outlines of expectations are still needed; more sophisticated versions of each step in the research strategy require instruction; and some skills will need to be introduced, such as footnoting and the use of direct and indirect quotations. This K-7 research strategy lends itself, though, to an extension at the secondary level, with the addition of Stage IV and perhaps V leading to independence and a high level of sophistication in research. Secondary stages would involve increased expectations in terms of complexity of sources, quality and quantity of research and sophistication of standard formats and presentation techniques. Skills needed for doing research from primary sources would also be introduced.

RELATED SKILLS

The nine steps in the strategy are skills clusters rather than separate, discreet skills (see K-7 Research Strategy: Related Skills, page 97).

1. **Identification of Topic** is a sophisticated process involving the broadening or narrowing of a topic within a range of possibilities. Brainstorming and clustering (see Glossary) are introduced at the earliest stages, usually as large group activities, to give students experience in expanding and narrowing topics and organizing information searches.

2. **Webbing** (see Glossary) is a means of organizing and focusing research. Clusters of ideas developed during brainstorming are organized in a visual format which the student refers to, and modifies as necessary during the research process. Webbing allows students to make decisions about the scope and direction of research and helps to classify information. Webbing also limits the student's impulse to copy. With a clear idea of the kind

of information required the student is less likely to resort to the "quantity vs. quality" approach to research. The web also serves as a guide for developing an outline and for preparing the final presentation.

3. **Selection of Suitable Materials** is essential for success. At Stages I and II materials are preselected by the teacher and teacher-librarian and student choice takes place within this set of materials. Independent selection at Stage III should involve monitoring and guidance. The selection of materials involves much instruction regarding varieties of sources, selection of materials with an appropriate reading level and suitable, relevant content, as well as the many locational skills; involved in use of the resource centre (see Related Skills). The "5-finger rule" facilitates selection at Stages I and II, while the technique of scanning is stressed at Stages II and III (see Glossary).

4. **Selection of Needed Information** involves a wide variety of skills (see Related Skills) which require instruction and frequent practice in many varied contexts. At Stage I, required information is clearly specified and dictated by the brainstorming session and the web format, so choices for the student are obvious. At Stage II, the needed information is clearly defined during large group brainstorming and web development, but more scope is involved and the student must read more carefully to identify appropriate information. At Stage III the process is much more open-ended as it is expected that the student will have developed the skills and confidence necessary to select information independently.

5. **Recording Sources of Information** is included at all stages, but a simplified standard bibliographic format is expected only at Stage III.

6. **Notetaking** from both print and non-print resources follows the web format. Notes are organized by subtopics as they are recorded. In Kindergarten and early Grade 1, pictures are drawn to record information. Later, key-word notetaking is introduced, followed by a combination of key words and phrases.

7. **Outlining** facilitates the organizing of information gathered and the preparation of the presentation. At Stage I, the research form (see Glossary) provides the outline and, in fact, becomes the presentation in booklet form. At Stages II and III formal outlines are prepared using both the web and notes, moving from a simple outline to a more sophisticated standard format (see Glossary). While the web may appear to be a good organizer in itself, the process of developing an outline involves the editing and reorganization of information gathered. The student has been encouraged to modify the web as research proceeds and it is at the outline stage that the final decisions regarding content of the presentation and sequencing of information are made. The outline is less necessary for visual presentations.

8. **Preparation for Presentation** varies according to the medium of presentation (see The Three Stages and Sample School-Based K-7 Research Strategy). Where the presentation is written, emphasis is placed on the writing process, including drafting, editing and proofreading skills.

9. **Presentation** may be written, oral or visual or some combination of these. Options should be varied to include things such as posters, dioramas, slide-tape or dramatizations, as well as written reports.

Process writing (see Process Writing and the Research Strategy) is a logical extension of this approach. The research strategy is the writing process applied to the gathering, recording and processing of information rather than to creative writing. A school-wide commitment to the writing process is not essential to the development of a research strategy but the benefits to the student of using the parallel processes are significant.

The school-based K-7 research strategy is based on the three stages and breaks the developmental process into specific elements for each grade level, providing for a logical progression of skills and expectations. Like the continuum of information skills, it is essential that there be total staff involvement in and commitment to the development of the school-based strategy to ensure common goals, logical progression and suitability to the needs of the students. Staff involvement also clarifies the teacher's goals and responsibilities and reemphasizes the cooperative nature of the program and the desirability of teacher/teacher-librarian partnerships in program development. The research strategy can be implemented in schools which have not developed a school-based continuum of information skills; however, the strategy works best where it is seen as being a step beyond the information skills already designated appropriate at each grade level. In addition, teachers are more likely to see the inherent logic of developing a school-wide strategy where the information skills continuum has already been developed and implemented.

The teacher-librarian interested in developing a school-based strategy may choose several different paths towards this goal. It is possible to begin using the strategy with certain interested teachers or at certain grade levels, with the aim of demonstrating its effectiveness and drawing in other staff members. Where staff is receptive, where a continuum of information skills has already been developed and/or where the writing process is in place, an in-service presentation to staff may be appropriate, followed by grade-level meetings to develop specific expectations and goals.* Using the Three Stages outline, and if possible, the information skills continuum, staff decides which aspects of the strategy will be emphasized at each grade level. In the sample school-based

---

*For further suggestions regarding the development of a school-wide program, see *Developing the School Resource Center Program: A Systematic Approach* (*EL*, 12:1) and *Information Skills in the Curriculum: Developing a School-Based Continuum.* (*EL*, 13:1).

strategy, movement from one stage to another is not lock-step; some developmental stages require more emphasis than others.

In addition, an interim version of the strategy, providing for "catch-up" in later grades where a formal process has not been previously used school-wide, may be necessary before the final K-7 research strategy can be put in place.

Yearly review of the strategy is essential to ensure its continuing effectiveness. Teachers may find that students can move more rapidly through the stages to an even more sophisticated level by Grade 7. Alternatively, the developmental process may be slower and expectations may need to be adjusted accordingly.

Consideration must also be given to the evaluation of the process. Evaluation is based on the student's ability to apply the overall strategy in a variety of situations as well as to use the many component skills. It is important to stress that evaluation must be of the process and not of the final product alone. Evaluation must be on-going and based on frequent contact with the student at all steps. Once again, cooperatively planned and team taught programs facilitate such evaluation as both teacher and teacher-librarian are available to guide the students. The step-by-step progression of the strategy also makes evaluation of the process easier, as do the checkpoints which are built in to Stage III assignments. The student should be aware of expectations and evaluation criteria before beginning research so that the aims and responsibilities are clearly understood.

A school-wide program has many advantages:

- Guided sequential development ensures that students grasp the strategy and can internalize the process for application to research in many subject areas.

- Success is built in at all steps and stages. Expectations are clearly defined, the process is familiar no matter what the subject area or grade level or who the teacher assigning the project, and instruction and monitoring of progress are an integral part of the strategy.

- The strategy provides for the introduction of skills and processes in the early grades and therefore permits relative sophistication and independence by Grades 6 and 7.

- Numerous opportunities are provided for students to apply skills and attain mastery and transference.

- A school-wide program developed in cooperation with the staff ensures that teachers remain aware of skills required at each stage and that they incorporate skills instruction into their programs.

- A school-wide strategy *limits* assumptions teachers may make about the scope of an assignment and the abilities of the students. Teachers will be more inclined to tailor the assignment to the developmental stage of the students. On the other hand, a school-wide commitment to a research strategy *permits* teachers to make assumptions about the skills background of students and to proceed to expand expectations and instruction. Consistency of approach and working cooperatively towards goals mean clearer objectives for the teacher and for the students.

- A K-7 research strategy developed by the total staff in cooperation with the teacher-librarian ensures this consistency and, equally important, ensures commitment and participation at all levels. Students can then become secure in their approach, as expectations and processes are consistent.

Teacher-librarians are effective when they plan and develop units of study with classroom teachers to integrate information skills, and then teach these units together. The school-based research strategy builds on the information skills continuum to assure well-planned, well-integrated, team taught programs for young people.

Elementary Research Strategy: The Three Stages

The Nine Steps	STAGE I Introduction	Stage II Development	Stage III Application
① Identification of Topic (Brainstorming, Clustering)	Assigned by teacher and teacher-librarian; topic could be the same for all students or differ for groups or individuals. Brainstorming: "What do we want to find out about our topic?"	Student choice of a specific topic from a given list. Brainstorming: "What do we want to find out?" Clustering: "Can we group our ideas into clusters (subtopics)?"	Student choice of specific topic from a range of topic areas, with the option to develop own topic. Assistance, as necessary, in narrowing topic, deciding suitability. Independent or small group brainstorming, clustering.
② Webbing (Organization of Research)	Provided by format; group discussion to clarify specific areas of investigation.	Teacher - led discussions to develop webs of increasing complexity; moving towards student independence in completing webs.	Student develops web independently or with other student(s). Checked by teacher, teacher-librarian.
③ Selection of Suitable Materials	Selection by teacher and teacher-librarian.	Selection by student from a set of given materials (print, non-print). Student makes decisions re suitability of content, reading level, according to learned criteria.	Independent selection using knowledge of types of materials available, locational skills, learned criteria for deciding suitability.
④ Selection of Needed Information	Resource format (Web) dictates information required; preselected materials permit easy identification. Students move from finding information in pictures to using captions, reading simple text, using simple indexes.	Student applies skills within the context of the web. Scope limited. More sophisticated skills introduced (headings, subheadings, skimming etc.) Skills for using non-print materials developed. Process monitored frequently by teacher, teacher-librarian.	Student applies skills within the context of the web. Scope is broader. Teacher and teacher-librarian monitor at check-points.
⑤ Recording Sources of Information	Simple recording of author, title, on a given format. Introduce publisher, copyright date as appropriate.	Recording of bibliographic information given "Fill-in-the-blanks" forms for various media. Information compiled according to simplified standard format.	Student records and presents bibliographic information independently, following standard format.
⑥ Notetaking	A picture or key word is recorded on a given format.	Key words or phrases are recorded on a given form. Information recorded by subtopics.	Notetaking cards used; students record information by subtopics as dictated by the web.
⑦ Outlining (Organization and Evaluation of Information)	Research format is both web and outline.	Teacher - led discussions to develop outlines which correspond to webs. Increasing complexity and student independence in completing webs.	Student develops outline independently from web and notes, following standard format.
⑧ Preparation for Presentation (written, oral, visual)	Dictated by format, age, skill level. Drafting and editing introduced in written work. Planning for oral and visual presentations via group discussions.	Partially dictated by format; much direction via group discussion, instruction. Drafting, editing of written work. Guidelines established for oral, visual presentations. Frequent monitoring by teacher; moving towards independence.	Guidelines provided; progress monitored at checkpoints. Independent editing of written work. Speaking cards prepared for oral presentations. Visual presentations planned on paper. Frequent opportunities for practice.
⑨ Presentation	*Will vary according to choice of presentation medium. Criteria are established for presentations; frequent opportunities for feedback from teacher(s) and students; audience expectations are set. Guidelines become more sophisticated, with increasing complexity and independence expected.*		
LEVELS	Early Primary ⟷ Middle Primary	Late Primary ⟷ Early Intermediate	Middle Intermediate ⟷ Late Intermediate

Sample School-Based K-7 Research Strategy

	K	1	2	3	4	5	6	7
① Identification of Topic (Brainstorming Clustering)	Teacher decision Brainstorming to establish criteria: "what do we want to find out?"	Teacher decision Brainstorming established purpose, guidelines for choosing key words.	→	Teacher decision. Group brainstorming, clustering led by teacher. Number of sub-topics determined by teacher	Students select from a range of well-defined topics. Teacher-led brainstorming, clustering.	→	Students select from a range of topic areas; narrow topic with assistance. Small group brainstorming, clustering.	Students choose and narrow topic given guidelines and assistance where needed. Option to choose own topics. Individual brainstorming, clustering.
② Webbing (Organization of Research)	Provided in the form of booklet or research page.	→	→	Teacher directed with web outline provided for students to complete. (Two subtopics) Second tier of web added.	Teacher-directed with web outline provided (3-4 subtopics). Second tier of web added	Sample web developed as large group; students develop own webs from model.	Review of webbing techniques. Students develop own webs to second or third tier.	→
③ Selection of Suitable Materials	Selection by teacher, teacher-librarian. Students have limited choice. →	→	Selection by teacher and teacher-librarian, provision for range of reading levels. Students choose appropriate materials using 5-Finger Rule & simple scanning techniques.	Some selected by teacher and teacher-librarian; some independent selection, using established criteria and techniques. Non-point materials introduced. Two sources required.	Guided independent selection where appropriate for skill level of students. Two-three sources required.	Guided independent selection. Variety of sources required (ie. book, encyclopedia, filmstrip)	Independent selection, monitored by teacher, teacher-librarian. Variety of media.	
④ Selection of Needed Information	Webbing format dictates information required. Pictures as information sources.	Webbing format dictates information required. Pictures and simple texts as information sources.	Web provides strict focus for identifying needed information. Simple indexes introduced.	Web limits scope but student must make more decisions in selecting significant information. Skimming introduced. Teacher monitors closely.	→	Independent selection monitored by teacher at checkpoints.	→	Independent selection
⑤ Recording Sources of Information	Record title of book.	Record author, title.	→	Record author, title of print or non-print materials, alphabetically.	Recorded on "fill-in-the-blank" forms. Compiled according to simplified standard format.		Student records and presents bibliographic information independently, according to standard formats.	→
⑥ Notetaking	Pictures to illustrate concepts in web.	Pictures or key words, recorded on "web."	Key words recorded on notetaking form.	Key words recorded on notetaking form by subtopic.	Key words, phrases recorded on notetaking form by subtopic.	Key words, phrases recorded on notetaking cards by subtopic.	→	→
⑦ Outlining (Organization and evaluation of information)	Provided by format. →			Boxed on web: main point outline developed in teacher-led group discussion.	Based on combination of web and notes: main point outline in standard format developed as a group. Increased independence in completing.	Based on web and notes. Simplified standard format, developed independently with assistance as needed.	Standard outline format developed independently. Monitored at checkpoint.	→
⑧ Preparation for Presentation — Written	Booklet or other research form completed. →		Draft prepared by writing sentences from key words (notes). Student and/or teacher editing.	Draft prepared for each subtopic. Paragraphing introduced. Introductory, closing statements added. Student and/or teacher editing.	→	Draft prepared for each subtopic, with introductory, closing statements incorporated. Student editing, monitored at checkpoints.	Draft prepared in standard essay format. Edited drafts monitored at checkpoints.	→
— Oral	Practice presenting booklet after group discussion of criteria for presentation.	Group discussion to establish criteria. Student decides two or three sentences to tell about booklet. Opportunity for practice.	→	Student practices using key words from notetaking sheet to speak to topic. Booklet or other visual aid.	Student uses notetaking cards or prepares speaking notes; practices presentation.	← *Increasing complexity expected* →		
— Visual	Booklet is visual presentation. Guidelines established through discussion. →		Details from notes represented in visual form (picture, model etc.) Description can be added. Guidelines established through discussion.	→	Guidelines established. Student plans visual presentation with guidance.	Guidelines established. Student plans on paper. Monitored at checkpoints	*Increasing complexity expected*	
⑨ Presentation	Booklet is presented with prepared comments.			← *Will vary according to choice of presentation medium. Can combine written, oral, visual presentations. Criteria are established for presenter and audience. Frequent opportunities for feedback from teacher(s) and students. Expectations become increasingly sophisticated.* →				

Process Writing and the Research Strategy

Process Writing	Research Strategy
1. Prewriting • identification of topic, genre • brainstorming • clustering • use of pattern books, realia, experience as source of ideas	1. Identification of topic, • brainstorming • clustering 2. Webbing 3. Selection of suitable materials 4. Selection of needed information 5. Bibliography 6. Notetaking
	7. Outlining 8. Preparation for presentation • drafting
2. Drafting 3. Editing 4. Proofreading 5. Publication 6. Presentation	⟶ • editing ⟵ • proofreading 9. Presentation

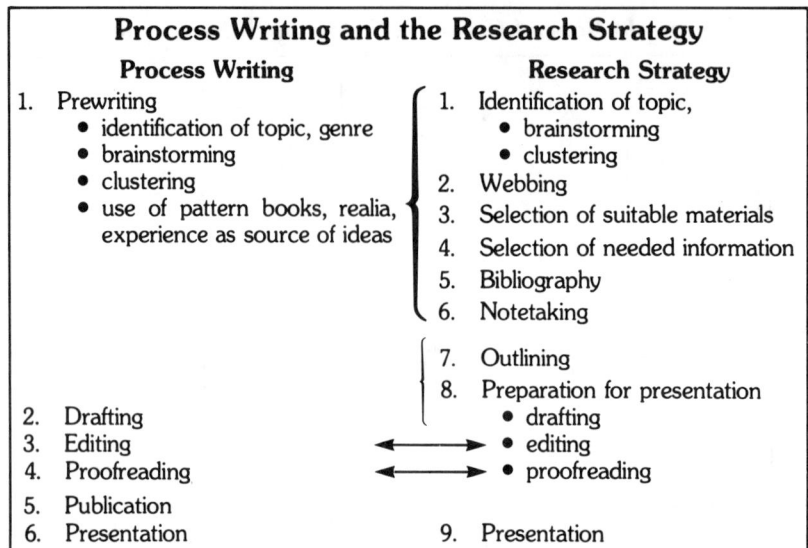

K-7 Research Strategy —
Related Skills

Identification of Topic
- brainstorming
- clustering (ability to group ideas, concepts)
- narrowing or broadening a topic

Webbing
- recognizing subtopics as parts of the whole
- recognizing most significant concepts, ideas
- structuring a web

Selection of Suitable Materials
- scanning
- use of tables of contents, indexes, headings, subheadings
- recognition that copyright date can indicate usefulness of information
- analysis of reading levels to judge suitability of materials
- knowledge of a variety of media (i.e. books, encyclopedias, magazines, audiovisual material)
- locational skills (use of catalogs, knowledge of Dewey Decimal System, etc.)

Selection of Needed Information
- use of indexes
- skimming
- distinguishing fact from fiction
- selecting significant information (information appropriate to web)
- reading captions
- interpretation of charts, tables, diagrams

Recording Sources of Information
- knowledge of reasons for recording sources
- identifying author, title and subtitles, titles of articles, chapters, publishers, city of publication, copyright date
- knowledge of standard formats (from simplest to most complex) for citing various media
- alphabetization

Notetaking
- identification of key words, phrases
- recording key words, phrases
- organizing information gathered
- notetaking from both print and non-print sources

Outlining
- knowledge of outline format
- recognition of subtopics as parts of a whole
- recognition of logical sequence of information
- editing out of inappropriate or less significant information
- organizing information in logical groupings (This will have been covered at the webbing and notetaking steps as well.)

Preparation for Presentation
(A very wide range of skills needed, depending on medium chosen)
- writing sentences from key words
- paragraphing
- writing introductory and closing statements
- knowledge of essay and paragraph formats
- editing
- proofreading
- preparation of notes for oral presentations
- preparing illustrations, diagrams, charts, graphs
- planning presentation (i.e. sketch of visual presentation, plan for oral presentation)
- layout, lettering and other "artistic" skills

Presentation
Many presentations will be a combination of the following:
Written
- paragraphing
- essay format
- ability to present information in an attractive manner

Oral
- ability to speak from prepared notes
- voice control
- use of illustrative material or objects
- ability to respond to questioning

Visual
- technical skills, depending on medium chosen

Research Strategy - Glossary

Brainstorming is a pre-research activity to help the student establish the scope of research and to develop some areas of inquiry which will be appropriate. In brainstorming, the student is asked or asks "What kinds of things should I find out about this topic?" All possibilities are recorded.

Checkpoints are points built into an assignment at which the student working independently through the research strategy, must check in with the teacher or teacher-librarian to ensure satisfactory completion of a step in the strategy. This permits the teacher to provide direction, encouragement, and individual review and/or instruction. Checkpoints also help to clarify the steps in the strategy, as checkpoints are at the end of each step.

Clustering is the intermediate step between brainstorming and webbing, in which the student groups the ideas from the brainstorming session in logical clusters in order to provide a focus for research. Clusters become subtopics on the web.

5 Finger Rule is a means by which students can quicky evaluate the suitability of reading level. The student chooses a "typical page" and reads, recording the number of unknown words on fingers of the hand. If three "problem words" are found, the student should question the usefulness of the material. If more than three words are found, the material is probably too difficult.

Notetaking is the recording of key words or key phrases in the student's own words to the greatest extent possible.

Outlining is based on a web, or a combination of a web and notes. An outline provides a guide for drafting, paragraphing and editing a report, essay or oral presentation. At Stage I, the outline is provided by the research format. At Stage II outlines are developed through the teacher-directed discussions. At Stage III the student develops an outline independently, following a given standard format.

Scanning is perusing materials to decide on suitability by looking at such things as tables of contents, headings, subheadings, indexes, and reading level.

Skimming is quick reading of appropriate sections of material, looking for key words related to the web topics and subtopics. More detailed reading of significant sections following skimming.

Webbing is a technique for establishing clear goals for research by defining and limiting the direction the research takes. The web becomes the student's guide to locating significant information. It is also helpful in writing outlines, as the web is, in effect, a research outline.

Outlining

Stage I — Format provided.

Stage II — A simple outline is developed as a group activity, based on a web. The next stage is to develop an outline format to the subtopic level as a group, then allow students to work independently to add details to the outline in logical order.

Topic — Black Bear
A - Subtopic — Appearance
B - Subtopic — Habitat
	I **Topic — Black Bear**
	A - Subtopic — Appearance
	  1. (detail) — Size
	  2. (detail) — Coat
	B. - Subtopic — Habitat
	  1. (detail) — Home
	  2. (detail) — Food
	C. - Subtopic — Reproduction
	  1. (detail) — When it has its young
	  2. (detail) — Where it has its young
	  3. (detail) — How it cares for them

Stage III — Students develop an outline independently, following a given standard format and basing the outline on a combination of the revised web and notes.

I. Topic
  A. Subtopic
    1. Detail
      a) Additional detail
      b) Additional detail
  B. Subtopic
    1. Detail
    2. Detail
      a)
      b)
	II. Topic
	  A.
	    1.
	      a)
	      b)
	  B.
	    1.
	    2.

Web Development

Stage I
The web is provided by the research format.

Cover (Topic)	(Illustration) Key word
(Illustration) Key word	(Illustration) Key word
(Illustration) Key word	Bibliography

K-1

Cover (Topic)	Table of contents
Key word or phrase & Illustration	Key word or phrase & Illustration
repeat	repeat
Index	Bibliography

Grades 2-3

Students work on a large sheet of paper divided into 6 or 8 sections. Sections are set aside for cover, bibliography, table of contents, etc. Information to be recorded in the remaining sections is defined in the brainstorming session. Notes are recorded either on the research paper (K-1) or on a separate note-taking sheet (Grades 2-3). When research and illustrations are completed, the sections are cut apart and stapled to form a booklet.

Stage II
The web is developed in a large group, teacher-directed discussion. Individuals use the web generated by the group.

(1 tier web)

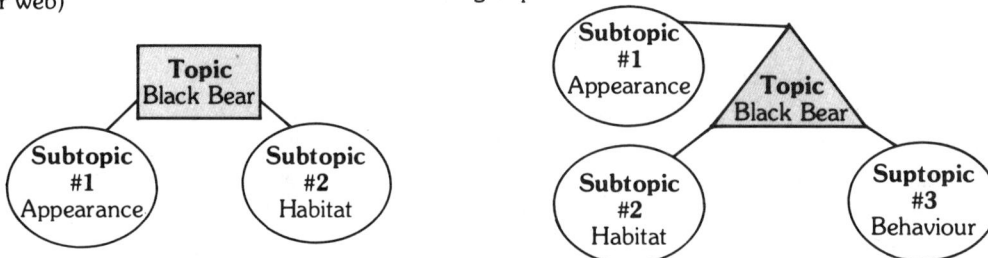

(2 tier web)

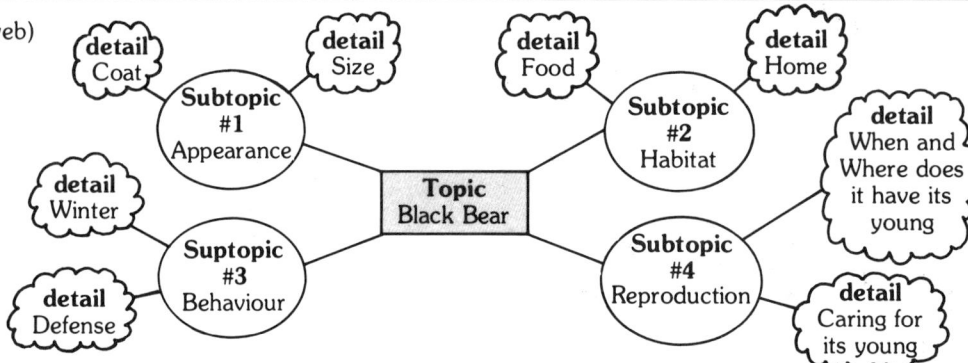

Stage III
Independent (individual or small group) development with guidance and/or checkpoints

(3 tier web)

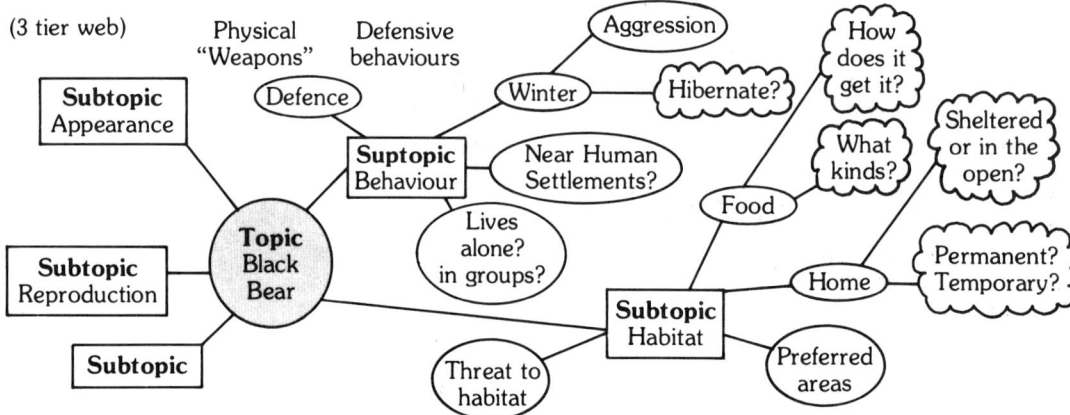

Student Strategy for Research: A Developmental Approach

Iris Spurrell

Integration of research skills into regular classroom units of study is now recognized as the most effective means of transmitting those skills. This integration is achieved through cooperative planning and teaching by the teacher and teacher-librarian. While joint planning and shared teaching do much to enhance the learning in a project, their presence alone does not ensure either maximum use of the library facilities or the development of a useful strategy for research which students can repeat at all levels of their education. All too often, jointly planned units are successful in themselves, but tend to be isolated experiences with not enough attention given to building continuous experiences year by year.

If one of the goals of a library program is to impart to students a knowledge of the research process, then the program must be structured to foster that end. Because the acquisition of research skills and strategies is developmental across the grades, successful achievement of the "research goal," requires the cooperation of the total school staff. The approach to research can then become a sequenced one, with the various stages of the research process being introduced at appropriate grade levels along the way.

EXPECTATIONS

Our goal at Glamorgan Elementary School (Calgary, Alberta) is to develop grade six students who can (1) use the card catalogue to locate and retrieve all the resources available in the library resource center on a given topic, (2) use these resources to extract pertinent information, and (3) reorganize this information for presentation. This three-part expectation assumes gigantic proportions upon closer examination. Not only does it entail a working knowledge of the card catalogue and library organization, but it also assumes grade six students are familiar not only with books, but also with filmstrips, pictures, records, videocassettes, and the verticle file as sources of information. Traditionally, card catalogue and location skills have been taught by the teacher-librarian who can verify that, by the end of grade six, students have been exposed to these basic library skills. However, our program's expectation is to teach children to *use* these library resources — at once a much broader and more difficult goal to achieve. In the case of print resources, skills pertaining to the use of table of contents, index, subject headings, graphs, charts, and illustrations, are included. In the case of non-print media, using the library's resources requires proficiency in the handling of the various pieces of equipment. Here in the second part of our three-part expectation, teachers can begin to see the need for co-operatively planned and taught library-based units. After all, why teach the use of these resources, if there is no need for this knowledge in the school's programs?

Following from this is the expectation that grade six students should be able to extract pertinent information from whichever resources they retrieve. This is the most difficult expectation of all — the one which often yields the least satisfactory results from students, with the most common complaint from teachers being verbatim copying from the resource. Yet, this expectation of extracting pertinent information traditionally receives the least consideration in actual teaching strategies. It is as though we expect the students to learn the process almost by osmosis.

Finally, there is the expectation that by the end of grade six, students should be able to synthesize the information they have collected to meet the requirements of the method of presentation selection for a particular project, be it a written report, or a series of diagrams or graphs. Again, the team of teacher and teacher-librarian face a great challenge to assure that this expectation is achieved.

It is with regard to the second expectation, the whole matter of extracting pertinent information from resources, that a developmental approach to the research process has its greatest merit. Within this context, a series of staged research-based projects, one each year, jointly planned and co-operatively taught, has the potential to produce grade six students who are well on the way to becoming effective and independent researchers.

DEVELOPMENTAL APPROACH

Total school involvement in a developmental approach to the research process is not easy to achieve. Regardless of the teacher-librarian's commitment, the principal's active support must be present to attain success. While the task of presenting the specifics of the long range plan for library research may fall to the teacher-librarian, the principal *must* speak in favor of this approach.

In our school, the research goal of the library program was first discussed with the staff as part of a professional development day in a joint presentation given by the teacher-librarian and the principal. The teacher-librarian talked about the long-range goal of a developmental research program, the objectives of each stage along the way, and the kinds of materials and activities best used at each stage. The principal first reiterated the long term benefits of such a program, and then reminded the staff that the plan being presented should not be viewed as something extra being added to their workload. The skills to be practiced were already requirements of various curriculum areas. The difference would be that, with a long range plan in place, these skills would be practiced in a different setting, the library resource center, and with a helper, the teacher-librarian, to share the work of teaching these skills.

During this same professional day several decisions were made about the approach to be taken. The first was that in grades one, two and three, the library-based projects would familiarize students with a variety of resources. The focus for grades four, five and six would be the employment of the resources to extract and synthesize information for an assigned topic. The final decision was that, to achieve the broad goal of acquainting students with a variety of resources, a stations or centers approach would be employed as a common format through all the grades. Each station would bear the name of a source of information, regardless of the topic being studied. Given that a whole class would be involved in each project, seven to nine different stations would be required. Possible stations for units would include Books, Magazines, Pictures, Encyclopedias, Filmstrips, Sound Recordings, Atlases, Vertical Files, Special Reference Books (Almanacs, Biographical Dictionaries, etc.), and Machines (overhead or opaque projectors). This plan was based on the assumption that over a six year period students would internalize a check-list approach to researching in a variety of resources. As well, each exposure to these resources would heighten their understanding of the research potential of each resource, and familiarize them with using these resources.

During this same session it was agreed that in the upcoming year each teacher would participate in a library-based project. We realized that our long-range goals could not be achieved in the first few years, but it was important to make a beginning. It was never stated, *"You must do this, or else...."* However, with the principal's support, the proposal to teach the research process developmentally gained enormous credibility. Moral support became more tangible when the principal personally covered classes for teachers so that they were free for an initial planning session with the teacher-librarian.

Given that for each of these projects, an entire class and its teacher would be working in the library, much time went into the preparation of activities for each unit. Fortunately, we were able to work in teams by grade, which considerably lessened the number of projects to be developed. By working to meet the deadlines in place in our year-long timetable of research projects, every child in the school participated in a library-based unit the first year.

In grade one a library-based unit that has worked successfully is an author study of Dr. Seuss. We plan this unit for early June so that the students' independent reading skills are at their best. The unit involves work at nine stations. In addition to one period at each station, the project requires a number of introductory or "tour" periods. During these periods the locations of stations are shown, and the materials at each, presented and explained. Besides the teacher's help, one grade six helper is assigned to each station. The helper's task is to set up equipment, verbalizing each step in the process, and to assist with instructions.

Throughout this unit the activities at each station are very open-ended in nature, allowing the greatest possible flexibility in finished work. At the Filmstrips station, for example, the children watch a short biography filmstrip about Dr. Seuss's real life. Their worksheet asks them simply to write some interesting facts about this author that they learned from the filmstrip. Responses tend to vary greatly depending upon the children's own interests and experiences. The next station—Special Reference Books—uses *Something About the Author*.

The children are shown further information about Dr. Seuss and his work, and the address at which he can be reached. At this station each child is then assisted in writing a letter to Dr. Seuss.

With the rotation through nine stations such as these, the students increase their knowledge of Dr. Seuss and his work, and more importantly, they achieve the beginning of familiarity with a variety of library resources. Although no formal research is undertaken, the foundation is laid for the next project.

With grade two the basic format of the previous year is repeated, but with several additions. The topic used is Christmas, and again materials are provided at various stations, each of which represents a type of library resource. As before, the children learn about their topic through whatever suitable resources are available. However, in grade two an attempt is made to extend the children's knowledge of the resource center. For example, the project includes a tour to show the location of the resources which will be used. Since the collection is not integrated, the children are surprised and intrigued by the extensive filmstrip, record and study print collections. As well, the children are encouraged to work more independently at this grade level. Instead of a grade six helper at each station, each of the nine small groups is assigned a group leader. Chosen by the teacher, these leaders are responsible children with good reading skills. Throughout the unit they interpret instructions and help the group share the materials and the reading to complete the tasks set at each station. These same group leaders are trained in advance of the project to set up and clean up the equipment.

The most important addition to this second unit in development of the research process is that at each station the tasks are much more skill specific. Generally, the tasks at each station are based on the Q.S.R. (Question, Skim, Read) technique. This technique emphasizes a particular process; that is, when searching for information, first, know the question to be answered and keep in mind the key words from the question; skim through the material to locate these key words; then, read carefully to find the answer. At each station questions keyed to the resources are provided for the children. Working together using the Q.S.R. process, the children formulate answers to these questions.

The grade three unit provides a further opportunity to acquaint students with the use of a variety of resources, using the Q.S.R. technique to gather information about a topic. As before, the questions to be answered and the materials required to locate the answers are present at each station. However, this unit emphasizes even greater independence in research. The topic is a country study, and, in all, five countries are under study. At each station no two children are working on the same country. Since each child within each small group is working on a different country of the five under study, there is no sharing of resources, of reading, or of formulating answers. Furthermore, each child is now required to set up the filmstrip viewer and tape recorder independently. At this time proficiency with these skills is taught.

By the end of grade three, all the children have had exposure to a variety of resources through three different library-based units. They have acquired familiarity with these resources and are able to use them independently to extract information required to answer questions set by the teacher and teacher-librarian. With a firm grounding in these skills, the students are now ready to proceed with the next step in the research process: the inculcation of research strategies.

With the grade four library-based unit, the focus changes quite significantly from that of the previous units. At this point the emphasis is on developing a strategy for research that can be useful to students through the various stages of their education. This change in emphasis greatly enlarges the scope of the project and requires even more co-operative planning and teaching on the part of both the teacher and teacher-librarian.

The goal of the fourth grade unit, as with those units in grades five and six, is to develop the skills of extracting pertinent information on a given topic and reorganizing this information for presentation. This broad goal at once brings to mind a host of reporting skills. Rather than setting out different specific skills to practice with each of the research units, our plan is to work on all research skills as they arise throughout the course of the project.

The key to the success of these units lies in setting a topic and then pre-selecting resources to use with it. Remembering that a stations approach will be used and that the children will be required to gather information from as many as seven to nine different sources, it is imperative to determine before-hand which resources are available. The children do not have free choice of whatever they wish to study. If the topic is dinosaurs, they will have to choose from four or five identified dinosaurs. The restricting of choice is justifiable considering that the emphasis is on the process rather than the end product. A further advantage of pre-selecting resources is that unsuitable resources (whether of too difficult a reading level, or lacking an index) can be excluded from the unit. Once the resources have been screened and included in the directions provided at each station, they are returned to the shelves for retrieval by the students as required during research periods.

At this point a series of lessons is begun which develops a strategy for research. As an extension of the Q.S.R. technique, the children are reminded of the starting point for their work—the basic question—"What do I need to know about this topic?" In a brainstorming session with the whole class, the children share questions they might ask to find out every-thing about a dinosaur if the topic is dinosaurs or a bear if the topic is bears. Such a session produces fifty to sixty unedited, haphazardly arranged questions. The second lesson focuses on the classification of these questions under appropriate headings elicited from the children. This is followed by a session in which the questions are weeded, extended, and rewritten under their headings, forming a rough outline of the report. This outline will serve as a checklist as the children rotate through the stations, the idea being that questions already answered in notes may be crossed out, thereby helping the children to focus more clearly on the details still to be located.

This set of three lessons keys the children's thinking to the questions they are hoping to answer during the research. The more familiar they are with these questions, the more time-on-task research is produced. Without these questions, many children cannot readily identify pertinent facts within a chapter or article, and hence verbatim copying often becomes the only way to manage note-taking. When these questions are known, however, the children seem to connect their key words

in the text or on the filmstrip, and note-taking, by virtue of its brevity, becomes a much more desirable way to record the facts. For these reasons, each research project begins with the three lesson format described above.

The next session (or sessions as required) deals with the skill of note-taking. Each child is given the same information from several different sources about a sample dinosaur or bear not included in the list under study. The children are taught to collect information and write notes under appropriate headings. Experience has shown this lesson to be of prime importance as the children come to see what is involved in research. They are shown that skimming is crucial to it and that as they read they must consider each and every piece of information presented in their source, asking themselves with every fact: "Is this an important detail for me to include?" "Under which heading does it belong?" "Do I have this in a note already?" As well, even grade four students become aware of the problems encountered in research. For example, often there will be disagreement among sources. Perhaps neither source provides answers to some of the questions on the outline. Perhaps information is included which the students were not aware of when the questions were developed. In this lesson there is an opportunity to discuss these and other matters before they become problems during the actual research time.

Now the children are introduced to the next stage of the research process—"Where am I likely to find out what I need to know about this topic?" At this point the children begin their tour of the research stations for this particular unit. This tour acquaints them with the actual location of each station and more importantly allows the teacher-librarian an oppor-tunity to present instructions for each station and review skills which are required. For us, the tour really is a review of the skills taught previously. Generally speaking, the specific skills needed at each station have been incorporated in Q.S.R. units through the primary grades. At this stage the materials needed are listed on the instruction sheets but must be retrieved by the students. With this in mind, card catalogue and non-fiction retrieval skills are pre-taught in the context of choosing pleasure reading materials. Consequently, the "tour" is not interrupted by in-depth skill lessons. However, teachers and teacher-librarians attempting this sort of project for the first time should be prepared to stop and spend as much time as is necessary at each station to acquaint the children with the means of locating the materials designated to that station.

Upon completion of the tour the students are ready to begin research in the next lesson. Then, for seven to nine consecutive days they come to research their particular aspect of the broad topic under study, be it triceratops, Captain Cook, the python, or whatever. Each day they move to a new station and research from a different type of library resource. By restricting the time with a particular resource to only one period (usually 60 minutes), a certain urgency to work with that resource is present, and the children work intently every day. This part of the research process may be thought as stage two—collecting the information.

Upon completion of these research periods, further lessons take place in the classroom with the final stage of the process—reorganizing the information for sharing. Depending on the product of the research, the teacher-librarian may or may not be involved.

Within the context of a developmental approach to research skills, the above format, once established with children, needs only further practice and an accompanying refinement in various skills and strategies to establish itself as a pattern for research in the minds of the children. In our program, repetition of this process occurs at least once in each of the two following elementary grades. Only minor changes are made to the various facets of each project.

With regard to the brainstorming session, this may be done in small groups in a grade five class, rather than as a large group lesson. When each small group has completed its question list, all questions from all groups are shared to make one long master list for the whole class. This small group set-up has also been used for lessons in classifying. In grade six brainstorming and classifying lessons have been treated as individual seatwork assignments before being shared with the whole class. When handled this way, the approach definitely takes more time, and for some this may be a reason to continue brainstorming in large or small groups. However, when children go through the process of listing questions by themselves, they become more actively involved in the topic being researched as the station work is done.

Similarly, within the stations the children are expected to be a little more independent at the grade five and six level. With the Books station, for example, by grade six they are expected to use appropriate subject headings to locate and skim materials on their own. This of course makes planning less time consuming for the teacher and teacher-librarian as they are not pre-selecting which resources will be used. They are still scanning all resources to ensure that the topic can be covered but the onus is now on the children to locate suitable materials for the stations.

STUDENT PERFORMANCE

Regardless of the grade or research topic, we have made certain observations about student performance which support the validity of this format for research. The main one is the feeling of success it affords everyone involved. The pre-selection of materials allows the inclusion of materials at an appropriate level to meet the needs of students. The notes taken resemble the response to an open-ended question, with students answering at their individual reading and understanding levels. Also, with both the teacher and teacher-librarian to give help, students (and even teachers) can practice resource retrieval skills in a meaningful context.

Another aspect of this format for research which has helped sell it to our teachers is that note-taking under headings using a variety of sources all but eliminates plagiarizing. This

may be simply a by-product of time constraints imposed at the beginning of each project—the children know they have a maximum of one period (usually one hour) at each station. Therefore, they feel a great pressure to skim all the material at that station during that single period. That goal is quickly lost if they begin copying verbatim, a fact which they seem to realize without being told. All the teachers who have used this format have commented how pleased they are with the time-on-task shown by the students. The finished products may not be as clearly polished as copied encyclopedia articles tend to be, but at least they are the students' own words and ideas!

From a teacher-librarian's perspective, this developmental approach to research has an overwhelming advantage. This advantage is in knowing what the students have been exposed to previously when planning the next year's unit. Without a developmental approach in place it is difficult to sort out which students in one of this year's grade four classes participated in which activities with which grade three class last year! If all grade three classes have covered the same research skills, the co-operative planning process is greatly facilitated.

One final observation is that there does seem to be a great degree of carry over of the basic steps of this plan for research from project to project and from year to year. This has come to us in parents' comments about children who have gone through our school and on to junior high. It is also evident in the way our current students handle research. For example, a grade six group has recently had to do an *independent* mini-report on an ecology-related topic in science. It was very encouraging to watch them individually go through the steps on their own.

It is our hope that in the near future we will be able to carry out some performance testing to provide more tangible evidence that our own developmental approach to research-related skills has helped make successful and independent researchers of our students.

EL EXTENDERS

"Developing the School Resource Centre Program—A Systematic Approach." *Emergency Librarian*, Volume 12:1 (September-October, 1984), pages 9-16.

"Information Skills in the Curriculum: Developing a School-Based Continuum." *Emergency Librarian*, Volume 13:1 (September-October, 1985), pages 11-17.

"Developing a School-Based Research Strategy, K-7." *Emergency Librarian*, Volume 13:1 (September-October, 1985), pages 19-26.

Part 5
SECONDARY SCHOOL APPLICATIONS

Too often on district outlines of research and study skills or information skills, the secondary grades are characterized by the terms "reinforce" or "extend" whatever was done at the elementary level. Secondary teacher-librarians tend to undertake this with small groups and students on independent study. Liz Austrom applies the basic principles outlined in previous sections and builds appropriate units of study with colleagues. Although we prefer to emphasize guiding principles, processes and strategies we include specific units here to demonstrate the type of teaching program which is feasible and desirable in secondary schools. It is important to recognize that these secondary school assignments have been cooperatively planned and taught in a "real" school and a "real" situation.

Debra Simmons takes a teaching strategy more common at the elementary school level and applies it successfully with colleagues at the secondary level. The conversion of a secondary school skeptic to a stations approach to learning may provide some alternatives for you to consider in your school.

the stages of your project

- **what do I
  need to do?**

  what topic should I choose?
  what is the topic?
  what do I already know about
  this topic and what must I find out?

- **where could
  I go and
  when?**

  what sources exist?
  how accessible are they?
  how appropriate is each one to
  the topic?
  where do I go first?
  do I need to create my own information?

- **how do I get
  at what I
  want?**

  what procedures should I follow?

- **which shall
  I use?**

  how should I choose?
  what resources are there?
  how can I tell which to select?
  what other sources could they lead me to?

- **how shall
  I use them?**

  what will help me to find the
  information I'm looking for?
  what strategies
  could I use?

- **what should
  I make a
  record of?**

  what is important?
  how could I record it?
  how should I arrange it?

- **have I got the
  information
  I need?**

  what have I got?
  what do I think?
  what does it all add up to?
  have I got what I need?
  should I look further?

- **how should
  I present it?**

  in what form could I present it
  (if choice allowed)?
  who is my audience?
  how should I report it?
  how could I structure it?

- **how have
  I done?**

  in my opinion?
  according to others?
  what knowledge have I learned?
  what skills have I learned?
  what should I improve and how?

THE INQUIRY FRAMEWORK
From the Information Skills in the Curriculum Research Unit
Inner London Education Authority, U.K. Project Director: Terence Brake
Reprinted with Permission in Emergency Librarian

Secondary School Assignments: Cooperatively Planned and Taught

Liz Austrom and Colleagues

It is not usually possible to transfer a unit of study or assignment from one situation to another without at least some adaptation, modification or revision, based on the needs of the specific program and the group of students to be taught; nevertheless, it is useful to examine what has been developed by others in order to ascertain the relative value of the approach used, the elements of the particular design and the structure of the assignment for one's situation. The units and assignments outlined here have proven successful in more than one setting and may provide inspiration or insight to develop something just that much better. *We trust that readers will make a similar commitment to sharing the results of their efforts in cooperative program planning and teaching.*

INDUSTRIAL REVOLUTION PROJECT SOCIAL STUDIES 9

The Industrial Revolution Project was planned to develop and reinforce basic skills in report writing (specifically taking notes and organizing information) in the ninth grade. These skills have been taught and assessed in the previous grade by teachers and teacher-librarians in a developmental reading program.

This unit was initiated by the teacher-librarians after group discussion about the lack of report writing skills exhibited by students. An hour in-service with the social studies department was held, focusing our presentation first on the teacher-librarians' role in materials supply and then on team planning and teaching. We ended by sharing our negative observations about student report writing abilities. The teachers shared concerns and commented on student tendencies to copy directly from encyclopedias. As a result of this discussion, most of the ninth grade social studies teachers decided to work with us on a unit designed to improve report writing skills. Together we selected the Industrial Revolution as the content area, basing our decision on the availability of a wide range of materials at many reading levels, since the students in our population exhibited a wide range of prior achievement.

We established the following unit plan:

Period One – The introduction of the unit in the classroom. The teacher may already have spent several periods on the topic, but this period focuses on the requirements of the assignment and on the selection of individual topics, as well as reviewing the use of key words and indexes, particularly of encyclopedias.

Period Two – Whole class instruction in the resource center. In the first half of the period the teacher-librarian explains the purpose, offers encouragement and reassurance, and demonstrates the process of using the sheets that each student is given in a folder, using overhead transparencies of the sheets.

The **Research Record** is worth 30 percent. Students are told to include every book they look at so as to get credit for the search as well as the notes. This sheet was included so that all students would have a chance to succeed. It is usually done significantly better than the bibliography and pulls up the average mark. In a school where students are less varied or where they have had a lot of prior experience with reports, it might not be necessary. It does have the advantage of telling the teachers whether or not students are using the indexes. All of the possible bibliographic citations are noted on cards on a ring, and each includes a notation about whether there is a good index or table of contents. This is available for teachers and teacher-librarians; it makes marking the sheets much easier.

Outline – Worth 20 percent. Students are advised that the final period instruction will show them how to do the outline. The teacher-librarian in this period merely emphasizes the need to have all the notes done by the final period, shows how the note slips will be cut apart, sorted by topic, organized in order, and stapled in order in clumps which correspond to the paragraphs in the final outline. A reminder sheet on the process is stapled to the inside back cover of the folder so that students can check there if they forget which step comes first.

In the second half of period two, the social studies teacher, or the reading teacher if you have one in the school, reviews the Preview/Question steps in the SQ3R (Survey, Question, Read, Recite, Review) study method, using class sets of a

ASSIGNMENT SHEET

I. **Introduction.** Briefly, the Industrial Revolution means the shifting from hand tools to power machinery and the application of power driven machinery to manufacturing. The Industrial Revolution began about 1750 and is still in progress.

II. **Purpose.** To gain an understanding of inventors or scientists who made significant contributions to the Industrial or Scientific Revolution and to develop skills in researching and organizing information.

III. **Materials** Materials in the school library resource center will be on overnight loan for your use in this assignment.

IV. **Organization and What To Do.** Following is a list of inventors or scientists who made significant contributions to the Industrial Revolution in the fields of transportation, communication, manufacturing, medicine and engineering.

17th and 18th Century	*19th century*	*20th Century*
Eli Whitney	George Eastman	Wright Brothers
James Watt	Carl Benz	Henry Ford
Robert Fulton	Isambard Brunel	Vlasimir Zworykin
George Stephenson	Nicholas Otto	Ferdinand de Lesseps
Sir Humphrey Davy	Rudolf Diesel	John Deere
Elias Howe	Heinrich Hertz	Justus von Liebig
John Kay	Samuel Morse	John Dalton
Richard Arkwright	Alexander G. Bell	Werner von Braun
Johna Gutenberg	Thomas Edison	John Rockefeller
Benjamin Franklin	Guglielmo Marconi	Frederick Banting
Edward Jenner	Charles Goodyear	Alexander Fleming
William Harvey	Louis Pasteur	Ernest Rutherford
Isaac Newton	Alfred Nobel	
	Robert Koch	
	Sandford Fleming	
	Joseph Lister	
	Thomas Telford	
	James Simpson	
	Gregor Mendel	

Choose *one* of the assignments listed below.

1. **Inventor.** Choose one inventor from the list above. Identify the person's invention, explain its importance to the Industrial Revolution and its effect on the way people lived. If your chosen inventor produced a number of inventions, choose only the one that you consider to be most important.

2. **Invention.** The most significant impact on changing technology has come about as a result of inventions that have been developed and refined by a number of inventors over the years, e.g., the automobile. Choose an invention and explain how it has evolved and improved to its present state. Discuss in more detail the work of two inventors involved in the invention's refinement and explain their contributions. Be sure to mention the machine's impact or significance.

3. **Field of advancement.** Select a field in which technology has improved rapidly over the last 200 years, e.g., manufacturing, transportation, communication, medicine or engineering. Summarize the improvements made in the field of your choice and explain its impact or significance on people's lives today. Include details of work of two or three inventors/scientists who contributed to this area.

During the six periods you are in the resource center, you will be expected to complete your notes, a bibliography, a report outline and a research record form. You will be given instructions for each and you will be given marks for each.

When you return to the social studies classroom you will be expected to write an in-class report using your notes and outline to assist you. The report will also be marked.

Remember:
It is *your* responsibility to have the assignment completed on time.

(SAMPLE)

Research Record   **Name** _____

                              Topic _____

I used the source materials listed below	complete call number	I used the index or table of contents	I found this source useful not useful	not on my topic

Notetaking Sheets — worth 30%. Students were told to use one side only, to use one main idea only in each section, to record the necessary information at the top of each section, and to paraphrase only. Although the slips have a section to check "direct quote", students ar advised not to use it. The same forms are used by senior students and they are allowed to use quotations. Each sheet contains six notetaking sections with the following layout:

Reference #_____Page # _____Paraphrase _____Direct Quote _____

Resources Used and **Preparation of Essays and Bibliographies** — worth 20%. Students are told that they will be taught in detail the next period how to do a bibliographic citation or description. In this period the teacher-librarian simply emphasizes through demonstration that if the column headed "Useful" was checked on the **Research Record**, then a bibliographic description should be written before the notes are taken. The reference number on the notetaking sheet is also related to the reference number on the **Resources Used** sheet. Students are advised that they may have many notes from one reference, or they may have only one - depending upon the number of relevant ideas they find in the book. Reference numbers are assigned arbitrarily, 1 for the first book used, 2 for the second, etc. A **Resources Used** sheet sample normally contains space for six references but has been abbreviated for inclusion below.

Topic _____ Student Name _____

    Resources Used: Write down in **Correct Form.**Use the
                             Preparation of Essays and Bibliographies
                             as a guide.

REFERENCE #		CALL#

Terms: _____

Corollary Information to be checked: _____

Definitions: _____

THE OUTLINE	EXAMPLE	NOTES

An outline is a *plan* for your report. It should follow this pattern.

1. Put your notes in order.
2. Make your outline from the key words in your notes.

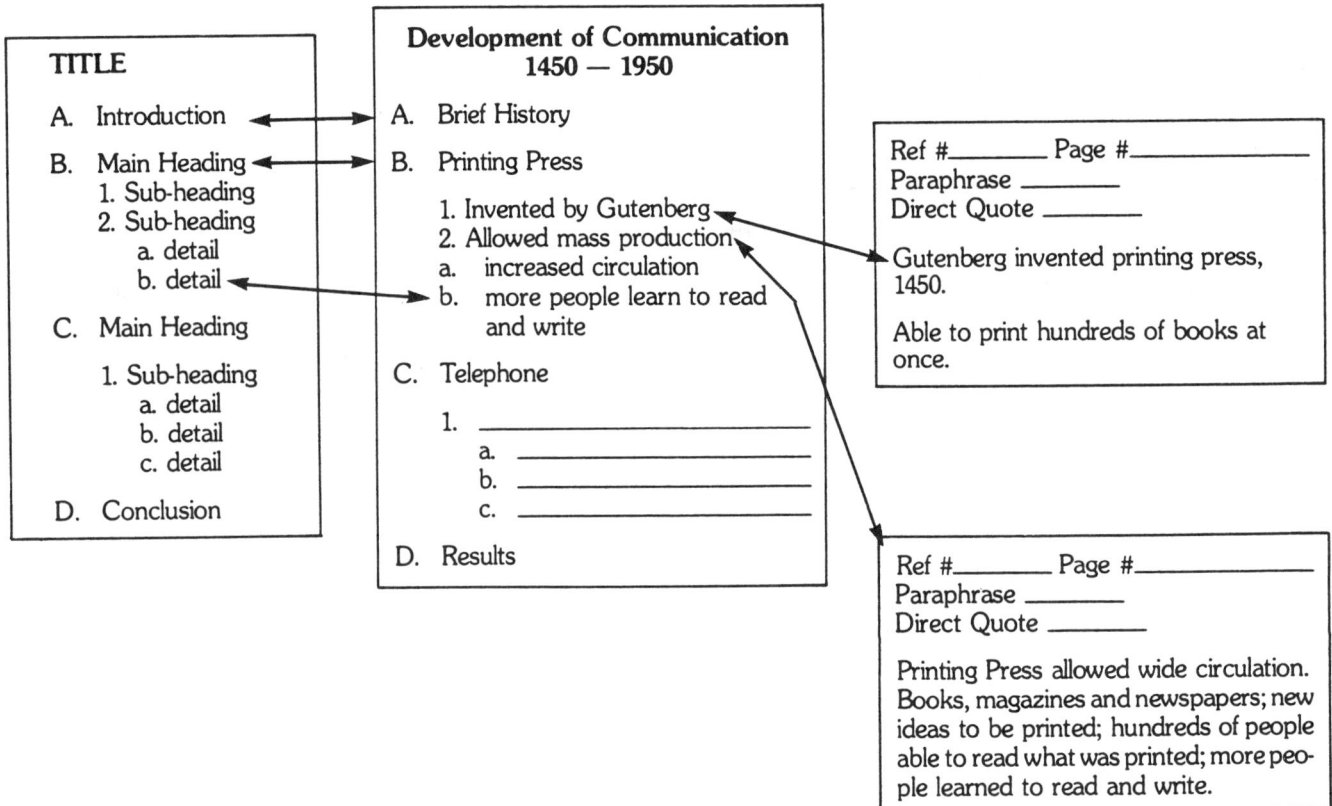

TITLE

A. Introduction

B. Main Heading
   1. Sub-heading
   2. Sub-heading
      a. detail
      b. detail

C. Main Heading

   1. Sub-heading
      a. detail
      b. detail
      c. detail

D. Conclusion

Development of Communication
1450 — 1950

A. Brief History

B. Printing Press

   1. Invented by Gutenberg
   2. Allowed mass production
      a. increased circulation
      b. more people learn to read and write

C. Telephone

   1. _____
      a. _____
      b. _____
      c. _____

D. Results

Ref # _____ Page # _____
Paraphrase _____
Direct Quote _____

Gutenberg invented printing press, 1450.

Able to print hundreds of books at once.

Ref # _____ Page # _____
Paraphrase _____
Direct Quote _____

Printing Press allowed wide circulation. Books, magazines and newspapers; new ideas to be printed; hundreds of people able to read what was printed; more people learned to read and write.

---

chapter from *Carl Benz and the Motor Car* by Doug Nye, and a page from *Merit Student Encyclopedia* on the history of the automobile. The focus is to have the students develop questions which will direct their reading. The same handouts are then used, in conjunction with a one page summary of skimming techniques, to practice key work skimming and topic sentence skimming. Some classes do not require the full hour to complete these activities. When this happens, students are encouraged to begin the search on their topic by looking in encyclopedia indexes and identifying sections that they can use in subsequent periods.

Period Three — The class is split into two groups which are designated on each folder beside the student's name. Instruction is for thirty minutes and then the groups switch and receive the second half of instruction. In one group the social studies or the reading teacher uses the chapter from *Carl Benz and the Motor Car* for a directed reading exercise where students take practice notes on notetaking sheets. The emphasis is

- **Skim** to locate the answer,

- **Read** the specific section carefully, and

<table>
<tr><td colspan="2">Grade 9 Research Project Marking Code
Industrial Revolution</td></tr>
<tr><td>Paraphrased Notes</td><td>Possible Mark</td></tr>
</table>

1. Completed reference details	2
2. Information complete and relevant to the topic	8
3. Paraphrasing skills:	
uses key words, omits unnecessary words	3
uses own words	3
information makes sense	3
one idea per strip	3
4. Organization of information	6
5. Legibility of notes	2
Total	30

The Outline

1. Topic complete (Title, headings for introduction, conclusion, etc.)	10
2. Organization of ideas	6
3. Correct format (numeration, indentation, etc)	3
4. Neatness	1
Total	20

Research Record

1. Correlation with bibliography and notetaking (including quantity)	10
2. Variety of resources attempted	5
3. Complete call number	4
4. Complete title	4
5. Used index and/or table of contents where appropriate	5
6. Legibility and neatness	2
Total	30

Bibliography

1. Correct form	
completeness	3
order	2
spelling	2
punctuation	3
capitalization	1
indentation	1
2. Variety of resource	3
3. Complete call number	2
4. Legibility and neatness	2
5. Reference number	1
Total	20

- **Paraphrase** the information using **key** words.

Recording the Reference #, and Page # at the top of the strips is stressed, as is writing only one idea per strip, and using abbreviations and note codes where possible.

In the other group, the teacher-librarian teaches students how to use the style guide for bibliographic citation which is stapled to the inside front cover of the folder. It is based on the idea that there is a basic pattern and several variations that cover most book materials. Students each complete one practice bibliographic citation for a preselected book, then modify it for a series. All preselected books are from the Wayland/Priory Press series *Pioneers of Science and Discovery*. Next, the format of an encyclopedia article is taught and practiced. Everyone must be right on task if this is all to be accomplished in 25-30 minutes!

Periods Four, Five and Six — A quick reminder of the process and then everyone gets to work, using the books which have been pulled and are located on a trolley, plus the encyclopedias which are not pulled into a separate collection. Students who need help are given it by whichever teacher is nearest and not helping someone else. The idea is to supervise closely enough so that students are not practicing errors, but are shown the correct method as quickly as possible. Some never need much help, while others need constant assistance at first. The social studies teacher can often identify the most needy and spend most of the first working period with those few students while the teacher-librarian handles the rest of the class. Students are advised that they must do homework, and all materials are available to be checked out overnight but must be returned before school the following day. We usually put a limit of two regular books or one book and one encyclopedia per student per night. Even so, circulation figures often reach 100 + per night, and the recarding task each morning is a heavy one.

Period Seven — Students must have their notes complete for this period. Whole class instruction takes approximately 20 minutes, and emphasizes the process of cutting the strips, sorting them into categories, sorting each category clump into logical order, stapling in clumps which correspond to paragraphs, and making an outline from the notes. Overheads and prepared outlines on chart paper are used to demonstrate, and students are given the one page sample outline format. The bulk of the period is spent with teachers assisting students to organize their notes and get started. None of the students finish their outline within the period. In the last five minutes the teacher-librarian summarizes what must be handed in, what it is worth in marks, and the expectation that the bibliography will be rewritten in alphabetical order on another sheet before it is handed in.

Period Eight — Most teachers give their students some time back in the classroom to finish their outlines. Others do not. However all teachers allow one or two periods before the student must write their in-class essays using only their notes and essay outlines. This allows students to perfect their organization and also to take a few more notes if they feel they do not have enough or if they have a weak area.

Evaluation is shared by all teachers participating. The social studies teacher marks the reports. When we have had a reading teacher participate, she has marked the notes and outline, while the teacher-librarian has marked all of the process sheets. The process sheets are worth twice what the "end product" is worth and all marks become part of the social studies mark. We use marking code sheets so that a standard level of expectation is maintained no matter who marks. When marking is completed, a library volunteer records the marks on a class list and the folders are returned to the students. Excerpts of the marking code are given on page to indicate the range and value of the various concepts evaluated.

Industrial Revolution, Grade 9			
Plan For the Project - Time And Content			
A. Classroom	1 period	Introduction to Industrial Revolution Unit. Preview of assignment. Quick review of skills learned in developmental reading e.g., skimming, scanning, previewing techniques. Students look at list of topics - make choices	Subject teacher Reading center teacher or Teacher-librarian
B. Resource Center	6 periods	Lesson 1. Introduction Purpose & process of assignment Skimming; SQ3R technique	Teacher-librarian Reading center teacher

		Lesson 2.
		    Class in two groups
		    Group A. Paraphrasing, Bibliographies
		    Group B. Bibliographies; Paraphrasing
			Teacher-librarian
			Reading center teacher

		Lessons 3,4,5.
		    Collection of information
		    Organization of notes & bibliographies
			All assist

		Lesson 6. Instruction on report outline	Teacher-librarian
		Organization of notes Writing of outline	All assist
C. Classroom	1 or 2 periods	Writing report Review of unit	Subject teacher

In general, students do quite well on this assignment. It must be noted as well that the most difficult part of the assignment is the outline. Composing an outline is a high-level thinking task and is one which needs repeated practice. One danger of doing the unit year after year is that the personnel involved somehow begin to feel that student performance should somehow drastically improve. We have done it so many times that we forget that the students are doing it for the first time. And we forget that it is a sophisticated task which requires repetition to be mastered.

We provided for that repetition by establishing a second unit which is done with *all grade nine science students* each year, and which includes the use of the periodical index. Further followup is provided by an *English research essay in grade 10* which adds the use of footnotes via the Harvard system of referencing. These two repetitions of the same process in different subject areas ensure both mastery and transfer of learning. Since we know all students have had the previous instruction we do not have to commit the ultimate sin in students' eyes of reteaching what they have already "had." We simply remind them of what they have already learned and then we add something new to the process. Students then perceive a reason for doing another research project and they are not turned off! The subsequent units do not need to be as lengthy as the original unit, since we are building on the prior instruction. New students in the school are easily identified and given the necessary extra help.

These assignments might be seen to add to the work load of the teacher-librarian, but they are worth the work. Students are so much more capable of handling assignments and they do appreciate the help given them. They also view the teacher-librarian as a source of future assistance and some become "regulars." Some have come back to the school and said that the one facet of their university experience that they felt totally prepared for was writing essays. When we recall our own experiences in that area, we feel that the work involved in these units is the best, most valuable work that we have ever done. Other teachers and teacher-librarians who have been involved all feel the same way.

PEOPLE PERSPECTIVE ART 8

All too often library-based assignments in art rely on the old standards of writing a biography of a famous artist or a report on a period of art history. This particular assignment maintains the integrity of art objectives while integrating specific information skills.

This segment of the grade 8 art program is designed to change students' attitudes toward drawing and image making. Many students come to a class feeling that they cannot draw because they always compare their work to other people's work and find their own inadequate. If students' abilities are to develop, then a primary goal must be to assist them to gain more assurance and to feel more comfortable with drawing as self-expression. Students must be willing to take risks in their drawings. Risk-taking is where all the exciting things happen.

When students say they cannot draw, they are really saying that they are not satisfied with their drawings. To help them become more satisfied, we can do two things. First we can teach them a technique which will give them a method of approaching the task. The contour line drawing is one such method. It becomes a seeing tool for students to use. Secondly we must emphasize the individual nature of any art experience: we are all different; we are all important, unique and special; our unique experiences and perceptions affect the way we see and feel about things, therefore our drawings should reflect that uniqueness. Students' drawings must be accepted as a personal individual expression.

Goals

- to give students a method of approach and a skill which will enable them to draw a portrait.

- to build students' confidence and an acceptance of their own work as valuable.

- to broaden students' view of portraits by establishing a context of the variety and uniqueness of expression found in portraits.

Learning Objectives

- the student will make several contour line drawings.

- the student will complete a contour line drawn portrait from life.

- the student will examine and react to six portraits drawn from a representative list of portraits.

- the student will utilize the card catalogue, tables of contents, indexes and list of illustrations to find the selected portraits.

- the student will evaluate his own portrait.

Unit Plan

Periods 1 and 2: Art classroom

1. Teacher introduces drawing, with an emphasis on contour line drawing.

2. Students complete a minimum of four blind contour line drawings per period.

Periods 3 and 4: Art classroom

1. Students complete several contour line drawings, looking at the drawing for reference points not more than half of the time.

Period 5: Art classroom

1. Students complete a figure drawing from a live model, and using contour line drawing.

2. Drawing must fill a paper 24 by 18 inches. Lines running off at least 3 sides of the paper.

Period 6: Art classroom

1. Students complete the drawing, including background, and transfer to black paper.

Periods 7-10: Art classroom

1. Students complete pastel of the portrait on black paper; color choice to be determined solely by the students.

Period 11: Art classroom

1. Teacher critique of work, emphasizing the individuality of expression and uniqueness of interpretation of each portrait. (All portraits to be hung on the wall for display.)

Period 12: Art classroom

1. Teacher discusses work of Maxwell Bates, using slides. Teacher emphasizes the communicative skill of the artist in spite of a technique which students might perceive to be crude.

2. Teacher introduces sheet for library assignment, *People Hunt.* Emphasis is put on looking and interpreting.

Periods 13 and 14: Library Resource Center

1. Teacher reminds students of discussion of assignment previously done in class, stressing the individual, thoughtful response required.

2. Teacher-librarian introduces the Resource List, emphasizing:

   — use of subject side of card catalogue.

   — difficulty of last names with "Van" or "De" and suggesting that if a two part name is not found under one of the parts the student should try the other part.

   — process of not looking for the title of the painting until they find the book, then they use the index and list of illustrations.

3. Students complete the worksheets, with assistance as necessary from both the art teacher and the teacher-librarian.

Evaluation

1. Students evaluate their own pastel, assigning letter grades according to established criteria, e.g., anyone who has made a genuine effort should not get below a C.

2. Teacher marks the original drawing on which the pastel was based, assigning letter grades. Both teacher and student letter grades are recorded.

3. Library assignment is marked either "acceptable" or "not acceptable," depending upon the thoughtfulness of the work done.

People Hunt - Art 8

1. Select six portraits from the list you will find in this package of materials

2. Using the Resource List and the subject catalogue, locate books or pamphlets which have pictures of your selected portraits.

3. Use the *index* or *list of illustrations* in the book to help you in your search.

   Note: a. You should find a color picture, not a black and white one.
   b. Make sure that what you have is not a "detail" study of only a part of the whole portrait.

4. Fill in one section of the attached worksheet for each portrait you have selected. Base your answers on what you observe and feel about the person shown in the portrait.

The student assignment sheet (above) is accompanied by a three page worksheet with the following form repeated six times, the only differences being the painting number, which goes from one to six.

Painting #1: _____   _____
                        Artist   Title of Painting

1. What kind of person is this? _____

2. What does this person do for a living? _____

3. What did the artist think of this person? _____

4. Would you like to meet this person? _____

Why? _____

Note: The portrait list which follows is the one used by students to make their selections of 6 portraits to find and comment upon Another Teachers' Reference Sheet, which students do not have access to, gives the name of the painting, the name of the artist, the complete call number of the book, and the title of the book. If we run into difficulties during a class we can always consult the list. Also if there has been heavy circulation of art books just prior to the assignment the list can be used for a quick check to ensure that needed titles are indeed on the shelves.

Of course, all portraits were originally checked to make certain that they did appear in books, and that there was relatively easy access to them via the subject catalogue. Many additional subject cards for the painters had to be added to our subject file the first time we did the assignment.

People Hunt Portrait List

Name of Painting	Name of Artist
A. Durer's Self Portrait	A. Durer
Absinthe	Degas
Anna Christina	Wyeth
Bacchus	Caravaggio
Battista Sforza	Piero Della Francesca
Cafe Singer	Degas
Cardinal Leger	Lemieux
Clown	Rouault
Comtesse D'Haussonville	Ingres
Don Fernando Nino De Guevara	El Greco
Dr. Gachet	Van Gogh
Farm Girl	Soutine
Federigo Da Montefetro	Piero Della Francesca
Genivra Di Benci	Leonardo Da Vinci
Gertrude Stein	Picasso
Girl with Braids	Modigliani
Girl with Veil	Vermeer
Half Past Three (or "The Poet")	Chagall
In a Private Room at the Rat Mort	Toulouse-Lautrec
Jew in Green	Chagall
La Goulue Entering the Moulin Rouge	Toulouse-Lautrec
La Muta	Raphael
Lacemaker	Vermeer
Le Beau Major (Dr. Devariagne)	Modigliani
The Loge	Renoir
Madam Matisse	Matisse
The Madwoman	Soutine
Malle Babbe	Frans Hals
Man in Armour	Rembrandt
The Man with a Pink	Van Eyck
Margaretha Van Eyck	Van Eyck
Marilyn Monroe	De Kooning
Marilyn Monroe	Warhol
Mme. Ines Moitessier	Ingres
Mme. Rene De Gas	Degas
Miss Olson and a Kitten	Wyeth
The Old King	Rouault
Old Peasant	Van Gogh
Ortukaryooak the Inlander	Winifred Marsh
Oscar Wilde	Toulouse-Lautrec
Page Boy at Maxims	Soutine
Pere Tanguy	Van Gogh
Portrait of a Man	Antonello Da Messina
Portrait of a Man 1512	Titian
Portrait of a Man with a Medal of Cosino	Botticelli
Portrait of a Nurse	Soutine
Portrait of a Woman (c1900)	Bonnard
Portrait of a Woman (La Schiavone)	Titian
Portrait of Cardinal Nicholas Albergati	Van Eyck
Portrait of Jean Cocteau	Modigliani
Portrait of Jules De Jouy	Monet
Portrait of Sculpture Miestchaninoff	Soutine
Portrait of Vava	Chagall
Queen of Hearts	De Kooning
St. Jerome as a Cardinal	El Greco
Self Portrait	Degas

(People Hunt Portrait List continued on p. 116.)

People Hunt Portrait List — *Continued*

Name of Painting	Name of Artist
Self Portrait	Durer
Self Portrait	Gauguin
Self Portrait 1895	Munch
Self Portrait in Blue Jacket	Beckman
Self Portrait 1901	Picasso
Self Portrait 1656	Rembrandt
Self Portrait 1629	Rembrandt
Self Portrait with Palette	Cezanne
Self Portrait with Palette	Gauguin
The Tipsy Woman	Manet
Weeping Woman	Picasso
Woman Ironing 1904	Picasso
Woman I	De Kooning
Woman with Fish Hat	Picasso
Young Canadian	Charles Comfort

People Hunt Portrait List - Teacher's Reference Sheet

Name of Painting	Name of Artist	Call #	Title
Absinthe	Degas	759.4 DEG	Degas
Anna Christina	Wyeth	759.13 WHE	Two Worlds of Andrew Wyeth
Bacchus	Caravaggio	759.5 CA	The Complete Painting of Caravaggio
Battista Sforza	Piero Della Francesca	709 HAR VOL.II	Art, A History of Painting, Sculpture, Architecture
Café Singer	Degas	759.4 DEG	Degas
Cardinal Léger	Lemieux	759.11 DU	Four Decades
Clown	Rouault	759.4 ROU	Rouault
Comtesse D'Haussonville	Ingres	709 HAR	Art, a History of Painting, Sculpture, Architecture
Don Fernando Nino de Guevara	De Guevara	759.6 THE	El Greco
Dr. Gachet	Van Gogh	759.05 Plg	Post Impressionists pg. 53
Ella	Thomas Cook	759.11 HAR	A Peoples Art pg. 91
Farm Girl	Soutine	759.4 SOU	Soutine
Federigo Da Montefetro	Piero Della Francesca	709 HAR Vol II	Art, A History of Painting, Sculpture, Architecture
Genevea Di Benci	Leonardo Da Vinci	750.5 LEO	Leonardo Da Vinci
Gertrude Stein	Picasso	759.6 PIC	Picasso
Girl With Braids	Modigliani	759.5 MOD	Modigliani
Girl with Veil	Vermeer	759.94 VE	The Complete Painting of Vermeer

(SAMPLE ONLY)

Look up headings in the

Subject File —

1. The name of the artist

   eg. **Gogh, Vincent Van**

2. **Painters**, followed by the nationality of the artist

   e.g. **Painters, Dutch**

3. Other headings:

   Artists
   Painters
   Painting - History
   Portraits

Write the complete call numbers of useful books in the spaces above. Then - take your list to the shelves and look for the books.

* **Remember:**

1. R above the call number means the book is in the Reference section.
2. The Card Catalogue will tell you if there are pamphlets on your topic.

_____

_____

_____

_____

_____

_____

Special Reference Source:

McGraw-Hill Encyclopedia of World Art.

— includes information on a wide variety of artists throughout history. As well, it has many color plate of famous works of art.

* **Important:**
  Use the
  Index,
  Volume XV

McGraw Hill Encyclopedia of World Art
Gogh, Vincent van (Dutch ptr., 1853-90) 14 694-700', plate 286 292
Les Alyscamps 14 697
and Anquetin 14 696
Apples 14 696
L'Arlesienne 14 697
Back Side of Old Houses 14 696
Basket with Crocuses 14 696
La Berceuse 14 697, 699, plate 292
and Bernard 14 696
Cezanne's comment on 9, 33, 34
Les Chaumieres 14 698

ART 8

PEOPLE HUNT

The resource list on the previous page is meant to be folded like a greeting card and looks very attractive if printed in color. The subject heading *Portraits* is included on the list but students are advised that it is the least useful of the headings, in spite of the fact that it might seem like the best heading. Having students strike this heading off the list reinforces the fact.

From the teacher-librarian's point of view this assignment reinforces the use of the card catalogue very well, without much "talking to" on the part of the teacher-librarian. It also emphasizes to grade eight students that search skills are necessary in subject areas other than those termed "academic."

The best part is that while working with the students you are able to see their reactions to some wonderful portraits. Almost as exciting is working with a teacher on a simple project that is fully integrated into the classroom activity and hence has full value and meaning for all participants. John Denver sings about "Rocky Mountain high"! This is just as great a feeling!

SIMULATING INTERNATIONAL RELATIONS POPULATION CONTROL SOCIAL STUDIES 11

While the topic of this assignment may not suit every situation the approach is an interesting one and the design elements well worth replicating in this and different subject areas. This assignment builds in a research strategy, one of the most important of information skills but one of the least common. Students do not actually begin "research" until a number of preliminary steps are completed.

Staff scientists of the Canada Research Council are reported to have perfected a new form of contraceptive drug. The drug is effective for one year with only one dose and may be taken by either a man or a woman. There are no harmful side effects and it is soluble and so can be added to water systems. The drug is one hundred percent effective, but an antidote is available.

Unfortunately the drug is expensive to manufacture and, until a commercial plant can be built, only a limited supply will be available. The Canadian government has decided to offer this contraceptive to the world. However, because of the small amount produced so far, only one country will be able to receive the drug.

Your group has been called together by the Prime Minister and Minister for External Affairs. Briefly, your task is to decide which country should receive the drug. You should look at possible countries from these points of view.

1. Which country has the msot need? Some factors to consider are:

   • Population per arable acre or hectare.

   • Food availability

   • Growth rate

   • Density

   • Degree of urbanization

   • Degree of industrialization

   • Gross National Product or Gross Domestic Product

   • Health facilities

   • Distribution of income

   • Potential for future development

2. What factors will work against widespread acceptance of the drug? These are mainly cultural and religious beliefs, e.g., local customs, need for large families, etc.

Procedure

You will work in groups of three to four people. Use Country Choice Process Sheet and note-taking form to help you choose your country.

When you have chosen your country you must let me know. Each country may only be done by one group per class.

As a group, you will be required to make a three to ten minute report explaining your reasons for choosing a particular country. This report must also contain visual materials. Each group member must participate in the oral presentation.

The teacher and the rest of the class will listen critically as members of the Cabinet. Be prepared to defend your choice during the question period after your presentation.

Card Catalog

Look under general subject headings and under specific subject headings.

Reference Materials

General encyclopedias such as

World Book Encyclopedia
Merit Students' Encyclopedia
Encyclopedia Britannica

... and special encyclopedias such as

Peoples of the Earth
Lands and Peoples

Evaluation

Possible
Marks

1. Note sheet
   (if completed during period) 5

2. *Teacher evaluation as follows:*
   Factual information 20
   Concluding argument 8
   Visual (or audio) materials
   (classroom size charts, graphs, maps, etc.) 18

3. *Student evaluation:*
   Argument
   (What did they say, how convincing were they?) 7

   Presentation
   (Manner, clarity of voice, use of visuals) 7

These marks will be averaged from each student's evaluation

Total 65

(Late Deduction) 25%

Bonus: 5 marks for most convincing presentation
Time: — Resource Center— 3 periods only
  — Books will be available during class time as well as for overnight loan.
  — Presentations will begin _____

Country Choice Process Sheet

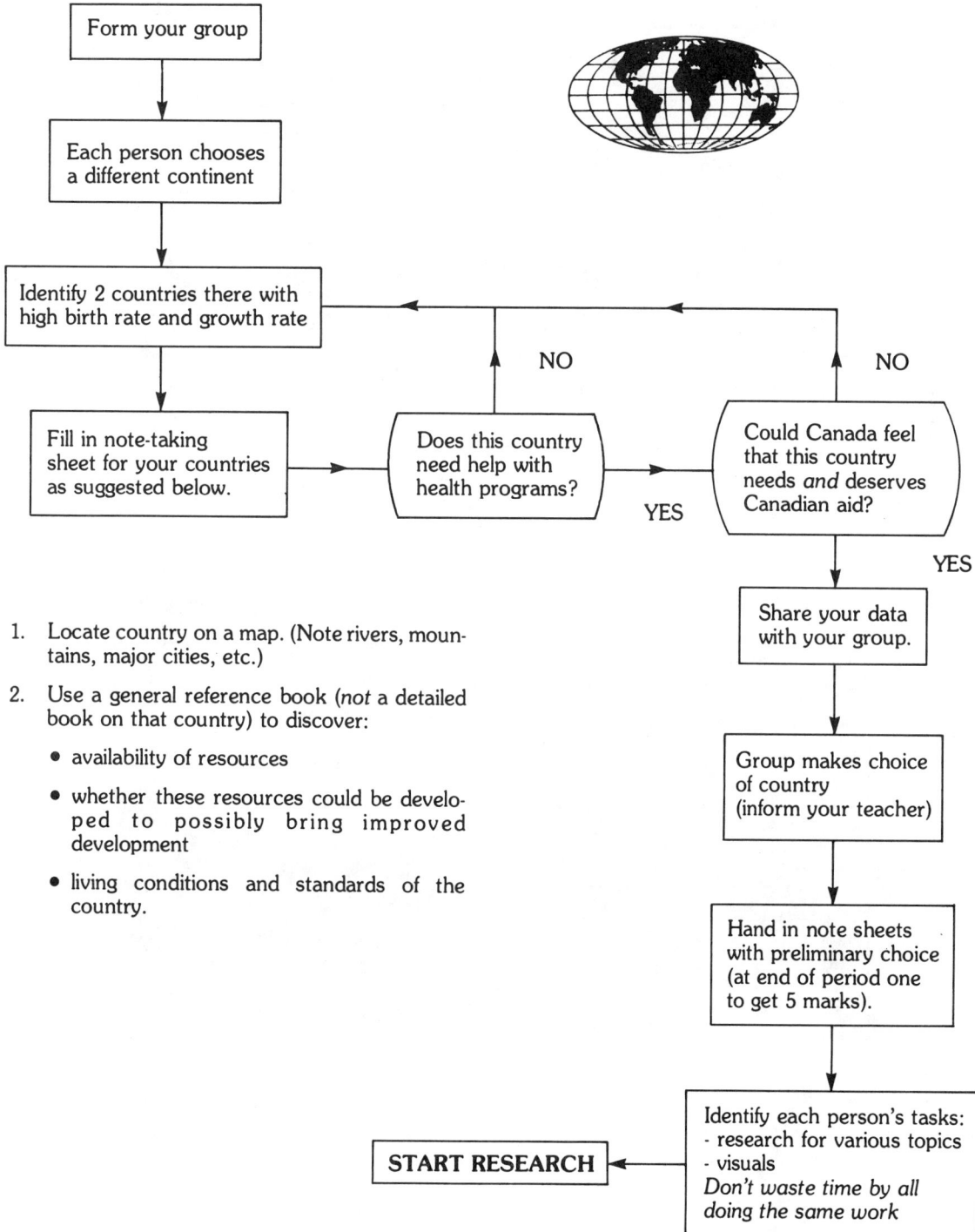

Form your group

↓

Each person chooses
a different continent

↓

Identify 2 countries there with
high birth rate and growth rate

↓

Fill in note-taking
sheet for your countries
as suggested below.

→

Does this country
need help with
health programs?

NO ↑

YES →

Could Canada feel
that this country
needs *and* deserves
Canadian aid?

NO

YES ↓

Share your data
with your group.

↓

Group makes choice
of country
(inform your teacher)

↓

Hand in note sheets
with preliminary choice
(at end of period one
to get 5 marks).

↓

Identify each person's tasks:
- research for various topics
- visuals
*Don't waste time by all
doing the same work*

→ **START RESEARCH**

1. Locate country on a map. (Note rivers, mountains, major cities, etc.)

2. Use a general reference book (*not* a detailed book on that country) to discover:

   • availability of resources

   • whether these resources could be developed to possibly bring improved development

   • living conditions and standards of the country.

Population Control
Note-Taking Form

Student Name _____

Country _____ **Country** _____

BR _____ GR _____ GNP _____   BR _____ GR _____ GNP _____

Map   **Map**

   Rivers _____   Rivers _____

   Landforms _____   Landforms _____

Resources   **Resources**

_____   _____

_____   _____

_____   _____

Potential for development   **Potential for development**

_____   _____

_____   _____

_____   _____

Living standard   **Living standard**

_____   _____

_____   _____

_____   _____

Group members: **Possible choices:**

_____   _____

_____   _____

_____   _____

                            _____

      Group choice:

_____

Worldmark Cyclopedia of Nations
Encyclopedia of Social Sciences
McGraw-Hill Encyclopedia of Science & Technology

... other reference materials

Deadline Data on World Affairs
Clements Encyclopedia of World Governments
Europa Yearbook
Statistical Yearbook
Oxford Economic Atlas

Almanacs & Yearbooks—including

Demographic Yearbook

Periodical Indexes

Will guide you to magazine articles on your topic.
Look under headings such as:

Population
Population Increase
Food Supply
Birth Control

... and under specific countries e.g.,
India—POPULATION
China—FOOD SUPPLY

Pamphlet Files

Look in the grey filing cabinets for pamphlets and newspaper clippings, etc.
To locate, use the **Subject** side of the card catalog.

Audio-Visual Items

If there are filmstrips, etc. on your topic, they will be listed in the card catalog and their location given.

A Stations Approach to Learning; the Conversion of a Secondary School Skeptic

Debra Simmons

A "stations approach" to learning can be defined in the most sophisticated educational terms or can be described more simply as a series of activities, and supporting resources, designed to develop student knowledge and/or skills; each of these activities, or "stations," is physically separated one from the other. Each student moves through these stations following the instructions at each location in order to complete a task or solve a problem.

The first introduction I had to units based on stations convinced me that this approach was like a workbook that walked. In working through these stations, students were asked to examine a number of books on a given subject and to perform tasks using the books. The intent was to expose students to a variety of materials and through using them to learn how information is arranged within these books. But it seemed to me that the questions were not related to anything immediate or useful since reference books come and go, arrangements in books differ and idiosyncrasies abound. Filling in the blank became the primary object for the students much as filling in the blank in workbooks becomes the end for students. If felt there must be a better, more meaningful and quicker way to teach kids a procedure for locating information

than making them go through a three hour exercise of locating how many ships used the St. Lawrence Seaway in a given year or comparing population density for two countries. I acknowledged that some students made reference at a later date to a book they discovered during the exercise, but I was not convinced that stations could be useful for anything other than finding answers to questions for which the overlying objective of the unit was lost to most students.

Three years ago I worked with another teacher-librarian who bullied and cajoled me into creating a series of stations for a grade 8 class studying the Renaissance in Europe. We had a great time locating materials, thinking of questions related to these books, digging out inviting, interesting and "awesome" facts about the period.

My colleague taught me how to administer such a lesson. She passed on those seemingly insignificant details that separate success from failure. For instance: having students use only pencils so that marks in books can be erased; having answer booklets instead of sheets to reduce the possibilities of copying; physically separating stations as much as possible to ensure individual work. But like previous stations units, there was no purpose other than general exposure. The kids liked it because the situation was different from the usual classroom. They worked in isolation yet could move about. And they, like most people, were intrigued by the pictures, facts and fun of handling a variety of materials. What I felt was lacking was a focus—a purpose. This focus came eventually from classroom teachers. We should have employed cooperative program planning and teaching techniques from the beginning. But we learned. Subsequent stations were planned cooperatively with subject teachers.

What began as a walking workbook has evolved into a sophisticated approach to learning that caters to the content needs of the classroom teacher while integrating information skills and employing every level of Bloom's taxonomy of the cognitive domain. This has come about because of the cooperative and demanding nature of unit development within the social studies department at our school. The stations approach began in social studies but is about to spread to science now that we know how to make it work and how to ensure the combination of content and a development of skills.

The transformation began with the restructuring of the grade 8 social studies curriculum. A unit on the Middle Ages in China, India, and Japan was dropped into the middle of the course. There were a number of problems with this unit: teachers were unfamiliar with the material; students lacked a background; the desired concepts were lost in the mass of dates and names in the text.

Because our grade 8 teachers had used the Renaissance stations, they were receptive to developing a series of stations on the Middle Ages in these areas. They provided us with specific content goals and learning objectives. To these we added a variety of information skills that needed to be reinforced. The end product was a unit of 43 stations using books, cassettes/filmstrips that had a focus and could be used in a variety of ways. The unit allowed for a number of follow-up activities, and was more adaptable because it focused on course content. It could be used to replace, to supplement and/or to clarify the text. It has been used to review note-taking skills, it has led to further research, it became a foundation for discussion, and it has been used later as a basis in comparing this period with the Renaissance in Europe.

In preparing the questions and activities for this unit, we created a matrix of content and skills to ensure that the students were exposed to all the content concepts and used a variety of information skills. The matrix shows content goals and skills used. Most of the questions were of the lower cognitive levels—comprehension and application, with some analysis. Examples of the kinds of activities the students were asked to perform include:

- Using a physical map, imagine a land trip from China to Europe. Would the trip be easy or difficult? Give two reasons for your answer.

- Using specific photographs of castles of the Middle Ages in Scotland and India, identify the country, climate, decoration, construction; give your preference and reasons.

We viewed these stations as a means for teaching complex concepts using basic location skills. Talking among the students was not allowed. The intent was individual discovery.

Last year, the second teacher-librarian and I worked with a teacher to develop a stations approach to the physical regions of Canada. The teacher provided us with very specific concepts related to these regions. We decided that a visual approach would be best so that students would leave the exercise with a visual image of these regions. As a result, these grade 10 students do very little textual reading. There is also less emphasis on interpretation and analysis.

The 25 stations consist of pictures, slides, maps, pamphlets, graphs and a few books. There is more than one item at every station. Students are led to speculate, compare and apply knowledge. The unit has been used as an introduction to the subject of physical regions. It has also been used as a closing activity. It has been used with equal success with regular grade 10 classes, modified classes and with classes of English as a second language students.

There are important differences between this unit and previous ones. A major change is its size. Because we had time to develop and evaluate only 25 stations, we do not have one station per student as is usual. As a result, students frequently doubled up at some stations. The serendipitous benefit that came of this was the discussions which arose between students when the answer was analytical, speculative or unknown. Questions such as these stimulate discussion:

- Look at the physical map of British Columbia. What problems might there be in developing a transportation system?

- Look at a specific photograph. Make two statements about the climate of the area and speculate about what geographic region is most likely represented. Why?

When students were asked to evaluate the unit they wrote that they enjoyed it, liked not having a lot to read, and acknowledged their inexperience in "seeing" information. Because of the nature of the questions, the stations provide an excellent opportunity for one-on-one teaching and the teacher is frequently another student.

This year we have pushed the limits even further. In the past we have been able to develop stations that are content relevant, flexible in organization, and adaptable to a variety of materials and students. This year, we were asked to work with a teacher to incorporate the ability to see the relationship between evidence and conclusion into a stations approach to the Industrial Revolution. Instead of giving us specific content, the teacher wanted the stations to provoke the students to generalizing. The basic generalization that was sought was that "The Industrial Revolution continues today and affects your life beneficially and detrimentally." Stations were set up around eight areas: medicine; transportation; science; war; commerce; communications; personal life; technology. Each area had five stations and each student had to complete two subject areas. The materials were neither predominantly visual nor textual, but a combination of both. Since this was intended to be used with grade 9 students, once again basic location skills were reinforced. Each station was formed in such a way that a conclusion could be reached based on the data located. Students were asked to link a station with a given conclusion. The factual information and the conclusions reached led to an in-class essay about the impact of the

Industrial Revolution on medicine or war or technology. From these essays came a discussion of the advantages and disadvantages of continued technology in our lives.

This unit has not been as popular with teachers. The absence of specific content makes follow-up activities difficult. The abstract nature of the material requires careful guidance by the teacher. Also, making time in a crowded curriculum to discuss evidence and conclusion as well as the ethical, moral, political and economic aspects of technology requires a skill at juggling time as well as students. It is our intent to alter the unit somewhat and introduce it into the new grade 11 science and technology course. The prime objective of this new course is to help students evaluate and solve problems. The abstract reasoning abilities of grade 11 students is more developed than in grade 9 students and the older student will be better able to deal with this material. We will of course first involve the teachers involved and incorporate the principles of cooperative planning and teaching. We have learned the hard way that which is blatantly evident to many: working in isolation just doesn't work.

Now we are working on a grade 10 unit to supplement the study of physical geography. These stations will be similar in that they will be primarily visual. They deal specifically with the relationship between the physical and economic geography of British Columbia. Content matter has been provided by the teacher. Once again we have added information skills. Greater emphasis is being placed on incorporating the higher levels of cognition—evaluation and synthesis. Once again a matrix has been created into which we place information about which station covers the content and which cognitive level is employed. This unit is in preparation and will not be used until next September. We don't yet know how the students will respond to questions that require greater abstract thinking skills as well as locating skills.

I have become very enthusiastic about the possibilities of the stations approach. I have seen it work with modified students, large and small classes, classes of students with English language disabilities. It need not always use set questions, but can be used to lead students into formulating their own questions. It teaches information skills in conjunction with a content area; it can be used to stimulate imagination as well as to identify factual data. It is an adaptable and viable way to introduce, to enhance, to sum up. I'm convinced. I've been converted.

Grade 8 Social Studies—Patterns of Civilization

CONTENT: Aspects of life in India, China, and Japan during 500 - 1600 A.D.											
RESEARCH SKILLS		Skim Scan	Dictionary Vocabulary Enrichment	Table of Contents	Index	Intepretation of illustration, maps etc	Listening	Viewing	Comparing	Recognizing

INDIA
- blending of cultures
- influence of invasion
	1. Customs of daily life, food clothing, shelter, etc
	
	2. Arts - painting
	          poetry
	          theatre
	          puppetry
	
	3. Cultural accomplishments:
	  - gunpowder
	  - printing
	  - medical advances
	  - magnetic compass
	  - etc									

CHINA
- cultural accomplishments
- rise and fall of Empire
- isolation
	4. Warfare
	  - weapons
	  - leaders
	
	5. Education
	  - subjects
	  - rigors									

JAPAN
- adopt and adapt
- feudalism
- isolation
	6. "Riches of the East"
	  - spices
	  - silks
	  - jewels
	
	7. Architecture
	  - Taj Mahal
	  - Mosques/Temples
	  - other
	
	8. Religions
	  character of
	
	9. Personalities
	  - Genghis Khan
	  - etc									

BRITISH COLUMBIA - ECONOMIC AND PHYSICAL GEOGRAPHY

	RAW MATERIALS	SECONDARY SUPPORT	PRODUCTS	CONSERVATION	TECHNIQUES METHODS	MARKETS	EMPLOYMENT	PHYSICAL	CLIMATE	POLLUTION
FISHING										
MINING										
TOURISM										
FORESTRY										
AGRICULTURE										
MISC.										

	A	B	C	D	E	F
TOPIC	KNOWLEDGE tell label list locate cite offer choose name find say group show	COMPREHENSION translate propose define expand explain alter outline annotate restate infer offer contemplate	APPLICATION relate operate utilize try solve exert use put to use adopt take up employ handle	ANALYSIS break down check examine reason look into divide uncover deduce dissect include sift screen	SYNTHESIS create yield combine reorder make structure build cause compile effect blend form	EVALUATION judge accept decide reject rate criticize prioritize award rank umpire weigh settle

Part 6
ISSUES AND CONSIDERATIONS

There is no shortage of issues and considerations in teacher-librarianship! We provide some insight into only a few of them here. The obvious place to start is with Susan Casey's review of theory to determine her reality. Others do have stereotypes of the teacher-librarian and these are not going to be changed overnight. Evolution is the key to success, not revolution, but you can't start in the dark ages even if that is where people "are at." Step back and analyze where you are and where you are going; the road will be clearer and more accessible as a result. Mieko Nagakura surveys attitudes of teacher-librarians toward networking and teacher utilization of the resource center in a comparative study of ten countries. Her findings are based on a small sample but make for fascinating reading.

Critical thinking skills represent one of the current bandwagons in education. Is it what you mean by information skills? by library skills? It's worth finding out because a great many professional associations, school boards and departments of education are working on their versions of "critical thinking" and the teacher-librarian is nowhere in sight. Speak up and remind those involved of your expertise and willingness to "mainstream" their program and yours.

Microcomputers. Are they going to revolutionize everything and make life that much easier, more interesting and exciting, for both teacher-librarian and student? Perhaps. Although written five years ago (how quickly things change!), you may find the words of caution in our editorial on micros ("the new status symbol") still valid and worthy of your consideration. Let's at least stop to think about these issues before joining the headlong rush to every direction at once. Debra Simmons sounds a similar alarm from the association perspective in her look at the library, the computer and utopia. There are of course fine examples of outstanding use of microcomputers for student learning in resource centers and Bill McKinnie provides one such example in his description of online bibliographic searching in a secondary school resource center.

Are school assignments a public library responsibility as Nancy Black, Ken Roberts and Valerie White suggest? Not everyone agreed with their beliefs when this article was published. What happens in your community? What should happen?

In a major research study in school librarianship the Calgary (Alberta) Board of Education learned that its school library resource centers were definitely worth their keep. Bev Anderson reports on some of the more significant findings and the implications for professional practice.

The ten major issues in school librarianship facing teacher-librarians in one country bear a striking similarity to the major issues in every other country. Let's work together to overcome these and eliminate them from any future edition of this book!

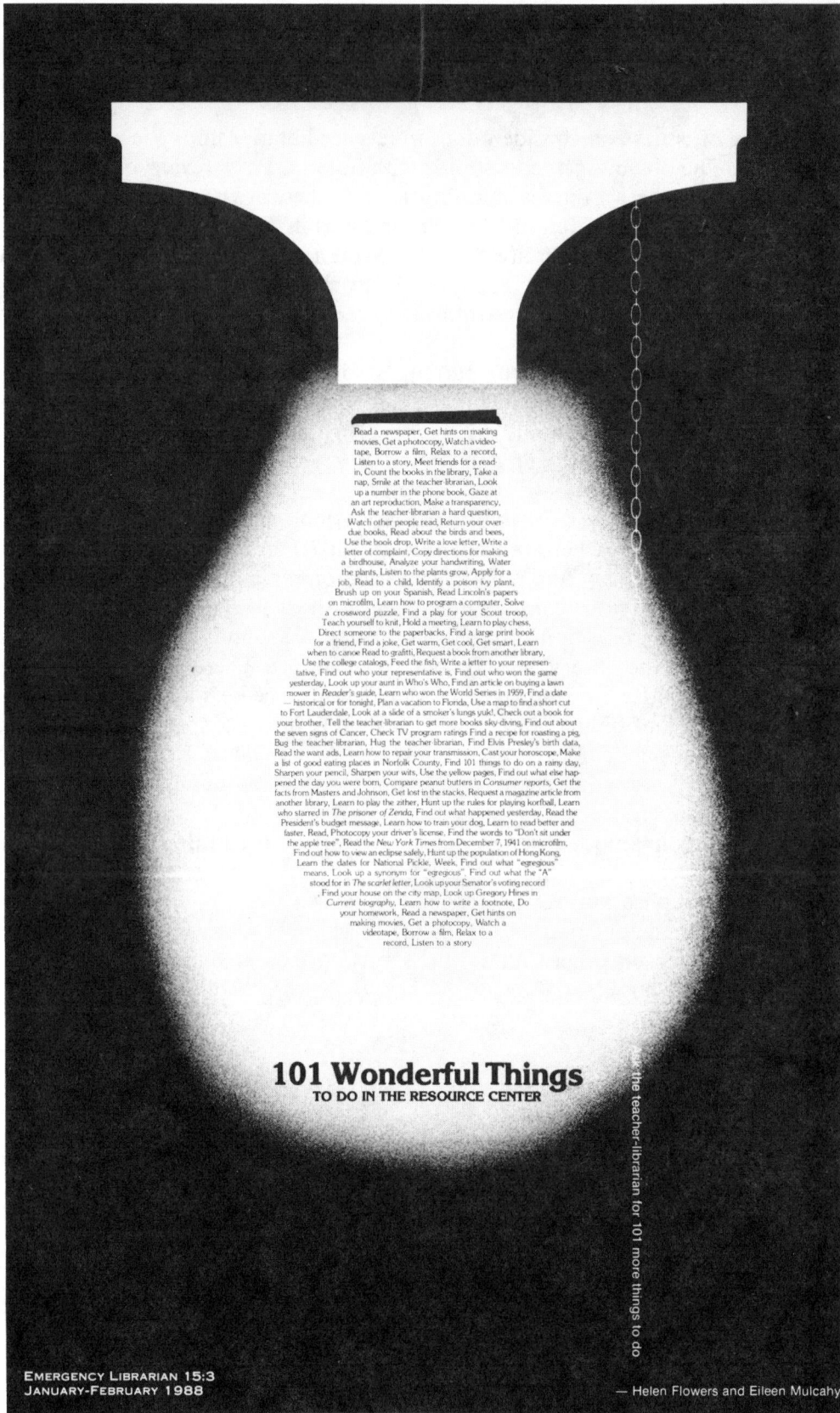

Read a newspaper, Get hints on making movies, Get a photocopy, Watch a video-tape, Borrow a film, Relax to a record, Listen to a story, Meet friends for a read-in, Count the books in the library, Take a nap, Smile at the teacher-librarian, Look up a number in the phone book, Gaze at an art reproduction, Make a transparency, Ask the teacher-librarian a hard question, Watch other people read, Return your over-due books, Read about the birds and bees, Use the book drop, Write a love letter, Write a letter of complaint, Copy directions for making a birdhouse, Analyze your handwriting, Water the plants, Listen to the plants grow, Apply for a job, Read to a child, Identify a poison ivy plant, Brush up on your Spanish, Read Lincoln's papers on microfilm, Learn how to program a computer, Solve a crossword puzzle, Find a play for your Scout troop, Teach yourself to knit, Hold a meeting, Learn to play chess, Direct someone to the paperbacks, Find a large print book for a friend, Find a joke, Get warm, Get cool, Get smart, Learn when to canoe, Read to graffiti, Request a book from another library, Use the college catalogs, Feed the fish, Write a letter to your representative, Find out who your representative is, Find out who won the game yesterday, Look up your aunt in Who's Who, Find an article on buying a lawn mower in *Reader's guide*, Learn who won the World Series in 1959, Find a date — historical or for tonight, Plan a vacation to Florida, Use a map to find a short cut to Fort Lauderdale, Look at a slide of a smoker's lungs yuk!, Check out a book for your brother, Tell the teacher-librarian to get more books sky-diving, Find out about the seven signs of Cancer, Check TV program ratings Find a recipe for roasting a pig, Bug the teacher-librarian, Hug the teacher-librarian, Find Elvis Presley's birth data, Read the want ads, Learn how to repair your transmission, Cast your horoscope, Make a list of good eating places in Norfolk County, Find 101 things to do on a rainy day, Sharpen your pencil, Sharpen your wits, Use the yellow pages, Find out what else happened the day you were born, Compare peanut butters in *Consumer reports*, Get the facts from Masters and Johnson, Get lost in the stacks, Request a magazine article from another library, Learn to play the zither, Hunt up the rules for playing korfball, Learn who starred in *The prisoner of Zenda*, Find out what happened yesterday, Read the President's budget message, Learn how to train your dog, Learn to read better and faster, Read, Photocopy your driver's license, Find the words to "Don't sit under the apple tree", Read the *New York Times* from December 7, 1941 on microfilm, Find out how to view an eclipse safely, Hunt up the population of Hong Kong, Learn the dates for National Pickle, Week, Find out what "egregious" means, Look up a synonym for "egregious", Find out what the "A" stood for in *The scarlet letter*, Look up your Senator's voting record , Find your house on the city map, Look up Gregory Hines in *Current biography*, Learn how to write a footnote, Do your homework, Read a newspaper, Get hints on making movies, Get a photocopy, Watch a videotape, Borrow a film, Relax to a record, Listen to a story

101 Wonderful Things
TO DO IN THE RESOURCE CENTER

Ask the teacher-librarian for 101 more things to do

EMERGENCY LIBRARIAN 15:3
JANUARY-FEBRUARY 1988

— Helen Flowers and Eileen Mulcahy

Theory—Where Is My Reality?

Susan Casey

I had always been interested in cooperative program planning—it seemed to me to be the major goal of a school library program. However from practice I knew it was not in place as widely as I felt it should be—including in my own resource center. At the time the study was completed, I was a teacher-librarian in a grade 6-9 open area school. I was convinced cooperative program planning and teaching, or curriculum development at the school level, as the process is often referred to in the literature, was an important part of my role, but how did I "measure up?" The literature made the process sound widespread—was I falling below the mark? How much was I already doing? How could I increase the amount of time I spent in this activity, and where would the time come from in an already hectic schedule? I decided I needed to examine how I was currently spending my time—both at school, and at home on those activities that related to my role as teacher-librarian.

I am assuming that most teacher-librarians are the "already converted," and believe, as I do, that cooperative program planning (CPP) should be the major focus of the teacher-librarian role—but the more I talk with practicing "in the field" teacher-librarians, the more I am convinced that CPP is not as extensively practiced as the literature would suggest. The most common problem for teacher-librarians wanting to engage in CPP is the lack of time.

I began by examining the role of the teacher-librarian as a whole—what aspects made up this role that is a combination of both teacher and librarian? This was a difficult process, but by becoming actively involved in examining what it is that I do, I came to a much clearer understanding of my role. It became much easier for me to set priorities for my time, increased my feelings of professionalism, and above all else had an extremely positive impact on my job satisfaction by allowing me more time to do what I think is important—CPP. It also increased my awareness of the role, and has allowed me to speak with more conviction to the administration and teachers at my school.

How did I arrive at these results? I have had the following saying on my bulletin board for years:

If you don't know what's important
then everything is important

If everything is important
then you try to do everything

If you are attempting to do everything
then people will expect you to do
everything

And in trying to please everyone
you don't have enough time
to find out what's important

I would like to thank the originator, but I have no idea where it came from! I originally stuck it up because I thought it was funny, but one day in the middle of this study, it jumped out at me, and since then it has become my creed. I willingly share it with those of you who find the element of truth in the statement! (See *Emergency Librarian* poster, 14:1!!!)

I also realized my own perceptions were a combination of what I believed, and the often deflating perceptions of friends and colleagues. When someone very close to you asks you why you need a Master's degree just to stamp out books to kids, it can have a rather depressing effect on your professional ego. It seemed I was always justifying my role, and I was beginning to wonder about it myself. Teacher-librarians are continually fighting the battle to be recognized as the professionals they are, and not just as clericals. Unfortunately most school systems do not provide enough clerical assistance to school libraries, and the teacher-librarian often must perform clerical duties. As a result of the examination of my role I found I was doing fewer clerical tasks than I originally believed. I think this was because I always felt guilty—clerical tasks were not a good use of my time and so they frustrated me. My attitude has changed in the last year as a result of the study. First, the strictly clerical duties I must do—for example dropping the

This article describes the research conducted by the author at the University of Calgary (Alberta) Faculty of Education in an area of interest to many *Emergency Librarian* readers—the relationship among the need for cooperative program planning and teaching, setting priorities and finding time.

filed cards in the card catalogue—I try to do when no one is watching. I have become a "closet cleric" if you will! Perceptions of others are often based on stereotypes, but those perceptions can be effectively altered if reality does not support them. I now do these unavoidable clerical tasks before the resource center opens, or after it closes. No one sees me doing them and I'm not resentful of the time because I "should" be working with kids or teachers. I think it is extremely important that the teacher-librarian stops and examines the role being perpetuated in the school.

Of course there are always some clerical tasks that must be done by the teacher-librarian during the course of the day. I found that by recognizing these activities and stretching the role beyond the clerical task, I can intensify my impact, perpetuate my role as a professional, and increase the job satisfaction I feel. (And the term clerical is not meant to be derogatory. I have been extremely fortunate to have had highly competent clerical assistants. By the term clerical I am referring to those aspects which are not of a professional nature—enough on that point.)

Let me share with you an example. I'm sure many of you have experienced the frustration of dealing with a teacher whom you've not been able to reach with the virtues of CPP. After five years he still asks you to pull all the books in the resource center on a certain topic for his grade 9 social studies class, and send them all to his room on a shelf! I find these requests to be exceedingly frustrating for a number of reasons—the main one being that I am not given the opportunity to help teach the process of information search, identification and synthesis. I feel as if I am spoon feeding, rather than working toward one of my main goals which is the creation of independent learners. The concentration on product, rather than process, goes against my fundamental educational beliefs. Until I completed this study, I would have tried to convince him of the positive benefits that could result for his students if we cooperatively planned an integrated unit using the resource center as a resource base for the students. He would have politely listened, and then reiterated his request, insisting he didn't have time for such "frills," and I would have gone and pulled the books, all the while muttering under my breath about the lost teaching opportunity, and the poor use of my time which didn't call on any of my specializations as I perceived them. This year, however, I was ready! The conversation began in much the same way—up to the point where I used to give in because "he has so much to cover before the exams"—a legitimate concern on his part no matter how frustrating for me! I compromised, I let him know that with my clerical assistant's time cut to half this year, I was also short on time, and could he please send three or four students to help pull the books—a legitimate concern for me. I also requested that the entire class come in for one period following the initial search to identify their specific needs. The four students came in, and received some intensive search strategy instruction from me while we pulled the materials. They were also able to assist me when the rest of their class came into the resource center. Those four students had obtained ownership of their problem, had a more positive attitude toward the resource center, and I had changed a clerical task of pulling books into a teaching function that had very positive side benefits. In addition I was no longer frustrated—better four students than none! All of these positive results merely by a creative

stretching of the clerical role, and only possible because I had taken the time to examine what I was doing.

This is just one simple example of how examining my role has led to positive changes in my performance of the teacher-librarian role. The process I went through was exceedingly helpful to me, and I'd like to outline it briefly for you.

First of all, it is important to discern the goals and objectives of your school's curriculum, and the philosophy of the school. Next, the teacher-librarian needs to carefully think through goals and objectives for the library program. I went through this goal setting and objective stating process under protest. I found it both a more difficult process than I had anticipated, and a more useful one that I had expected. I always knew I had my objectives "in my bones"—I knew what I was doing "instinctively." However, the process of thinking through my feelings, precisely wording my ideas, and committing them both to paper was extremely useful, and I would recommend it to those of you who, like me, are content to leave them unstated. I had to focus my ideas and, in the process, where I was headed with the library program became much clearer. It also gave me something concrete to discuss with my administration and staff. This was the next step, discussion with the rest of the staff. As well as opening discussion and allowing for school ownership of the resource center, looking at the goals and objectives provided an excellent introduction to the uninitiated staff members as to what the resource center could do. The goals were no longer my hidden agenda. They belonged to the school. It became our resource center, and I could work with staff members as a partner in the learning process.

It is important for the teacher-librarian and the administration to realize that the process of becoming a partner in the integration of classroom and library programs is a slow one. Gains will be small at first but a commitment to a school library program that supports all areas of the curriculum and development of the student, will have significant educational results. Small, solid steps, based on research, and an understanding of goals and objectives, are much better than huge leaps and bounds that ultimately result in a fall.

Becoming a full partner in curriculum development at the school level is a process of evolution, not creation. Where you begin the evolution will determine your success.

I was, at this point, even more committed to the idea of CPP, but I still didn't know where I would find the time. I decided to complete a five week study on myself as a teacher-librarian. Very real terror struck! What if it turned out I do nothing more than the clerical aspect, and somebody in power finds out, and I lose my job! Some research project! After being reassured that the results could not possibly measure up to my wildest nightmares, I began the time study.

I examined the role of the teacher-librarian, and attempted to divide it into the various aspects, or functions of the role. I read a great deal of literature on the topic, and finally chose the following functions as the focus for the study:

- **Administrative/Managerial**
  those activities which ensure the effective running of the physical plant.

- **Reference**
  those activities whose end product is information for its own sake—quick response items.

- **Clerical**
  those activities of a non-professional, or secretarial nature.

- **Teaching**
  this function was split into three categories:

  A. non-library related teaching

  B. teaching which is directly library related

  C. non-directive teaching—such as casual discussion with student "guidance."

- **Professional**
  activities which keep the teacher-librarian current in both the educational field and the field of school librarianship.

- **Cooperative Program Planning**
  those activities which draw on the unique expertise of the teacher-librarian in bringing students and resources together in the learning process.

This is a very brief outline of the six functions I used for the purpose of analyzing my time. I carefully thought through each of the functions, and made the description of each specific, with examples. In this way I had clearly delineated for myself the areas each of these functions encompassed.

I set up the study using a tape recorder and a pad of paper to note down everything I did during the day and madly transcribed both every night onto a data sheet. From there I was able to figure the amount of time spent in each function, and arrive at daily, weekly and complete five-week percentages for each of the six functions. I decided to keep track of the number of interruptions I received—that lasted for the first part of the first day. I quit counting when the total was over one hundred interruptions, and it wasn't even near lunch! I began to realize why I often felt frustrated because I wasn't getting anything accomplished! Few teacher-librarians just sit and wait for questions and therefore much of our role involves interruptions. I am now more realistic in my planning, realizing that interruptions are merely opportunities in a strange disguise. I find my frustration level to be much lower, and many of those "interruptions" lead to exciting opportunities for CPP and real teachable moments.

The study was successful in that it fulfilled the initial purposes I had set out, but it also had many side benefits, a few of which I have attempted to illustrate in the above discussion.

My first purpose was to find out how I was spending my time in each of the six functions at the time of the study. The chart fulfills that purpose in a very narrow manner. The results are neither right, nor wrong. They are merely mine and reflect how my time was spent during that five week period only. In no way do they reflect my average day, or week, nor are they able to be generalized to the way anyone else spends a "typical" day. They are, however, extremely useful when interpreted. They gave me a graphic representation of not only how I spent my time, but also the total time I spent—an average of 55 hours per week at work, or at home doing work-related activities. No attempt was made to account for every minute

spent at work, yet I was really amazed at the number of hours I put in. I think other teacher-librarians would find they have much the same results as far as the amount of time spent is concerned. It can give you a real boost when you wonder why you are so tired!

The results also led me to examine my yearly plan. I chose the particular time of year for the study because it was a traditionally low use time in our school library and I knew I would have the extra hours necessary to complete the type of introspection I knew would occur. Ideally I would have had an impartial observer follow me around and note how I was spending my time, but I am not sure that would have been as productive a learning situation as this was for me.

The high result in the category of *Administrative/ Managerial* activities was, at first, upsetting. Then I realized that as I had identified the time period as one of low use, I naturally left such activities as weeding, paperback purchasing and so on until that point in the year.

Figure 1 shows the final percentages for the five week study in each function.

By taking a look at the pattern of use, I was able to identify other traditionally low use times during the year, and was then able to begin slotting some new CPP units into these low use time frames. I also developed a large "year at a glance" chart where I mapped out all of the yearly type projects, like grade 7 CPP orientation to the library/social studies project for the last two weeks of September. This chart I have found to be invaluable for a number of reasons. It is visible and allows teachers to see what units I am involved with in the school as a whole. It allows for more effective use of the resource center and its resources (including me!) by creating a realistic timetable for units across the subject areas. I can also determine activities which should be delegated to the clerical assistant, volunteers, or student aides. Some of the things I was doing were just not a productive use of my time. I now find myself being much more aware of the activities I choose to do and those I choose to delegate. If there is someone else who can effectively do the task I am doing, it frees me to complete activities that I am specially trained to do.

In the year since I completed the study, my time spent in the *Clerical* function has increased. This is entirely the result of the administration's decision to cut my assistant's time from full to half. I know I now spend less time in some of the other functions, but I have kept this frustration to a minimum by stretching the clerical function at every opportunity. I am more aware of the clerical functions I choose to perform and make sure they involve a reasonably effective use of my time. I have also become much more aware of the role description I wish to perpetuate and keep the visibility of the clerical functions to a minimum.

This chart does not make a distinction between the time spent during and after school hours in the professional function. When I examined the data to discover the breakdown of time in this function, I found that 70% of this time was spent outside of school hours. Evenings and weekends I spent a great deal of time attending workshops, reading and pursuing other professional activities. I no longer feel guilty when I see another teacher on staff taking home a huge pile of marking. Teacher-librarians do their share of after hours work—and I have the stats to prove it!

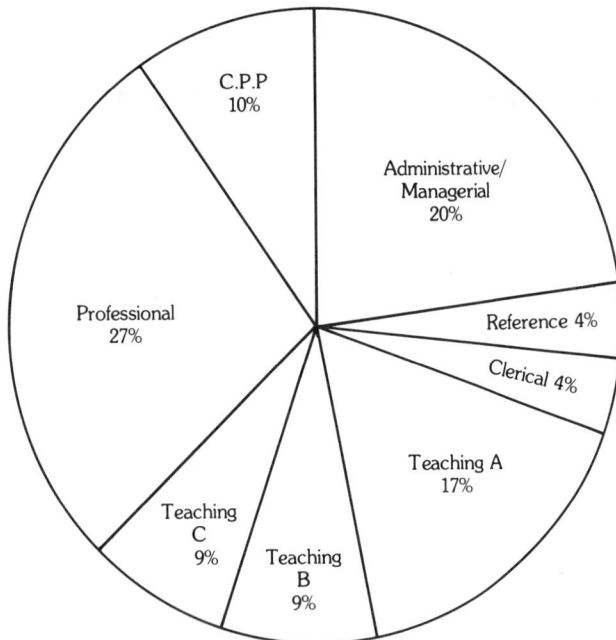

Fig. 1. Final percentages.

At first glance, I felt the percentage of time spent in the *Cooperative Program Planning* function was low. After reflecting on the data, I realized that this included planning time only, and that once a unit is moved from the planning stage to the teaching stage, the time spent became a part of the *Teaching B* function. As a result of examining my time, I was also able to include two new units of CPP in that time slot in the next year.

My second purpose was to determine which functions were basic to my role, and had to be in place before the other functions could occur. Through the course of the study it became obvious that the *Administrative/Managerial* function is fundamental. It must be in place and operating smoothly before CPP can occur, otherwise there just isn't time. Similarly classroom teaching assignments of a non-library related nature severely handicap the effectiveness of the implementation of CPP in an integrated teaching situation. The more flexibility that is lost in the teacher-librarian's daily schedule, the more difficult it is to implement a successful CPP philosophy.

I discovered how much CPP I was doing and, when I reflected on the results, it was much more than I had anticipated. I had taken a great deal of the cooperative program planning that I do for granted, not realizing that CPP was just a term for much of the work I was already doing with teachers on my staff. I also found ways of restructuring and prioritizing my time which allows for more integrated unit planning and cooperative teaching this past year and so my third purpose was realized.

My fourth purpose was an examination of my own working habits. The study was a process of reflection and so many of the results are not transferable to other teacher-librarians, but I believe the process I went through may be of benefit to others. I have been able to incorporate some time management skills and as a result I now have more direction. I have come to understand the need for quiet reflective time to set priorities and directions. Time to assess where I've been, what I have accomplished, and what is the next direction has become a priority.

My fifth purpose was to discover the impact I had on the school, both within and outside the curriculum. I found I had worked with over three-quarters of the staff during the five week study at some level of CPP. This was the area which was the real confidence booster. The extent of the guidance function I performed really surprised me—a great deal of my time is spent talking with students, something that we, as teachers, often forget to count as an important part of our day.

I have learned to concentrate on what I did accomplish on any given day, rather than focusing on the seemingly ever increasing pile of things that I didn't manage to get to. My goals are stated, realistic and therefore attainable. I've come to understand the necessity of reflective time. I now take the time to find out what is important, rather than trying to do everything because I thought it was all important.

So how does all of this relate to the title "Theory—where is my reality?" I found out what my reality was by stepping back and analyzing it with as much objectivity as I could muster. In doing so I realized the theory must become the goal. It is a goal that can be reached if it is backed up by introspection and the examination of where you are and where you're heading. It is a goal that can be reached with small solid steps. It is a goal that I have not fully achieved as yet. I don't engage in as much cooperative program planning as I would like to—but I am doing more than I used to and I'm continually working towards the theory becoming my reality.

Attitudes of School Librarians toward Networking and Teacher Utilization; a Comparative Study of Ten Countries

Mieko Nagakura

The Ministry of Education of Japan supported, through a Scientific Research Grant-in Aid, an international survey of school librarians to find out how school libraries in various countries serve teachers, and how school librarians in these libraries view educational information service and networking. The survey was divided into two parts: the first was concerned with present usage of school libraries by teachers, and the second with school librarians' attitudes or opinions toward regional/national educational information networking. In forming the questions, multiple choice and constructed response (essay-type) methods were both adopted.

Questionnaires were sent to a total of 124 school library specialists and librarians in Australia, Canada, Denmark, Finland, Norway, Sweden, the United Kingdom (UK), the United States of America (USA), and West Germany. Librarians were selected on the basis of participation in conferences of the International Association of School Librarianship (IASL) and/or identification by IASL as a contact for visitors from abroad. Japanese questionnaires were sent to 150 librarians of both elementary and secondary schools in each of 47 prefectures in Japan. The final response rates were 71.4 percent from abroad and 92.5 percent domestic.

UTILIZATION BY TEACHERS

It is important to note that the questionnaires asked whether teachers used the school library resource centre for particular services. The survey looks at which services should be expected and whether teachers generally take advantage of them.

To the statement that teachers use the school library to acquire reference materials for curriculum planning, 100 percent of respondents in the UK, Canada, and Australia, 89 percent in Scandinavia, 88 percent in the USA, 86 percent in West Germany, and 70 percent in Japan answered in the affirmative.

More than 70 percent of respondents in all countries except Japan answered that teachers consult with the library staff when planning curriculum. However, only 56 percent of Japanese librarians stated that their teachers consult with them about curriculum planning. One respondent in West Germany, where 71 percent gave affirmative answers to the question about teacher consultation with library staff, believed that teachers did not expect or want any assistance, especially not from "foreign" people who do not belong to their own profession. (In West Germany school librarians do not have teacher certification or training; they are usually librarians who are part of the public library system.) Similar attitudes

also exist among the Japanese teachers who do not look to their librarians for professional help in educational matters. Also, more than 75 percent of respondents in every country but Japan reported that teachers ask library staff to compile bibliographies or booklists necessary for class teaching, while only 30 percent of respondents in Japan gave affirmative answers to this question. The affirmative percentage was as little as 21 percent in Japanese middle schools. One Japanese teacher was quoted as saying that librarians whose duties are the handling of library routines do not have the "right" to evaluate books and to compile booklists which can be used in class instruction.

Do teachers come to their school libraries to acquire appropriate materials for use in the classroom? The same percentages as shown above for the question referring to the acquisition of reference materials on curriculum planning were affirmative in every country except the UK and Japan. Affirmative answers were 75 percent of respondents in the UK and 90 percent in Japan. Teachers in some areas of the UK can also go directly to public libraries in their vicinity in order to acquire books and other types of materials useful for their class teaching.

The school library should logically be the first place where teachers go to look up information needed for the preparation of class instruction. One hundred percent of respondents in Australia, Canada, the UK, and West Germany, 94 percent in Scandinavia, 91 percent in Japan, and 85 percent in the USA gave affirmative answers to the question whether teachers come to the library for this purpose. It is not clear from the survey responses why the respondents in the USA gave less percentage of affirmative answers than those in other countries; one possibility would be that teachers in the USA need not make a self-search inasmuch as the school librarians do this on their behalf.

Non-print materials such as videos, tapes, slides, models, and films are widely used in multi-media instruction. Do teachers ask school librarians to duplicate or produce these types of instructional materials? Affirmative answers were obtained from 44 percent of respondents in Australia and the USA, 38 percent in the UK, 33 percent in Canada, 22 percent in Scandinavia, 21 percent in Japan, and 14 percent in West Germany.

In Australia, approximately 55 percent of respondents reported that school library staff provide videos and tapes. About 31 percent of respondents in Canada answered that they provide these materials. For the provision of non-print instructional materials, Scandinavian scene is slightly different from those mentioned above. A respondent in Sweden reported that there are audio-visual centers in many districts for the provision of non-print instructional materials, while a Danish respondent wrote that their teachers go directly to "tape centers" to obtain videos and recording tapes. In Japan the school library treats only print media and a separate audio-visual department handles non-print media. Japanese teachers would obtain audio-visual materials from district "film centers" through the audio-visual department in their school.

ATTITUDES TOWARD INFORMATION NETWORKING

The school library is unique from other kinds of libraries in giving its first priority to educational functions. This unique nature justifies the result that the majority of the respondents in most countries surveyed gave affirmative answers to a willingness to join national, regional, and/or area information systems only "with some limitations." The affirmative percentages were 78 percent in Canada, 62 percent in Japan, 56 percent in Australia, 50 percent in the UK, 44 percent in the USA, and 28 percent in Scandinavia. In West Germany and Scandinavia, the percentages indicating a willingness to join information systems "without any limitation" were the highest among the countries surveyed. Another notable result is that the percentage of negative answers was higher than the affirmative answers to join area or regional information systems in New York. Thirty-nine percent of respondents in New York were in the negative, while 28 percent were absolute affirmative and 33 percent were in the affirmative "with some limitations." An intermediate school librarian in New York wrote that the involvement in regional and/or area educational information systems would put more burden on the library staff.

The majority of school librarians prefer to join national, regional, and/or area educational information systems "with some limitations." Then, in what ways do they think the school library is to be involved in wide area information systems? On the questionnaire, choices such as a document dissemination center, an information retrieval center with traditional reference tools, or one with telephone service, or one with computer terminals connected to the area data bank, and an in-school educational data processing center were suggested as appropriate school library functions.

Most respondents favored the school library as a document dissemination center, providing requested information through interlibrary loans and/or reprographic services. Eighty-nine percent of respondents in Canada, 88 percent in the UK, 81 percent in Japan, 78 percent in Australia, 67 percent in Scandinavia, 56 percent in the USA, and 43 percent in West Germany were in the affirmative. Some librarians in the USA and West Germany suggested that teachers may go directly to public libraries and other information sources when they need information not held in their school libraries.

In the USA, Canada, and Japan, more affirmative percentages were attained for the school library as an information center equipped with telephones than one with traditional reference tools. On the other hand, the affirmative percentages were less in Australia, the UK, and West Germany. I could not find from the essay-type responses any reasonable reasons why such contrasting attitudes toward telephone services were

expressed by school librarians. The affirmative percentages were 78 percent in Canada, 75 percent in the UK, 67 percent in Australia, 61 percent in Scandinavia, 56 percent in both the USA and Japan, and 29 percent in West Germany.

Should school libraries install computer terminals which are connected to national and/or regional data banks? This question received the greatest difference of opinion among the respondents. The affirmative responses were 56 percent in Canada, 50 percent in the UK, 44 percentin Australia, 35 percent in the USA, 28 percent in Scandinavia, 21 percent in Japan, and 14 percent in West Germany. Several librarians in the USA would install a computer terminal for information retrieval in the school library, if it were financially possible. On the other hand, one librarian in the US indicated this is "a fantasy for almost all American school libraries." The high cost of computer installations was also referred to by the respondents in Australia and Scandinavia. Some specialists in the UK and the USA suggested that the computer terminals connected to national and/or regional data banks should be installed at district level centers.

Five extraordinary functions for school libraries were presented on the questionnaire as examples of possible extended services in the future. None of these functions was approved by the survey respondents. The affirmative percentages were less than 14 percent in every country. Most of the respondents did not agree that the school library should assist school administration or counselors by doing accounting, record-keeping, scheduling classes, computing test scores or educational measurement results, and providing reprographic services. Many librarians indicated that the utilization of mini or micro-computers and reprographic apparatus in school libraries should be strictly limited to the purposes of library management and services.

For the function to keep and disseminate personal information on students, such as I.Q.'s, personality and interests, family conditions, and academic records, the percentages for the affirmative attitude varied from 0 percent to 29 percent. The highest affirmative percentage was attained in West Germany, while all respondents gave the negative answer in Canada, Denmark, Sweden, Norway, and the UK. Those who indicated the affirmative attitude in the USA and Japan supplemented their answers by defining the student's personal information only as handled in the library, such as information which largely affects reading habits, interests, and ability.

In general, the majority of respondents agreed that the function of the school library is in the area of instruction based on the needs of both students and teachers.

To complete this survey, respondents were asked about the appropriateness of school librarians offering in-service training for teachers. Two major attitudes were distinctive. In Canada, Australia, the UK, and the USA, the affirmative responses were more than 56 percent. In Japan, it was 46 percent, while it was less than 28 percent in Scandinavia and West Germany. Such contrasting attitudes might be interpreted in light of the appropriateness of placing in schools librarians who have enough professional training and justified status for such a responsibility. Only the school library specialists in Vancouver and Winnipeg, Canada, reported offering such in-service programs for teachers at the district level.

TABLE I

Question Items / Respondents By Country	JAPAN	USA	CANADA	AUSTRALIA	DENMARK	SWEDEN	NORWAY	FINLAND	SCANDINAVIA	WEST GERMANY	UNITED KINGDOM	TOTAL JAPAN EXCEPT
NUMBERS OF ALL RESPONDENTS	136	34	9	9	5	8	2	3	18	7	8	85
Utilizations Of School Library By Teachers												
To acquire necessary reference materials for curriculum planning	95 (70%)	30 (88%)	9 (100%)	9 (100%)	5	7	1	3	16 (89%)	6 (86%)	8 (100%)	78 (92%)
To consult with school library staff on curriculum construction	76 (56%)	29 (85%)	9 (100%)	8 (89%)	5	7	0	2	14 (78%)	5 (71%)	7 (77%)	72 (85%)
To acquire appropriate instructional materials	123 (90%)	30 (88%)	9 (100%)	9 (100%)	5	7	2	2	16 (89%)	6 (86%)	6 (75%)	76 (89%)
To search knowledge, facts, & data needed for class teaching preparation	124 (91%)	29 (85%)	9 (100%)	9 (100%)	5	7	2	3	17 (94%)	7 (100%)	8 (100%)	79 (93%)
To send students to the library for library instruction by school librarian	76 (56%)	32 (94%)	7 (78%)	9 (100%)	4	8	2	3	17 (94%)	7 (100%)	8 (100%)	80 (94%)
To send students to the library for independent study	101 (74%)	30 (88%)	9 (100%)	9 (100%)	4	8	1	3	16 (89%)	7 (100%)	7 (88%)	78 (92%)
To send students to the library for free time utilization due to to unexpected teacher's absence	98 (72%)	18 (53%)	4 (44%)	6 (67%)	3	7	1	3	14 (78%)	5 (71%)	6 (75%)	53 (62%)
To use library facilities & premises for class teaching	89 (65%)	19 (56%)	5 (56%)	8 (89%)	2	6	1	2	11 (61%)	4 (57%)	5 (63%)	52 (61%)
To ask library staff to compile bibliographies	41 (30%)	29 (85%)	8 (89%)	7 (78%)	4	6	2	2	14 (78%)	6 (86%)	6 (75%)	70 (82%)
To ask library staff to duplicate printed materials for instructional use	24 (18%)	5 (15%)	0 (0%)	1 (11%)	1	1	0	0	2 (11%)	1 (14%)	1 (13%)	10 12%
To ask library staff to duplicate or produce non-print materials for instructional use	28 (21%)	15 (44%)	3 (33%)	4 (44%)	0	1	1	2	4 (22%)	1 (14%)	3 (38%)	30 (35%)
To utilize school library as information center for teachers' professional research	74 (54%)	29 (85%)	5 (56%)	7 (78%)	3	5	1	3	12 (67%)	6 (86%)	4 (50%)	63 (74%)
To utilize school library as information center for teachers' personal activities	78 (57%)	29 (85%)	6 (67%)	8 (89%)	3	5	1	2	11 (61%)	5 (71%)	5 (63%)	64 (75%)

TABLE II

Question Items / Respondents By Country	JAPAN	USA	CANADA	AUSTRALIA	DENMARK	SWEDEN	NORWAY	FINLAND	SCANDINAVIA	WEST GERMANY	UNITED KINGDOM	TOTAL JAPAN EXCEPT
NUMBERS OF ALL RESPONDENTS	136	34	9	9	5	8	2	3	18	7	8	85
School Librarians Attitudes Toward Information Networking												
To join a national, regional, & area educational information network — a.	43 (33%)	10 (29%)	0 (0%)	3 (33%)	4	3	1	0	8 (44%)	2 (29%)	1 (13%)	24 (28%)
a. To join without any limitation. — b.	84 (65%)	15 (44%)	7 (78%)	5 (56%)	0	2	0	3	5 (28%)	0 (0%)	4 (50%)	36 (42%)
b. To join with some limitations.												
c. Oppose to join. — c.	3 (2%)	9 (26%)	0 (0%)	1 (11%)	0	3	0	0	3 (17%)	0 (0%)	1 (13%)	14 (16%)
Function as document dissemination center in a school	110 (85%)	19 (56%)	8 (89%)	7 (78%)	3	5	1	3	12 (67%)	3 (43%)	7 (88%)	56 (66%)
Function as information retrieval center with with traditional reference tools.	70 (54%)	14 (41%)	6 (67%)	7 (78%)	3	5	1	2	11 (61%)	3 (43%)	7 (88%)	48 (56%)
Function as information retrieval center with telephone service.	76 (58%)	19 (56%)	7 (78%)	6 (67%)	3	4	1	3	11 (61%)	2 (29%)	6 (75%)	51 (60%)
Function as information retrieval center with computer terminal connected to national/regional data bank.	29 (22%)	12 (35%)	5 (56%)	4 44%)	1	3	0	1	5 (28%)	1 (14%)	4 (50%)	31 (36%)
Function as in-school educational data processing center.	19 (15%)	4 (12%)	1 (11%)	1 (11%)	0	1	0	1	2 (11%)	1 (14%)	0 (0%)	9 (11%)
Assist school administration department with mini-computer	8 (6%)	8 (24%)	2 (22%)	1 (11%)	1	2	0	1	4 (22%)	1 (14%)	0 (0%)	16 (19%)
Assist school administration department by printing service.	19 (15%)	3 (9%)	2 (22%)	2 (22%)	2	1	0	1	4 (22%)	2 (29%)	3 (38%)	16 (19%)
Function as in-school data bank by keeping school records, statistics, & etc.	15 (11%)	5 (15%)	2 (22%)	2 (22%)	0	1	1	1	3 (17%)	1 (14%)	1 (13%)	14 (16%)
Function as in-school instructional information center by keeping all kinds of students' data	16 (12%)	1 (3%)	0 (0%)	1 (11%)	0	0	0	1	1 (6%)	2 (29%)	0 (0%)	5 (6%)
To offer in-service training for teachers on educational information.	60 (46%)	20 (56%)	7 (78%)	7 (78%)	2	1	1	1	5 (28%)	1 (14%)	5 (63%)	45 (53%)

PROBLEMS OF AN INTERNATIONAL SURVEY

In any survey, it is essential to choose specimens or respondents based on logical sampling methods. Therefore, the most difficult problem encountered in any international survey is to locate enough respondents who are qualified to represent the referring countries and/or areas.

For this survey, respondents from abroad were limited to 150, because of the cost and the manpower involved.

Some respondents refused to answer the survey, stating that they were not in a position to represent their country or region. The respondents were identified through participation in IASL activities because, for a foreigner, it is almost impossible to locate the proper person who represents a particular country or region.

International research is essential for improved school library service in every country. Committees or groups of specialists from each country should cooperate in planning questionnaires, and analyzing and interpreting survey results. International cooperation in research will provide a better foundation for the development and extension of school librarianship throughout the world.

Secondary Schools and Critical Thinking

Ken Haycock

You might be thinking that this podium column is going to deal with the movement to develop critical thinking skills in students and you would be partly right. More importantly, I want to address the development of critical thinking skills in secondary school *librarians* and lament the possible loss of yet another program opportunity.

When I relinquished my editorial page for this "shared" position, I felt that I had had my say and it was time for others to have theirs. Certainly there has been no shortage of readers to come forward with viewpoints to present and discuss with colleagues. However, for this particular *Emergency Librarian* issue, I felt an overwhelming urge to withdraw the column going forward and to insert my comments instead—not because the alternative wasn't valid and valuable, it was and is; indeed, it will appear in our next issue. More to the point, however, I couldn't bear to focus debate (the purpose of this page) on management concerns in an issue dealing with secondary school librarianship.

You see, too many of our secondary school colleagues have been convinced that they are librarians and managers, but have forgotten that they are also trained, hired, experienced and paid as professional teachers. And professional teaching does not limit itself to teaching little lessons out of the context of classroom subject matter, or running around a library like a shop clerk (can I help you? can you find what you're looking for?). So, although I have initiated a move from personally writing five editorials a year to this podium column to be written by others, there will be an occasional lapse like this during the "transitional" period.

Teacher-librarianship has come a long way, with a solid and developing research base. There are many things that we know will better guarantee a quality program, not only in the eyes of the teacher-librarian, but also in the experiences of teachers and students and the concrete support of administrators. Let's just go through a short checklist and determine whether our programs meet this standard:

- The school has a stated aim for the program, focusing on assisting students to develop a commitment to informed decision-making and the skills necessary for life-long learning.

- The teacher-librarian is viewed as an equal teaching partner in the school, with a strong involvement in cooperative program planning and team teaching.

- The school has a coordinated curriculum: the school or each department has a department-based continuum of research and study skills or information skills, which specifies the skills and processes to be developed from year to year in a developmental, sequential way, such that each youngster is taught the *basic* information skills outlined in the curriculum guides, leading to increasing independence of action and judgment.

- The teacher-librarian does not teach library media skills on an isolated continuum or to individuals only but plans with subject teachers to integrate the skills which the department has specified as important at each level; units of study or assignments are clear, specific and team taught; the students know in advance what they will be taught and why.

- Student progress is monitored jointly by the teacher and teacher-librarian using checklists and observation to ensure that each student is in fact learning what we determined to teach.

• Units of study are recorded and left for successors so the program builds and grows, so that more and more choices are available to integrate skills (if history teachers and the teacher-librarian agree that the department continuum will include footnoting in the 10th grade, there may be a choice from three existing library-based assignments, jointly planned by teachers and teacher-librarian, which integrate the teaching of the skills involved).

The fact of the matter is that it *is* possible to develop a strong program; it's been done in many places, in many unique ways. It does seem impossible, however, to shake the complacency of some secondary school library managers who do not identify learning needs, plan and teach with colleagues to address them, and monitor and adjust for student performance, the basics of teaching.

So often in teacher-librarianship the world of the classroom teacher has skirted around our resources and talents when dealing with important issues. Will critical thinking be yet another one? Curriculum developers and other educators are placing increasing emphasis on the process-oriented curriculum, something many secondary school librarians have urged for years. Information skills, problem solving skills, decision-making skills, are all a part of this concern, now joined by critical thinking skills.

Elsewhere in this issue is a paper developed for the National Council for the Social Studies, a leader in this area. Nowhere is it mentioned where the teacher or student will locate the information to be used in defending a logical point of view or in analyzing different interpretations of the same events. Nowhere is it pointed out that many of these programs are floundering in spite of the best intentions of teachers, because a process-oriented curriculum is difficult to implement alone, without intimate knowledge of both the necessary resources and the means of accessing and using the information therein.

Perhaps we could afford to let knowledge of the changed teaching methods which necessitated library resource centers slip by us, and perhaps we could afford to let knowledge of the appropriate use of technology for information management and searching slip by us to the control of others, but can we afford to let the core of our professional being and status go too? Are we central to the resolution of the problems inherent in information skills and critical thinking skills teaching hidden in our school's curriculum? Or are we essentially still pleading professional ignorance of our resources, the foundations for their effective use, and the joint planning and team teaching necessary to making them essential?

Critical Thinking in the Social Studies

John J. Patrick

Critical thinking was the theme of the 1942 Yearbook of the National Council for the Social Studies. It is highlighted today in various statements and publications of state education departments, local school districts, and professional associations. Research and commentary on critical thinking have increased greatly during the last ten years. But it has not been taught extensively or satisfactorily in most social studies classrooms. Goodlad's nationwide study of schooling found little evidence of critical thinking and concluded that "preoccupation with the lower intellectual processes pervades social studies and science as well."

Current efforts to promote critical thinking in the social studies will fail unless we know what it is, why it is important, and how to use it. This summary treats the (1) meaning of critical thinking, (2) primacy of critical thinking as a goal, (3) inclusion of critical thinking in the curriculum, and (4) means of teaching critical thinking to students.

WHAT IS CRITICAL THINKING?

Definitions of critical thinking vary in breadth or inclusiveness. Broad definitions equate critical thinking with the cognitive processes and strategies involved in decision making, problem solving, or inquiry. According to Robert Ennis, "Critical thinking is reflective and reasonable thinking that is focused on deciding what to believe or do."

Limited definitions focus on evaluation or appraisal; critical thinking is formulation and use of criteria to make warranted judgments about knowledge claims, normative statements, methods of inquiry, policy decisions, alternative positions on public issues, or any other object of concern. Critical thinking, defined narrowly, is an essential element of general cognitive processes, such as problem solving or decision making, but is not synonymous with them.

Critical thinking, whether conceived broadly or narrowly, implies curiosity, skepticism, reflection, and rationality. Critical thinkers have a propensity to raise and explore questions about beliefs, claims, evidence, definitions, conclusions, and actions.

Many proponents of critical thinking stop short of evaluating the most basic criteria, or values, by which they or their students make judgments. They would teach critical thinking only within conventional frames of reference of a society. A more profound view encourages appraisal of frameworks or sets of criteria by which judgments are made. This deeper level of critical thinking counteracts egocentric, ethnocentric, or doctrinaire judgments, which result when thinkers fail to appraise fundamental assumptions or standards.

WHY IS CRITICAL THINKING A MAJOR GOAL OF EDUCATION?

Critical thinking is necessary to achievement of good citizenship and scholarship in a free society, two major aims of education in the social studies. A basic value is freedom to think and express ideas—even if they are unusual, unpopular, or critical of prevailing practices and beliefs. The civil liberties of individuals and minority groups are guaranteed against the tyranny of ruling elites and the tyranny of majority rule. Good citizenship involves responsibility to be an informed and rational participant in civic affairs, which implies capability to think critically about public issues, candidates for public office, and decisions of government officials.

Lessons that stimulate questions and criticism in pursuit of truth, which are commensurate with the cognitive and personal development of students, should be encouraged in the schools of a free society. In contrast, a closed or totalitarian society never permits critical examination of prevailing and sanctioned ideas. Ability to think critically can free students from the fetters of ignorance, confusion, and unjustified claims about ideals and reality. It can contribute to dissatisfaction with tyrants or totalitarian societies and to the improvement of democratic government and free societies.

Strategies and skills in critical thinking are keys to independent judgment and learning, which can be transferred to subjects and objects of inquiry within and outside of school. Students gain enduring intellectual abilities, which can be used long after particular facts have been forgotten. They are empowered as learners and as citizens to think and act more effectively.

HOW CAN CRITICAL THINKING BE INCLUDED EFFECTIVELY IN THE CURRICULUM?

All students, regardless of social class or presumed limitations in ambition or ability, have some degree of potential to think critically. This potential can be developed to the fullest by embedding critical thinking in the core curriculum, school subjects required of all students. Thus, critical thinking would become an essential element in the general education of citizens rather than the privilege of intellectual or social elites. If so, opportunities for academic achievement, socioeconomic

advancement, and effective citizenship will be spread more widely and equitably in our society.

Students' capabilities to think critically are likely to be increased if they practice strategies and skills systematically and extensively in all subjects of the social studies curriculum, and in a manner that is consistent with their cognitive development and prior learning experiences. Subject-specific teaching of critical thinking may be the most effective means to develop students' abilities to transfer strategies and skills to similar subjects in school and problems in life outside of school. By contrast, separate courses on critical thinking seem to be rather weak means of developing cognitive strategies and skills.

HOW CAN CRITICAL THINKING BE TAUGHT EFFECTIVELY?

Effective lessons on critical thinking interrelate subject matter and cognitive strategies and skills, because critical thinking cannot be done meaningfully unless the student knows certain concepts and facts related fundamentally to the question under consideration. A successful critical thinker is also aware of differences in criteria and evidence used to justify propositions in different subjects, such as history, economics, and geography.

Effective teaching and learning of critical thinking involves practice of skills with recognition of how they fit together as part of a strategy or process. By contrast, practice of discrete skills is a relatively ineffective means to developing capability in critical thinking.

Development of critical thinking strategies or processes requires continuous practice under the direction of a skillful teacher. Direct or didactic teaching is a useful means to introduce strategies and skills, but reliance on this method is insufficient. Students must be stimulated to think critically on their own to resolve dilemmas, take stands on issues and judge propositions about knowledge or ideals.

Learning to think critically involves multi-faceted intellectual activity involved in complex processes, such as decision making. Effective teachers challenge students to apply interrelated knowledge and skills to decisions about what to believe and what to do. In the process of justifying and evaluating knowledge claims and value judgments, involved in decision making, students are able to develop propensity for and capability in critical thinking.

Teacher modeling of critical thinking and expressions of support for it are effective classroom behaviors. Teachers who promote and practice critical thinking in the classroom contribute strongly to their students' intellectual development. Furthermore, they are likely to engender a critical spirit, or positive attitude toward critical thinking, among their students.

Certain procedures in management of classroom discussions appear to foster critical thinking. Teachers who ask challenging questions and require students to give evidence or reasons for their conclusions and opinions are likely to develop critical thinking abilities and a critical spirit.

There is a strong relationship between an open, supportive, and structured classroom climate, where opinions on issues may be explored and expressed in a free and disciplined manner, and the development of critical thinking and attitudes supportive of it. Effective teachers challenge students to examine alternative positions on controversial topics or public issues, require justification for beliefs about what is true or good and insist on orderly classroom discourse. In this manner, they provide powerful lessons on responsible scholarship and citizenship in a free society.

RESOURCES

Browne, M. Neil and Stuart Keeley. *Asking the Right Questions: A Guide to Critical Thinking.* Prentice-Hall, 1985.

Cornbleth, Catherine. "Critical Thinking and Cognitive Processes." *Review of Research in Social Studies Education: 1976-1983*, edited by William B. Stanley. National Council for the Social Studies, 1985.

Ennis, Robert H. "A Logical Basis for Measuring Critical Thinking Skills." *Educational Leadership*, volume 43, number (October, 1985), pages 45-48.

Goodland, John. *A Place Called School.* McGraw-Hill, 1984.

Moore, W. Edgar, Hugh McCann and Janet McCann. *Creative and Critical Thinking.* Houghton Mifflin, 1985.

Parker, Walter and John Jarolimek. *Citizenship and the Critical Role of the Social Studies.* National Council for the Social Studies, 1984.

Sullivan, David. "Using a Textbook for Critical Thinking." *New England Social Studies Bulletin*, volume 43 (Winter, 1985-86), pages 31-33.

Wright, D. P. *Instruction in Critical Thinking: A Three Part Investigation.* ERIC Document 138518.

Micros: The New Status Symbol

Key Haycock

If you haven't got a microcomputer in your library you must feel terribly out of it. The profession has rushed headlong to embrace the latest technology—some suggest that it will not only revolutionize education and library service (remember ETV?) but may very well be the only road to survival since the holder of the keys to an essential service *is* essential....

Perhaps, as professionals, we should stand back and examine the role which the teacher-librarian might, and perhaps should, play in the use of microcomputers regardless of whether the equipment is located in the resource centre. We are exposed enough, I think, to the marvels of the micro in administrivia and are conversant with applications in the home and general office. (I confess that this editorial is being typed on one.) But perhaps we should be asking whether all of those technical and clerical tasks have to be done at all before we determine how to do them better with a micro. There is also just no question that we need to look more closely at the related issues affecting services to teachers and students.

Answers to difficult questions are hard to provide since only you know your own situation. What are your resource centre's objectives? Is the intended use of the micro consistent with those objectives? If the general aim for the resource centre program is to assist students to develop independent learning skills and a commitment to informed decision-making, will the presence and use of the micro enhance that? Obviously, it depends on what you do with it. Too many teacher-librarians have convinced administrators to place the school's sole micro in the resource centre only to find that their well-planned, well-integrated, cooperative teaching program was reduced to student scheduling, supervision and management of a new toy.

Surely there are some general functions of resource centres which apply to all media, including microcomputer hardware and software. For example, if the school has a computer literacy program (pretty soon we may be literate in everything but reading), then the resource centre will have a collection of materials and magazines, for young people about computers. Professional resources should also be provided for teachers, either through the district or the school resource centre. And the teacher-librarian should keep abreast of technology which is having an enormous impact on information storage and management.

At an awareness level, the teacher-librarian has access to a growing number of very good professional journals which provide current information about microcomputers in education and libraries. We provide teachers with evaluations of newer media and information about what is available and that should be provided for microcomputer software and hardware as well. Similarly, librarians are conversant with criteria and guidelines for evaluation of different media and are in excellent positions to provide leadership in the evaluation of hardware and software. If assistance is provided to parents looking for a good encyclopedia why is information not available on the strengths and weaknesses of different equipment? Skills in organization of materials will also provide students and teachers with access to the entire school's collection and perhaps even the district's and beyond.

And how will the collection be developed? As we rush to purchase software will we have serious, professional guidelines as a framework? A recent advertisement suggested that one could purchase 2500 public domain programs for $500. Is that a good buy or a waste of money? Are war games acceptable? Games of any sort? We no longer tolerate the workbook mentality in teaching but we seem prepared to encourage the new "electronic workbook" simply because it's on a screen. If it's not valid on paper, why on the screen? Only your objectives and guidelines will provide the answers.

Students will need opportunities to search data bases to retrieve information. To provide the utility to do this is one thing but there are many opportunities which may be lost if the technology is not used to enhance the role of the teacher-librarian. We know, for example, that one of the basic skills of research that causes problems for students is formulating important questions as an initial step in the search strategy— the use of microcomputers for searching data bases may alleviate this in a good cooperative teaching program. We may also have to push to make more elementary indexes such as the *Children's Magazine Guide* and the *Abridged Reader's Guide to Periodical Literature* accessible.

Who is to manage the program? Do we have time when there isn't time for other important services? How important, and political, is your involvement in your own school or district? This may be an overriding factor. Will a fee be charged for services? Why a fee for this service and not others if it is important and perhaps essential? Just because it's new? By charging a fee are libraries making the tools of survival less accessible to the disadvantaged who are also living in an information rich age? If fees for microcomputer use, can fees for storytelling be far behind? And then for borrowing materials? Are we insisting that professional development programs be provided to equip us with not only the skills to use well a newer technology but also knowledge of the issues and sources to find and provide answers to difficult societal questions.

Microcomputers may enhance the role of the teacher-librarian if any proposed introduction is well-planned and the implementation carefully thought out. If teachers and librarians get mesmerized by the technology, however, we will witness the new absurdities of books becoming "random access hard copy modules" and too many professionals thinking that putting young students on keyboards will ipso facto regenerate the world's great literature.

The Library, the Computer, and Utopia

Debra Simmons

In The Commonwealth Ballroom of the Holiday Inn, Saskatoon, on June 13, 1982, the Canadian School Library Association passed a motion that resolves CSLA to

advocate the following role for the teacher-librarian in the management and the educational use of computers: coordination of the selection, acquisition, cataloguing, and distribution of computer material; development of programs to assist other staff members in the effective use of computers and development of programs to assist other staff members in the effective use of computers and development of programs, cooperatively with teachers, to address: computer awareness, computer literacy, and computer science.

Teacher-librarians find themselves, once again, having a role thrust upon them, a role that revolves around a new technology. Once again, the role requires the teacher-librarian not only to disseminate information, organize and manage a new technology, select related materials, jointly teach a new literacy and awareness, but assist other professionals in introducing materials and in using them effectively. Once

again, teacher-librarians are expected to assume a role without sufficient evaluation of the place this new technology has in learning and, in this case, without establishing a clear relationship between the process of education, the computer, and libraries. It has taken teacher-librarians years to sort out the mess left behind by the "media revolution" and to use the positive features of audio-visual materials for education and fit these into resource centre programs. Now, again, assumptions are based on what has been rather than what should be. Before educators proceed further on the microcomputer bandwagon, consideration must be given to the difference between what we think computers can do for learning and what society and schools will allow them to do. This evaluation of computers in learning is of greater importance than evaluations of previous technologies because of the power of computers, their popularity, potential, and pervasiveness. And when all consideration is completed and discussions have ended, school resource centres may not be judged the best place for the computer.

Basic to this problem and, as a result, basic reading for anyone interested in the problems of computers and learning, is Seymour Papert's *Mindstorms*. Papert wrote *Mindstorms* in an attempt to demonstrate how computers can be used with children while they learn about language, mathematics, and thinking, to show how computers will affect the way people think and learn, and how, by carrying powerful ideas, computers can cut across traditional lines which separate learning into subjects. Despite the strong mathematical orientation and the technical nature of some of the chapters, Papert's book should be read by all educators if only to understand how a self-proclaimed educational utopian envisions the use of computers in learning. It will help teacher-librarians focus on the problems of how computers might be used in the future and how computers might or might not be used in resource centres. Papert is critical of current classroom teaching and argues that since computers are so universal in their ability to stimulate, they should be used to create an environment in which learning takes place in "a way a child learns to talk, a process that takes place without deliberate and organized teaching."

Papert also contends that "we're in the process of digging ourselves into an anachronism by preserving practices that have no rational basis beyond their historical roots in an earlier period of technology and theoretical development." Examples of this "QWERTY" way of thinking include using the computer for drill and remediation, using BASIC, and assuming that microcomputers belong in resource centres along with other media and hardware. Instead of responding to the computer's power to create situations, to make formal knowledge concrete and to simulate, the computer is used to make quantitative improvements over existing techniques instead of qualitative improvements.

The reluctance to change techniques that might result in qualitative improvements is due partially to the conservative nature of institutions, including schools, and partially to the commercialization of the technology. For example, BASIC was originally devised to accommodate machines with limited storage capacity. Despite the increase in the memory capacity of microcomputers BASIC is still *the* basic language of computers used in schools and homes. It is the language of most commercially produced programs because, Papert contends, it is the language most easily used by computer engineers not students. Most of the commercially available courseware consists of drill and practice. This "appeals to teachers because it resembles traditional teaching methods" and appeals to computer engineers because "drill and practice applications are predictable, simple to describe, efficient in use of the machine's resources." Using the computer in this way is an example of qualitative change.

Papert sees the computer as a way to gain integrated knowledge rather than departmentalized facts based on a predetermined curriculum. He suggests and gives examples of ways that the computer can stimulate ideas in a variety of school subjects: physics, mathematics, physical education, social studies, language arts. He contends that the process of programming computers and debugging the program changes a child's approach to problem solving in any area of learning, by teaching the child to adopt a procedure and to use "intuitive knowledge" rather than accepting the presence of a right answer. He argues that rather than using the computer to drill in the traditional way, the computer should be used to create a learning environment which is based on free access to the computer and which allows the child to manipulate the environment, play with its elements, explore the potential of both the environment and the computer, and function within an environment that is "discovery rich," that is new and exciting, participatory and that imitates adult life.

In the past two years, over 200,000 personal computers have been purchased in the United States alone. Over 40 percent of the school districts in the United States have purchased and use instructional computers. The use to which home computers are being put must be considered when planning for the use of computers in schools. If computers are used at home to produce a rich learning environment and in schools for drill and remediation, the breach between what the public wants and what it gets from schools will widen with little chances of establishing a public sympathetic to the growing needs and costs of education.

It is unwise for a teacher-librarian to accept the role proposed by CSLA without first discovering what the school, in which the resource centre is so intricately involved, intends for the computer. The computer used in the library for information retrieval, for technical services, and as a word processor is well established and poses no philosophical problems for the teacher-librarian. There is general acceptance of the teacher-librarian as organizer, purchaser, and disseminator of information and materials for computers. What is questionable is the additional task of developing programs to assist other staff members in the effective use of computers and addressing the problem of computer awareness, literacy, and science. What is meant by these terms? Is computer literacy merely the ability to understand and use computers or, as Papert suggests, "knowing not only how to make use of computers and computational ideas, but knowing when it is appropriate to do so." There is no substantive difference in the definition and these differences must be addressed by each teacher-librarian in the framework of the school situation.

Reading Seymour Papert's *Mindstorms* may help the teacher-librarian to approach the problem of computers, learning and the library, for until one knows how the computer will be used within the school, it is impossible to create programs for their effective use or, for that matter, to suggest whose responsibility these programs should be.

BIBLIOGRAPHY

"Canadian School Library Association" *Canadian Library Journal*. (October, 1982). Pages 339-40.

Mandell, Phyllis Levy. "Computer Literacy, Languages, and Careers." *School Library Journal*. (April, 1982). Page 19.

Papert, Seymour. *Mindstorms: Children, Computers, and Powerful Ideas*. New York: Basic Books, 1980.

Online Bibliographic Searching in Secondary School Resource Centres

William G. McKinnie

The growth of computer technology and the increasing availability of both source and data bases like the Toronto *Globe And Mail's* Info Globe, and reference data bases like the Educational Resources Information Center (ERIC), in electronic form, will have a significant impact upon the school library program. While there seems to be an increasing number of articles describing the use of microcomputers in school libraries,[5] there is very little in the literature which specifically describes online searching at the school level.

Wozny[7] describes a study of ninth-grade honors students who received training in online bibliographic searching as the last step in their research procedure for a science project. While her students reported that they recognized the value of online searching as a way to retrieve information, only 19 percent referenced materials retrieved from searching data bases online. Dowling[2] described a research program in which students taking advanced placement courses in Biography, English, American or European History were encouraged to submit requests for online searches. These searches were conducted at both the district and school level. Searches at the school level proved more satisfactory because students were given instruction in designing search strategies and they observed the actual search. Students quickly began to see how very useful a computer could be in aiding research. In an earlier article, Curley[1] described online searching in the school resource centre as a way of keeping the teacher up-to-date on the latest trends in education through the Canadian Selective Dissemination of Information (CAN/SDI) Program. Fenichel,[4] commenting about school resource centres, noted that "the time is right for research and demonstration projects in this area."

In the fall of 1981, the head librarian at The Guelph Collegiate and Vocational Institute, Guelph, Ontario, with the support and encouragement of the principal, began to make plans for the introduction of online searching as a special project. The objectives of this program were to provide a specialized reference service to staff and senior students, and to introduce staff and students to the capabilities of online searching through the resource centre's program of cooperative teaching. Both objectives were consistent with the school's program of promoting computer literacy.

Since a microcomputer and printer are already being used for administrative functions including overdues and several inventory programs in the resource centre, the necessary modem and modem software package were inexpensive additions to the system. Before the software package arrived, a data terminal with a built-in acoustic coupler and printer was rented because of its portability for practice sessions at home.

The microcomputer with its screen proved useful for giving demonstrations to small groups. For large groups it was hooked up to an ordinary large video monitor. The printer

proved essential to the system because it printed out references, provided the searcher with a copy of the search strategy for checking, and provided a copy of the charges for the search.

After the equipment was purchased, the next important consideration was the choice of an online search system which would provide access to the data base required to meet the needs of the resource centre's clientele.[6] An analysis of student and teacher requests and assignments revealed that any online information system selected had to be well-represented in the social sciences and the pure and applied sciences. As well, it had to provide coverage of core files in the humanities and coverage for the general reader.

The direct cost of searching was another consideration since a limited amount of funding was available for the project. The components of direct search costs were: the cost of communications between the user's terminal and the vendor's computer going through DATAPAC in Canada to TELENET or TYMNET in the United States; vendor fees for online connect time; and vendor charges for offline prints.

A comparison of the three largest online search systems revealed that BRS offered subscription prices while both DIALOG and ORBIT offered simple pay as you go plans. DIALOG files ranged in price from $25 to $300 per hour and ORBIT files ranged from $35 to $120 per hour. Full price of ERIC on DIALOG was $25 per hour. LISA was not available on BRS. The cost of ERIC offline prints on BRS was 6.5 cents per citation; on DIALOG and ORBIT the cost was 10 cents for each complete citation. All systems offered SDI (Selective Dissemination of Information) services and DIALOG and ORBIT provided an online document ordering service with access to an increasing number of vendors including ERIC.

Because of an initial reluctance to commit the resource centre to a subscription and because of DIALOG's potential search volume, an account was opened in January 1982 with DIALOG. The teacher-librarian attended a day and a half introductory session at Micro Media, Toronto. Two weeks of ONTAP (practice) files and $100 free online time for one month were also provided to encourage practice searching. As well, DIALOG manual and a Thesaurus of ERIC Descriptors were purchased.

In February, 1982, the program was implemented. During the next five months, presentations were made to six departments within the school. In each of the sessions the following outline was used: (1) brief history of online searching, (2) what a data base and a data system are, (3) searching a data base, (4) advantages and disadvantages of online searching, (5) value of online searching to teachers and to senior students undertaking research in their courses, and (6) a demonstration search. In all of these sessions it was emphasized that a search would be done only when all other standard reference sources available had been searched, or when a teacher or student wanted either very specialized information or information which required a broad coverage. Costs for the searches were to be charged against the resource centre's reference budget for the current year. These costs were to be closely monitored.

In addition to presentations to departments, one presentation each was made to senior classes in English, Sociology, Health and Physical Education, Mathematics, and Electronics. The presentations in Mathematics and Electronics were part of an assignment dealing with the applications of computer technology in society, and the presentations in the other subject areas were designed to demonstrate the capabilities of online searching and to retrieve relevant citations for assignments which students were completing. As a result of these presentations the resource centre had requests from teachers and from students who had been referred to us by teachers for online searches. These requests were carefully evaluated before a search was done.

The summaries which follow indicate the cost incurred in establishing the project and in searching data bases. They also indicate the nature and extent of the online searches. The average cost for a search was $5.02 and the most heavily used data base was ERIC. Since the user pays only for online time, costs were able to be closely monitored. A well thought out search strategy was essential before a search was begun. Of the 92 searches made in the first 7 months of the project, 63 percent or 69 percent were for staff and 29 percent or 31 percent were for students.

EXAMPLES OF ONLINE SEARCHES

1. *Student Requests*
   Surrogate mother
   Platonic relationships
   Home birth
   Effects of Vitamin E on athletes
   Housing for the handicapped
   The effects of altitude on atheltic training

Summary of Data Searches
P.G. Reid Resource Centre, G.C.V.I.
FEBRUARY - OCTOBER 1982

1. Direct Costs

Data Bases	File No.	No. Of Searches	No. Of Prints Offline	Total Costs*	Average Cost Per Search
Biography	88	9	-	$ 70.17	$7.80
Dialindex	411	3	-	13.50	4.50
Enviroline	40	2	-	16.38	8.19
ERIC	1	51	522	303.91	5.96
Excerpta Medica	72	6	-	8.13	1.36
Magazine Index	47	19	354	174.21	9.17
M.L.A. Bibliography	71	2	-	3.36	1.68
		92	876	$589.66	
Credit				−$127.50	
				$462.16	

Average cost per search = $462.16 ÷ 92 = $5.02

* Includes cost of prints and communication costs for Telenet or Tymnet.

---

2. Indirect Costs

September - December, 1981

Dialog Seminar	90.00
Dialog Binder	37.00
Rental Of Data Terminal	37.50
Modem	260.00
Modem Software	24.80
	$449.30

January - October, 1982

ERIC Thesaurus	35.00
Modem Interface	184.30
Dialog Kit	25.00
Dialog Publications	.74
Installation Of Phone Extension	40.25
Dialog Seminar	35.00
	$320.29

2. *Staff Requests*

  Reading skills in science
  Wildlife management and conservation
  Effect of class size on teaching
  ESL
  Cooperative education in secondary school
  Mainstreaming
  Teaching mythology in secondary school
  Articles by Willower (author)
  Designing report cards for the slow learner
  Teaching mathematics to the gifted student in
    high schools
  Self-concept and the slow learner at the secondary
    level
  Microcomputers in the school library
  Attitudes of students, teachers, employers to high
    school grads in Canada

While DIALOG provides an online ordering service for article reprints, it was not necessary to utilize this service to retrieve articles. Instead, copies of articles were retrieved from the school district's Education Library which has a large journal collection, from the Guelph Public Library, from the University of Guelph which has the complete ERIC file on microfiche, and through interlibrary loan with other cooperating libraries.

Online searching eliminated two of the problems identified by Drott and Mancall[3] in their bibliometric study of materials students use. In their analysis of bibliographies they observed that there was a strong preference by students for books as the major source of their information and that materials referenced were not particularly current; that is, they were not five years old or less. Online searching, on the other hand, introduced students to a wide variety of materials including articles from both specialized and general journals, from reports, and from books. During a normal search all the citations were printed out in reverse chronological order. It was also possible to limit a set of citations to a particular year or years.

Access to an online information system like DIALOG proved popular with both staff and students and offered many advantages. Reference tools which were too expensive or too impractical to buy given the demand for their usage were searched online at reasonable costs. The resource centre had access to resources beyond those conventionally made available. Online searching provided more access points to information than found in conventional indexes. Online searching was found to be a tremendous time saver. The computer proved to be accurate because it did not forget part of the bibliographic citation. The completeness of the data

base allowed the searcher to put together automatically the various components of the reference request in one phrase as opposed to flipping through various sections of the index.

Evaluating the relevance of citations generated for staff and students proved difficult. In general, user indicated satisfaction with the results and the demand for searches increased. However, a more quantitative measure like documenting the extent to which citations are included in project bibliographies will be examined as the project continues.

Online searching at the school level will no doubt have a number of unanticipated outcomes. Given the capabilities of the technology, the nature of the research assignment and student research methods will probably change significantly. As a result, teacher-librarians will need to learn the techniques of online searching and be prepared to teach these search techniques as part of their teaching programs. Student and staff use of online bibliographic searching should only serve to enhance the role of the teacher-librarian as a teaching partner.

REFERENCES

1. Curley, Elizabeth McDonald. "Online Reference Services and Teacher-Librarians." *Canadian Library Journal.* Volume 36 (October, 1979), pages 271-73.

2. Dowling, Karen. "The School Media Center Goes Online." *Catholic Library World.* Volume 53 (October, 1981), pages 120-21.

3. Drott, Carl M. and Mancall, Jacqueline C. *Materials Students Use: A Direct Measurement Approach.* Arlington, VA: ERIC Document Reproduction Service, 1980. ED 195287.

4. Fenichel, Carol H. and Hogan, Thomas H. *Online Searching: A Primer.* Marlton, N.J.: Learned Information, 1981.

5. Gillette, Meredith. "Micros Online: A Comparison of Available Citations." *Access: Microcomputers in Libraries.* Volume 1 (July, 1981), pages 10-19.

6. Harper, Laura G. "A Comparative Review of BRS, DIALOG, and ORBIT." *RSR.* Volume 9 (January/March, 1981), pages 39-51.

7. Wozny, Lucy Anne. "Online Bibliographic Searching and Student Use of Information: An Innovative Teaching Approach." *School Library Media Quarterly.* Volume 11 (Fall, 1982), pages 35-42.

School Assignments: A Public Library Responsibility

Nancy Black, Ken Roberts, and Valerie White

Last June the three of us ate lunch together at a conference and, as librarians sometimes do, we traded horror stories. The most memorable concerned a public librarian who conducted reference interviews with children and young people in the following manner:

Child: Do you have any books on calligraphy?

Librarian: Is this for personal use or for a school assignment?

Child: A school assignment.

Librarian: Then I can't help you. It is library policy not to support school curriculum needs. Next!

After we stopped groaning, we realized that this example, while extreme, was technically correct according to the official policy of many public libraries. Most public libraries do have policy statements denying support of school assignment needs. While these policy statements are explicit, they are interpreted quite differently.

In some public libraries this policy means they do not buy textbooks and do not buy sufficient duplicates to provide all of the students in Mrs. Johnson's class with three different books on koala bears. In other public libraries the policy means exactly what it says. Even though there may be regular juvenile requests for books on ancient civilizations, countries, animals, and many other subjects, no attention is paid to the development of the collection in these areas as the need is school related.

We believe there is a need for more discussion about public library policies and attitudes toward helping students find information for school assignments. We think it is, or should be, part of the mandate of the public library to provide reasonable support for this need.

In the past several years school systems in many areas have moved to a research approach. Instead of copying from textbooks, young people are more frequently encouraged to use resources, such as the public library, to find material on a subject. Lessons center both on the topic itself and on methodology. This is certainly a goal librarians should support. Ignoring finances for the moment, does it seem reasonable that public libraries should, by official policy, place roadblocks in the way?

School systems are also trying to make the point that information comes in forms other than encyclopedias. Again, this is a fact with which public librarians can agree. Yet encyclopedias are frequently all the public library can provide as a resource.

Does it seem reasonable that the public library throw resources into providing programming to attract children and young adults, much of it justified on grounds that we are creating an atmosphere which encourages them to return, and then turn these same people away when they come with a basic need? We find it easy to encourage young people to come to the library for the thrill of literature but not for their business—the business of education. The unofficial boundary which states that school libraries are responsible for curriculum needs and public libraries are responsible for personal reading is absurd. Public librarians should want young people to think of their institutions as information resource centres.

Imagine a child who has grown up in a community where the public librarians make no effort to provide assistance with school assignments. For twelve years that person listens to "No. We can't help you with that" and then becomes an adult. With no background of success, is that person likely to think of the public library when needing information about resumes, gardening, or cooking? Is that person, or the parents of that person, likely to sing the praises of the public library when a new building or budget increases are suggested?

Does it seem reasonable that the public library be the sole bastion of recreational reading? Studies such as Fasick's Regina report indicate that many parents do not take their children to the public library. Unless there are access points other than public libraries, these children will not read good fiction. School libraries can act as natural access points to literature. The roles of school and public libraries are not clear cut and distinct. Young people gain by some merging of responsibilities.

Obviously, one difficulty in dealing with school assignments is that they come in waves. One day every one wants information on India. The next day it might be information on Ancient Egypt or Halley's Comet. The waves keep coming, and public libraries deal with their own sense of frustration by washing their hands of the problem. And yet, when a new Stephen King or James Michener novel is published and the waves of adult readers begin to request it, we respond. We do not respond by buying copies for everyone, but we do not respond by denying responsibility. We respond rationally and seek a balance.

Public librarians should also seek a balance in their provision of service to students. What can public librarians do about school assignments?

(1) *Anticipate instead of react.*
Relevant public librarians should meet yearly with the subject co-ordinators of the school board. Curriculum does change and it is nice to know, ahead of time, that India or Japan is a planned focus for Grade Five students beginning

the following September. School personnel can also supply lists of "suggested reading" fictional titles for various grades. Teachers see and use these lists. So should public librarians. If *The Old Man and the Sea* is suggested reading for Grade Nine students, copies should be on the public library Young Adult paperback rack. The Children's and Y.A. racks can support school curriculum by making suggested titles available.

(2) *Plan.*

If students are constantly asking for information on Ancient Greece or on particular animals and it is known this is a yearly, multi-class assignment, do something. It may indeed be too late to do something for the current group of people standing in front of the desk, but it isn't too late to plan for next time.

Mark down the need for more material. When the material is back on the shelf, find a good book with clear headings and buy another copy for reference. This book will still be in the library when all others have left. It will not be an encyclopedia. It can be photocopied or used in the library. It changes the librarian from a person who says "no" to one who places responsibility onto the child to use material which is available.

Create vertical file material. Write to embassies. Buy paperback non-fiction material. Excellent, inexpensive paperbacks are available on subjects such as countries, various periods of history, and on many other topics.

Buy copies of both the multi-volume *Caxton's History of the World* and *The International Wildlife Encyclopedia* for reference use. Think about how you will deal with various school research needs and plan for what to say and where to turn when all books have left the library. Most importantly, remember that it is not the fault of the child in front of you that he or she is the eighteenth person to show up and ask for material on the inner ear. The eighteenth person has a right to the same courtesy as the first.

If students are constantly asking for information on countries, provide them with search aids which can be of assistance when all book information is gone. Search aids can explain the type of information found in *The Statesman's Yearbook* or in *Background Notes*. They can direct students to the vertical files and to periodical indices. They can do this in written, straightforward fashion so the librarian can show concern and save time with the interview process.

It seems to us that young people doing school research assignments have the same right as adults to expect, not success on every occasion, but a reasonable chance at finding valid information at their local public library. The provision of assistance to students need not be an expensive service. For the most part, it involves planning and respect for the validity of student needs.

TITLES MENTIONED:

Background Notes, United States Bureau of Public Affairs.
> Background Notes are up-to-date information sheets on all the countries of the world. They are purchased by subscription.

Caxton's History of the World, London, New Caxton Library Service, 1969.
> A multi-volume encyclopedia of History aimed at just the right level for many school projects.

Children Using Media, Adele Fasick, and Claire England, Reading and Viewing Preferences among Users and Non-Users of the Regina Public Library, Regina Public Library, 1977.

International Wildlife Encyclopedia, Marshall Cavendish Corp, New York, 1969.
> An excellent encyclopedia for school projects.

Statesman's Yearbook: A Statistical & Historical Annual of the States of the World, St. Martin's Press, New York.
> A one volume, up-to-date information source on countries.

On Book Exchanges

Carol-Ann Haycock

I find myself getting on a soap box more and more frequently these days as practices which I thought were long since dead keep raising themselves for discussion. Case in point—the weekly book exchange. I think that book exchanges are anti-reading, anti-enjoyment of books, anti-library, and probably even anti-educational.

Essentially, the only purpose that the regularly scheduled book exchange serves is one of teacher control—and, perhaps, librarian control. We have long since acknowledged that in any given grade level there is a possible, or even probable, 3 to 5 year span in ability ... the measure of that "ability" most commonly being reading level. Then, if students are reading at varying levels of ability and at varying rates, how can it be possible that every student in a third grade or a sixth grade class needs (or wants) a book at 9:30 a.m. on Thursday or at 1:00 p.m. on Tuesday?

"What," I ask, "are we promoting?" "What are children engaged in such a practice learning?" Please don't tell me "good library habits." The question that follows that line of thinking is "at what expense?" Lining up 20 to 30 students to exchange books for a period of 20 to 40 minutes does not allow enough time to provide individual assistance or guidance. Far too often, I have seen a primary child tug at a teacher and complain "I can't find a book," only to have a harrassed teacher grab a book from the shelf and say, "Here, take this one," while herding said child into the sign-out line.

"What about provision for individual interests and individual reading ability?" you ask. Well, these are certainly not guaranteed through a regularly scheduled book exchange.

But there are options. Book talks, the promotion of various genres, the recording of reading through a reading wheel, the sharing of titles read in class, can all be facilitated by cooperative planning between the teacher and teacher-librarian. The students can be taught techniques like the five finger test as a reading level check. Reluctant readers can, and probably should, be dealt with on an individual or small group basis by either the teacher or teacher-librarian. Obviously, more time may be necessary for promoting reading and facilitating a reasonable exchange of materials.

More opportunities can, and should, be provided for independent book selection as the need arises, either before and after school or at lunch time, or through the use of independent library tags during the school day. At least this will provide a better guarantee that a youngster is there to select a book because it is wanted or needed.

Most kids *do* want to read, but *when* they want or need something new to read can be no more dictated for kids than it can for adults. More options for individual selection and reading guidance, more cooperatively developed and implemented programs for promoting voluntary reading and more school-wide *proven* approaches such as USSR (Uninterrupted, Sustained Silent Reading), will lead to more realistic teacher expectations, better understanding and use by teachers of library resources, including the teacher-librarian, and better motivation to read for youngsters.

School Libraries – Definitely Worth Their Keep

Bev Anderson

When dollars are devoted to school library services, is there corresponding value for students? An evaluation of school library programs in the Calgary Board of Education suggests that the answer is "Yes!" The evaluation project measured the extent of library service, the skill level and attitudes of students and the resource allocation and background characteristics of 65 sample schools. Findings indicate that when there was sufficient staff time and resource budget, teacher-librarians performed a role of school-based consultant and were able to provide audiovisual services. When this expanded role occurred, there was corresponding increase in student skills, positive student attitudes and assistance for teachers.

BACKGROUND

In 1977, the Chief Superintendent of the Calgary Board of Education commissioned an evaluation of school library/ resource centre programs. The purpose of this evaluation was to investigate the question "Is the Board receiving sufficient value for the dollars that are/have been devoted to school resource services?" Specific direction was provided to include qualitative and quantitative data regarding the effects of resource services upon students. Rather than circulation statistics or reading preferences, the evaluation was to assess the relationship between provision of library service and learning outcomes for students.

The first phase of the evaluation was to establish base line information about resource centre programs. The second phase was to examine variations among programs and to assess their relative impact on schools. When dollars are devoted to school library services, is there corresponding value for students? There were two areas to explore: the role of teacher-librarians and the skill level and attitudes of students. To address the first area, a committee composed of the school principal, teacher-librarian, and two teachers in each school responded to the Liesener Inventory of Services.[2]

The Liesener Inventory was selected not only because it has been extensively field tested, but also because it stands as a major authoritative instrument in school library evaluation. This inventory is a refinement of the Gaver Inventory administered in Calgary in 1971. The inventory was used to describe the breadth of the resource centre program through a description of its events. District staff personally administered each inventory to ensure consistent interpretation at a regularly controlled pace.

A locally developed attitude measure was designed to determine students' feelings about their resource centres through responses to items such as:

Item 14: "The library is a favourite place of mine in the school."

An elementary school research skills test was developed locally, based on the district's scope and sequence research chart. It was subsequently pilot tested on two elementary schools that were not to be participants in the research project. A senior high school research skills test was based on a test developed and field tested by a committee of school and district personnel.

For both attitude and skill measures, two Year Six classes two Year Twelve classes were tested in each school, except in small elementary schools where there was only one Year Six class available. In each case, the tests were administered by district staff.

The above measures were used to gather quantitative data which was then coupled with qualitative data gleaned from all of the schools sampled. This was done through detailed observation in a wide variety of school resource centres using goal-free observation techniques such as those described by Barry MacDonald at the University of East Anglia[3] and Elliot Eisner.[4] An important consideration was that the past observations of the library media consultants could not be relied upon because those observations tended to be biased, as visits usually occurred on an individual basis.

Each case study involved a two-day observation period using unobtrusive observational techniques and interviews with students, classroom teachers, library/media staff and administrators. As the case studies progressed, it became obvious that background variables other than those described in the Liesener Inventory needed to be taken into account. These variables might enable, or limit, the capacity of the resource centre to provide the services listed in the Liesener Inventory.

The Liesener Inventory of Library Services includes items related to the existence of various types of library material, access to library production services, in-library instruction services and consulting services, contribution to school curriculum and teacher instruction.

Student skills and attitudes include library access skills, general book knowledge, instrumental value of the library to school work, and positive sentiment towards the library.

Background characteristics include personal qualifications of the teacher-librarian (e.g., education, seniority, teaching experience), size of the library program (e.g., time entitlement, library budget), size of the school (e.g., enrollment, budget), consultant visits, educational ability (e.g., student verbal and nonverbal, level of education in the immediate neighborhood), and others such as seniority of the principal and age of the school.

Analysis of the extensive data collected was directed by Dr. W. J. Reeves of the University of Calgary Sociology Department. His involvement as a methodologist was crucial to the project. A multivariate regression analysis was conducted to determine relationships between the objective data and background characteristics. With a possibility of approximately 30,000 correlations, this aspect of the evaluation project demanded the full capacity of the district computer. Only those findings that could be confirmed in both statistical and observational data are reported and, of these,

only findings which can be supported by correlation of .6 and more are included.

FINDINGS

At the first level of research findings, this study has confirmed what resource centres in Calgary look like. It is now known that even the basic core services offer support for teachers, opportunities for students, and a variety of general services including instruction for children. These "Baseline Library Services" do not, in and of themselves, represent an ideal nor complete program. What is amazing, however, is that in spite of dramatically different conditions in schools, resource centres are able to offer a broad list of common services.

When a service was offered in all or almost all schools, it was considered a program norm or part of a core of services offered throughout the district. Approximately fifty-five baseline services were offered by all resource centres. In addition, approximately thirty baseline services were offered by all or almost all elementary schools. Similarly, approximately thirty different baseline services were unique to senior high resource centres.

Core Services were clustered into four areas. Because the configuration was different at the elementary and senior high levels, they were labelled differently. The similarity of focus is, however, readily apparent.

BASELINE LIBRARY SERVICES

Elementary Schools	High Schools
The Child's Domain	Individual Instruction for Students
Reference Services for Individual Teachers	Group Instruction for Students
General Use Services	Teacher Services
	Library Administration

In the elementary school, the Child's Domain encompassed a variety of awareness and guidance services regarding resources.

Students had a wide variety of materials to choose from, in a variety of locations, and they were also alerted by the resource centre staff to materials and services in the library. Once students were cognizant of the existence of materials, they also received assistance from the teacher-librarian in locating and selecting materials most appropriate to their interests and needs. Renewal procedures were available in all elementary schools, should the student require this service. It was apparent that individuals and small groups of students used the library if the need arose in the classroom; in fact, small groups were regularly sent to the library to work with the teacher-librarian on assignments. Audio-visual equipment was available as required.

Student instruction occupied a large amount of resource centre staff time. Formal instructional program activities were evident in all elementary libraries. Individual instruction and guidance was offered to all students in all elementary schools, on request. This instruction occurred in the areas of reference materials and skills, research skills and the use and handling of audio-visual equipment.

Services clustered under the label "general use" in the elementary school centered around management of the library facility, collection and equipment, and awareness activities directed toward special events such as Book Week.

In the senior high schools, library administration was directed toward improving access to materials, including reservation systems and interlibrary loans.

Having identified the constants regarding school library programs in the district, it was noted that the role of school librarian as teacher and resource specialist was implicit. At this stage of the analysis only those items that varied in the sample (that is, where approximately half the sampled schools said "Yes!" and half said "No!" to the item) were investigated. Given the theoretical model of the research, it was important to know if it made a difference to the students whether the school had a particular library service or not—were the students in approximately half the schools who said "Yes" to a Liesener item more skillful or more positive than the students in the other schools who said "No!" From another perspective, was the existence or absence of a library service determined in any way by the background characteristics of the librarian, library, or school?

Examination of services which were found to be provided in some schools, and not in others, revealed an expanded role for the teacher librarian. This role is one of school-based consultant, with an additional program component dealing with audio-visual services. These two elements of consultation and audio-visual service manifest themselves differently at the elementary and senior high levels. Nevertheless, the pattern of development relative to individual schools and the district at large was remarkably consistent.

ELEMENTARY SCHOOLS

Initially, cooperation between teachers and teacher-librarians led to the selection of resources for teacher use *or* to extend and enrich experiences for students. At the next level, both these elements were present. A further stage of development was found when classroom teachers and the teacher-librarian engaged in a form of team teaching. In this case, the approach was frequently a division of labor, with the teacher-librarian entering the instructional sequence based on expertise. For example, instruction in the use of biographical reference works might be designed into a social studies unit. Fully developed consultation occurred when classroom teachers and teacher-librarian planned an instructional sequence, conducted instruction cooperatively and shared in student and program evaluation. Approximately 20 percent of the schools exhibited this level of development.

CONSULTATION INDEX LEVEL

Consultation leading to team lesson planning, and teaching cooperatively   5

Consultation leading to team teaching with classroom teacher   4

Consultation leading to selection of resources for teacher use AND for enrichment of student programs   3

Consultation leading to selection of resources for teacher OR for enrichment of student programs   2

No consultation with teams of teachers

Along with the consultative role of the teacher-librarian, the production of instructional materials was found to be a critical variable. This service element was not, at the time of the study, well developed. Typically, the library staff provided a video tape dubbing service for teachers.

It was important to consider what characteristics were related to whether or not the expanded role of the school library was present in elementary schools. Those with background and experience in libraries will not be surprised that the relationship was one of time (providing sufficient time for the teacher-librarian to work in the program) and money (providing sufficient funds in the library budget). What was gratifying about this finding, was the strength of the relationship and the precision with which we could establish cut points regarding variables. Because there was not a perfect relationship between school size and the amount of teacher-librarian time, some relatively small schools were able to exhibit the two variables and some large schools did not. Systematically, however, in small schools with less than half-time teacher-librarians and larger schools with less than two thirds of the teacher-librarian's time deployed to the program, the consultative role and production service was absent. Admittedly "small" and "larger" applied to school size are defined differently. At the time of the study, 14 elementary schools had enrollments of less than 150 students and the average size of school was nine classrooms. In addition, every school library has clerical staff and is supported by centralized ordering, cataloguing, processing, and a variety of school-directed services.

Similarly, data analysis revealed that, in terms of *1978* dollars, any school library budget which was less than $2,500 for materials, systematically exhibited no consultative or production role. Of particular interest was a further systematic relationship between the amount of time devoted to the school by library media consultants and production. When there had been five or more visits to the school, there was a strong positive relationship to the presence of the expanded role. This finding inspires much speculation and is deserving of more attention than can be paid in this article.

What about student outcomes in terms of skills and attitudes? Certainly, there were some items that stood out as bearing a strong relationship to the sentiments and skill development of children. For example, there was .8 correlation between the housing of photographs in the library and children declaring that the library was the most interesting place in the school. An interesting phenomenon, but hardly a significant one in the overall scheme of things. An equally strong relationship was one of socioeconomic status (SES) of the neighborhood to the importance which students assigned to the library. In lower SES schools, children systematically indicated that the library was important to their success in school. The reverse was also true; and this phenomenon was also related to the way the library was scheduled and the specific skills that were acquired.

The observational data collected during the case studies, together with the strong results regarding consultation, confirmed that the "first" clients of the elementary school library were the teachers who, in turn, sponsored children individually or in small and large groups to go to the library. Because the library program does not, nor can be expected to, have a mandated curriculum, the inconclusive results of skill measures were not surprising. There was, however, strong positive effect upon students' attitudes when teacher-librarians performed a consultative role with teachers. When this full partnership occurred, as was the case in 5 of the sampled schools, there was an obvious coordination and integration of the library program with classroom activities. Typically, the teacher-librarians in these schools were involved at the initial planning stages of the project, took part in cooperative or team teaching activities as the project progressed, and were certainly engaged in evaluation and follow-up at the project's conclusion.

In regard to the testing procedures, no attempt was made to test for library skill ability in subject areas, nor was performance testing carried out due to constraints of time. What is known, however, is that in schools where consultation did occur, library skills per se were not generally taught as a separate curriculum area, but instruction appeared to be given as the need arose in the classroom and after careful consultation between teacher and teacher-librarian. Furthermore, because only Grade 6 students were tested and knowing that teachers sponsor their classes to the library, it was not possible that the classes tested had not yet been sponsored for instruction in the skills that were being tested. Ideally, the entire school population should have been tested and those results examined in light of students being sponsored or non-sponsored to the library. The effects of the library program upon students is indirect, and is dependent upon teachers sponsoring student use of the services and resources that are resident in the resource program.

SENIOR HIGH SCHOOLS

Relationships between school library program development and student outcomes was more conclusive at the senior high school. In the area of extended library services, the elementary beginnings come to fruition at the secondary level. The continued importance of time in regards to consultation between teacher and teacher-librarian is, further, more specifically identifiable at high school to include the effects of specific kinds of consultation on student skills and attitudes.

Similarly, the audio-visual component which has its beginnings in the expanded teacher-librarian role at the elementary level, through the production of instructional materials for teachers, matures at the secondary level through more extensive audio-visual services.

In senior high, the expanded role can be obtained only when there is an adequate library budget and adequate clerical time which in turn manifests itself in two major areas inside the expanded role: the audio-visual component and differentiated consultative services. The audio-visual component, which includes services such as photography, has a significant impact on student attitudes.

At the secondary level, the existence and type of consultation are heavily dependent on how much clerical time is resident in the program. Since all senior high teacher-librarians work on a full-time basis, the operant variable, therefore, became the number of clerical staff and/or the amount of time spent in the program by the clerical assistant(s). This was a refinement in terms of the elementary program where not every teacher-librarian was able to devote full-time to the library program and his/her time then became the operant variable. In addition, at the secondary level, given an adequate number of clerical assistants, the resource centre was able to act as a media clearinghouse, and became involved in student-oriented consultation as well as in specific classroom projects.

Consultation was manifested in different ways, each of these having a strong positive relationship to specific student skills and sentiments. For example, when a classroom teacher and teacher-librarian cooperatively developed alternative learning situations for students (student-oriented consultation), the students systematically responded that the library staff was helpful and that the library was the most interesting place in the school. When team teaching occurred as a result of consultation, student reference skills were high. In the case of these items, the range of student scores by school was 30 percent to 78 percent on the administered skills test.

High scoring schools typically exhibited team teaching consultative behaviors. The range of student scores in the area of research skills, that is knowledge of how to begin a research project, was 47 percent to 80 percent. High scoring schools typically provided audio-visual services and the teacher-librarian was involved in developing and implementing class projects.

When school libraries provided extended audio-visual services, including listing, stocking and evaluating nonprint materials, and provision for photography, students systematically reported positive sentiments toward the library. These were manifested in students declaring that the school library was important to their success in school, that they used the library outside of class time, and that they used the library evenwhen this was not required for assignments.

The presence of the audio-visual component was, as one might expect, strongly related to significantly higher expenditure on nonprint materials. In these schools, students placed more instrumental value on the school library (it is important to my success in school) and exhibited higher scores in research skills. Interestingly, the presence of selection services in the area of nonprint was related to significantly higher expenditure on periodicals.

Consultation, particularly with regard to team teaching and the presence of a clearinghouse function, dealing with the widest range of school resources, was related to higher expenditure on books and the presence of two or more clerks. The number of clerks required to have an impact on this type of consultation varied directly with the size of the school.

LEADING EDGE PROGRAMS

When a service was offered by only a few schools, this service was at the "leading edge." These program elements are considered to be important in the field of school librarianship and may be common in other districts, but at this time, in Calgary schools, represented program extensions.

Examples of leading edge services included computer applications, identification of student learning styles and cooperatively developed resource centre goal and budget statements. However, this role was not well-defined at the time of the study. It is hoped that as programs progress, there will be a "collapsing towards the middle" whereby those services presently considered leading edge will move into the area of variable services and some of the variable services will shift into the area of core services. There had been some confirmation in this regard, available only one year later, in the area of microcomputers.

SUMMARY

The overall finding that important program elements have direct positive impact upon the students and that sufficient resources must be present in order for this to occur, will be no surprise to those intimately familiar with school libraries. As is always the case, the process of data gathering and analysis was, in itself, beneficial and stimulated some important activities. The Chief Superintendent accepted the conclusion that the Calgary Board of Education was receiving value for dollar in the areas of teacher support and positive student outcomes.

It is said that good research raises more questions than it provides answers. Many surprises were found and these bear further scrutiny. Among these are:

1. The training and background of the teacher-librarian was unrelated to the extent of the program or to student outcomes.

2. Verbal ability of students and socioeconomic status of the neighborhood was not related to the presence of extended services or positive student outcomes.

3. The Liesener Inventory is based on the assumption that "more is better." There are, clearly, some services that are more important than others. Indeed, the provision of some services was found to have a *negative* correlation with student outcomes!

CONCLUSIONS

Analysis of the findings yielded four major conclusions:

1. Library programs are an integrative resource in schools. Successful programs involve the teaching staff, school administrators, and central office functions.

2. The inconsistent deployment of staff time and materials budgets results in uneven program implementation from school to school. It appears that this inconsistency is related to administrative support and the teaching styles prevalent within the school.

3. The resource centre program is unlike a curriculum. Rather, it is a service that must be entrenched in the total school program, if students and teachers are to receive maximum benefits. When the program is dealt with as a residual of school resources, there is little provided that is meaningful for its clients.

4. Some schools do not have the necessary resources to support quality library programs without severely penalizing a curriculum area.

REFERENCES

1. Calgary Board of Education. *School Library Program Evaluation.* Office of the Chief Superintendent, Calgary Board of Education, 1981.

2. Liesener, James W. "The Development of a Planning Process for Media Programs," *School Media Quarterly,* I (Summer, 1973), pp. 278-87.

Liesener, James W. *Planning Instruments for School Library Media Programs.* American Library Association, 1974.

Liesener, James W. *A Systematic Process for Planning Media Programs.* American Library Association, 1976.

3. MacDonald, Barry. *Evaluation and the Control of Education.* Ford Foundation Safari Project. University of East Anglia: Centre for Applied Research in Education, 1974 (mimeographed).

4. Eisner, Eliot W. *The Perceptive Eye: Toward the Reformation of Educational Evaluation.* Paper presented at the meeting of the American Educational Research Association Division B, Curriculum and Objectives. Washington, D.C., March 31st, 1973.

Ten Issues in School Librarianship

Ken Haycock

1. The overriding issue in school librarianship is to ensure that the *role of the teacher-librarian* is both understood and supported by not only teacher-librarians but teachers, administrators and decision-makers. This necessitates a clearly defined and well-respected program for education for school librarianship in the country. Such is not the case at the present time.

2. If indeed, as the research suggests, teacher-librarians as a group do not convey agreement about their role then a major issue must be *colleagues who persist in offering peripheral services* (such as story reading and "library skills" in isolation, providing spare periods for teachers or working as a reference librarian rather than a teacher-librarian in a secondary school), rather than planning with teachers and team teaching. The transfer of thirty children from a classroom teacher to a teacher-librarian once a week is not a justifiable expenditure. Neither is the provision of simple reference services alone in secondary schools.

3. Teachers don't understand? Administrators don't understand? Then skills for *strategies for change* are essential. Each teacher-librarian should be ready, willing and able to provide formal and informal in-service education for colleagues.

4. Teacher-librarians are also recognizing new priority of *developing public understanding and support* for school librarianship as more and more taxpayers have no children in the public schools. Declining enrollments and declining financial support have made community understanding and involvement crucial.

5. A continuing issue in Canadian school librarianship is the nature and quality of *Canadian content in library collections*. Although publishers and professional associations have encouraged the selection and acquisition of Canadian materials, too many teacher-librarians (as well as both teachers and librarians generally) react in an all too common Canadian fashion of requiring the Canadian product to be twice as good as the foreign product before it is purchased. The logic of this escapes international observers but this is a phenomenon that pervades collection development (indeed life!) in Canada.

6. More and more teacher-librarians are faced with *French immersion programs* which require special knowledge of materials in another language when the teacher-librarian is often unilingual. Some school districts are developing guidelines and standards for teacher-librarians who work with French immersion programs.

7. With a large influx of immigrants and refugees in the past five years, teacher-librarians, as part of the general school setting, are faced with an increased number of *English as a second language (ESL) students and programs*. This obviously requires a certain type of material but also raises questions of the best ways of developing not only language fluency but also independent learning skills in ESL programs.

8. Many school districts are also facing the issue of *first language or heritage collections* when the research and leaders in the ESL program recommend the development of collections of materials in languages other than English while many professional practitioners, namely teachers of ESL programs, often prefer that only English language materials be available to students during the school day.

9. Like teachers and librarians everywhere teacher-librarians are struggling with the *application of newer technology* to resource centre operations and services. There is a growing concern that microcomputers and other, more available equipment support professional teaching services rather than being an outlet for administrative and technical interests alone.

10. Another issue, common more to the professional literature than the profession itself, is *resource sharing*. This will only be successful if structures incorporate the needs of students for immediate information and if developmental approaches to resource sharing with and without technological support are researched and implemented.

Part 7
CONCLUSION

Over the course of the past ten years I have clarified my thinking on the role of the teacher-librarian and the school library program. This has come through professional research and reading, dialogue with colleagues and most especially through the in-depth programs offered through more than 50 professional associations, school boards, universities and departments of education across the United States, Canada and Australia. There is nothing quite like three days of intensive training with committed professional teacher-librarians and administrators to challenge your philosophical positions and directions for effective professional practice.

This work was summarized at the request of the International Association of School Librarianship through the keynote address to their 1984 conference in Honolulu, Hawaii. The speech was subsequently published in more than a dozen professional journals in four countries. "Strengthening the Foundations for Teacher-librarianship" brings together basic beliefs on a solid premise aimed at deep structure for the program and significant infusion into the school beyond advertising and glitz. *Information Power*, the new guidelines for school library media programs calls the speech "an important statement on the role and change of directions for the library media center"; I hope that you agree.

"Children are the living messages we send to a time we will not see"

EMERGENCY LIBRARIAN 15:1
SEPTEMBER-OCTOBER, 1987

— Neil Postman,
The Disappearance of Childhood

Strengthening the Foundations for Teacher-Librarianship

Ken Haycock

As we consider the issues of school librarianship and gather program ideas, I would ask that you also consider the means by which the profession of teacher-librarianship itself might be strengthened and even enhanced. I use the term teacher-librarianship purposely here for the signs are clear that there is relatively little danger to the continued existence of school libraries. The issue today is the continued existence of school librarians. We have been successful in building facilities and collecting and organizing materials, but we have been less successful in developing an awareness and understanding of the role of the school librarian as a professional teacher, as an equal partner in the educational enterprise, and in developing strong support for that position.

As everyone in this room is well aware, this is a period of crisis in public education. There is evidence of considerable cuts in school library positions and cuts in materials budgets, and the prospects for 1985 and 1986 appear even bleaker.

There have also been a number of studies that show that the concept of the library as part of an instructional system responding to teacher and student needs, and even creating needs within that system, is perceived by relatively few school librarians and only dimly by most teachers and administrators. We are left with the fact that our school library resource centers are beauty spots on the body politic.

Now it would be all too common for us to sit here and bemoan the lack of understanding of our roles and our many contributions and wonder why the intrinsic value of our goods and services is not well-regarded and well-supported. But I would submit that while we know the answers to these questions, we just too often prefer to wring our hands, or reject difficult answers to easy questions. In the words of James Baldwin: "Not everything that is faced can be changed, but nothing can be changed until it is faced."

There is, however, a prescription for these ills. There are very simple, clear approaches which can be taken to ensure strong programs and their continued development. School resource centers, and teacher-librarians, can be educationally essential and economically justifiable. There are many school districts, including my own, where teacher-librarians are not "the first to go," even in times of dire economic restraint. Let's begin at "square one."

THE MISSION STATEMENT

Millions and millions of dollars are invested in school library resource centers each year. It would seem quite logical to me that the funding agency, whether the state or each school district, would have a clear, stated aim or purpose for the library program. Surely, trustees and school board officials, together with administrators and teachers, should know what the purpose of a program is before it is funded. This provides both a general framework for the program and a basic level of understanding. Seems logical.

Strangely, however, few school districts have a written statement of purpose for the program, or a "mission statement" if you will, thus leaving it in the never-never-land of the extra, the educational frill, good to have when you can afford it, but hard to justify when no one really knows what it's for; this mission statement must be clear, concise, and stated in educational terms. It is just not significant or defensible to state this aim as simply fostering a love of books and libraries.

The written purpose of library services in the Vancouver School District (Canada) is as follows:

> The aim of the school library program is to assist students to develop a commitment to informed decision-making and the skills of lifelong learning.

We know that to achieve this stated aim, teachers and teacher-librarians will have to cooperate to plan and implement units of study as teaching partners; these units integrate those skills necessary to locate, evaluate, organize, and present information from a variety of sources. Through such planning and cooperative teaching, students develop, master, and extend research and study skills in different subject contexts and at varying levels of difficulty. A secondary emphasis is placed on language improvement and enjoyment, and the promotion of voluntary reading through cooperatively developed programs.

The school library program should clearly be a partnership, involving the school district, the principal, the classroom teacher, and the teacher-librarian.

The school district is the public agency accountable to the community for the educational program. It has a specific responsibility to provide leadership in a number of areas, most of which cost little or no money. The school board, for example, should approve a stated aim for the library program that is clear to everyone; after all, if public funds are to be invested in this area, doesn't the educational community as well as the community at large have a right to know its purpose? If teacher-librarians are to be engaged, there should be a clear, written role description which stresses professional functions as well as minimum qualifications for that position.

The district should also have procedures in place to entrench or infuse research and study skills in the school curriculum. (In our case, research and study skill development and literary appreciation form part of the board's foundation or core curriculum which is every teacher's responsibility, and the roles for related staff, such as the teacher-librarian, are clearly spelled out.)

The district should also provide leadership by insisting on flexibly scheduled library resource centers, after planning between the teacher and teacher-librarian. The success of the library program rests on planning; if teacher-librarians are providing teachers with spare periods planning becomes impossible and the program doomed to failure, thus squandering public funds. Also, only the school district is in a position to organize support services for school libraries, such as central cataloguing and processing and central collections of backup materials.

Some districts virtually set up teacher-librarians and resource-based programs for failure due to benign neglect in the policy and support areas, and, as I have said, this leadership does not necessarily cost money; it does require a commitment from the teacher-librarian to work individually and through associations to advocate changes and necessary improvements, however.

As with the school district, the principal, as the professional responsible for the implementation of board policies and procedures, is accountable for the school program and has a responsibility to see that all school resources, including the teacher-librarian and library materials, are used as fully and effectively as possible.

There are a large number of things that the principal can do to support and enhance the program from querying prospective new teachers on how they would involve the teacher-librarian in their programs, to attending orientation and inservice programs put on by the teacher-librarian for staff members, through to including questions about the ways in which the resource center and teacher-librarian were used in instructional programs when evaluating teachers for written reports. The research on the principal is quite clear: the principal is the single most important factor in the development of a strong library program. In my experience, this is certainly true and points to a critical need for effective communication with administrators at all levels.

From the research we know that certain factors affect teacher use of the school resource center and teacher-librarian. We also know that the more that teachers make use of the resource center and the teacher-librarian, the better the program and the stronger the support. Those factors which affect teacher use are involvement in program planning with the teacher-librarian and team teaching, inservice programs organized by and/or put on by the teacher-librarian, administrative support for the library program, and the personality and qualifications of the teacher-librarian.

The classroom teacher bears considerable responsibility for the effectiveness of resource-based learning. Effectiveness is severely impaired if we simply transfer thirty youngsters from one teacher to another. The strength of the teacher-librarian lies in providing the classroom teacher with an opportunity to share not only planning but also preparation and implementation of programs. The teacher who chooses not to use the services of the resource center and/or teacher-librarian

is surely accountable for the development of research and study skills, especially if they have been outlined in the curriculum guides.

It is becoming increasingly possible to evaluate the teacher-librarian as but one component of the resource center program, and I think the more that we can recognize and reinforce this, the better that things will be for us. There are a great many factors which affect the quality of the program but for which the district, the principal and/or the teacher, the other partners, are responsible and should be accountable. For example, the teacher-librarian does not determine the quantitative aspects of the program such as the size of the facility, the size of the budget, the amount of time available, the amount of clerical support, and so on. Qualitatively, the district must provide some leadership in providing a framework for the implementation of quality programs—by stating the aim of the program, the role of the teacher-librarian, principal and teacher, the continuum of study and research skills to be developed, and by providing policies, procedures and services to support the implementation of the program. The principal is the key player in seeing that a program is developed, supported, and enhanced. The principal selects and evaluates the staff; the principal is accountable for the implementation of board policy; the principal can create the necessary environment to enable the teacher and teacher-librarian to work toward effective programs for resource-based learning. The teacher, of course, is responsible for the development of independent learning skills within the context of board and school guidelines and for seeing that all school resources are used effectively for student learning. If the program is a partnership, then the teacher has some responsibility to plan and work closely with the teacher-librarian.

If we can begin to evaluate resource *programs*, rather than simply teacher-librarians, if we can spell out each player's responsibility, there will be better understanding of the program as a joint effort and more commitment to it.

ROLE OF THE TEACHER-LIBRARIAN

This leads us, of course, to some determination of the role of the teacher-librarian. Many studies on the perception of educators of the role of the teacher-librarian have found that principals are amazingly consistent in their view of the teacher-librarian as having a strong role in the curriculum affairs of the school. Teachers are also consistent in their view of the teacher-librarian, but as a master at clerical and technical tasks, rather than teaching tasks (unless they have had experience in working with a teacher-librarian), while teacher-librarians themselves are terribly confused. The conclusion that these studies reach, of course, is that unless teacher-librarians start to speak with a unified voice about what the purpose of the program is and why they are in the school, there is never going to be a basis of understanding and support for that program and its continuation.

As I have stated, to develop the necessary programs to implement this stated aim requires a strong and close partnership with colleagues. Thus, we would do well to establish common bonds and eliminate unnecessary barriers. Let's start by eliminating unnecessary library jargon from our vocabulary. I, personally, feel that it may have been a mistake that we ever used the term school library and school librarian. Everyone has a personal vision of the purpose of a library because of personal experience in a public library or university library. I would submit that this is totally irrelevant. The school resource center serves quite a different function from other types of libraries, due to an emphasis on teaching young people how to process and use information. Even the subtle move to the term "teacher-librarian" designates the school librarian more clearly as a teacher and member of the teaching staff. And, of course, most school librarians are not professional librarians at all. We're teachers, professional teachers, and should be proud of it.

We also use terms like library skills—and I frankly don't know what they are, except perhaps shelving and dusting—when we could talk about research and study skills which are listed in a large number of curriculum guides as every teacher's responsibility. The term library skills simply denotes something that is taught in the library, by the librarian. In fact, a preferred term might be information skills since this is becoming an increasing concern in curriculum development. Instead of a library program, we could focus on resource-based learning, a viable and educationally sound approach. The card catalogue, which we insist on shrouding in mystique, is simply an index to the school's collection of curriculum materials. A vertical file is simply vertical, why not information file or pamphlet file? And why periodicals for what teachers, students, and the rest of the world call magazines? If we could break down some of these walls and establish common educational bonds, we could go a long way to entering the mainstream of educational thinking and decision-making.

The very nature of the role of the teacher-librarian is that of initiator and change agent. We talk of getting teachers to use the library when this is not the issue at all—what we are talking about is getting teachers to change the way that they teach and to adopt team teaching, resource-based techniques. This is why the job is so difficult and yet so challenging.

The school library program rests on teacher contact. The teacher-librarian must take the initiative to plan with colleagues. It isn't a matter of time, it's a matter of priorities. It isn't a matter of territory, it is a matter of commitment. The involvement of teachers is critical for successful, educationally viable program implementation.

I have asked the same question of hundreds of classroom teachers: "How many of you have ever been approached by a teacher-librarian, even very informally, to plan and teach a unit of study together?" The results are always the same. In every group of forty to fifty teachers, there will only ever be three or four who have been approached. We presume rejection and too often never even make the overture. We presume that teachers will view cooperation as interference. Perhaps we should extend to classroom teachers the right to reject us themselves—rather than doing it for them!

Then there are those who hold the view that we must start "where the teachers are at." Consequently, we tolerate programs determined by teachers who often see us in that subservient position and allow our roles and responsibilities to be determined by a colleague—something no one else would allow. Where is our professional commitment and integrity? The meek may indeed inherit the earth, but I can guarantee that the news of it will never get out!

The teacher-librarian's major task is to work with classroom teachers to plan, develop, and implement units of study which integrate research and study skills. I didn't say only task, I didn't say most time-consuming task, but I did say major task—and if this isn't the major task, what is? Teaching involves three professional functions—the ability to diagnose learning needs, to design programs to meet those needs, and to assess the degree to which the program has been successful. For the teacher-librarian to be successful, these are done in conjunction and consultation with the classroom teacher. Instead of having one teacher and thirty youngsters, we now have two teachers, the classroom teacher and the teacher-librarian, a range of carefully selected materials, and those same thirty youngsters. Research indicates that this is by far the most effective way of developing research and study skills in young people. In fact, if you believe in the class size issue at all, it stands to reason that two teachers working with the same group of youngsters are going to have a much higher level of success than one teacher.

We can no longer afford to waffle on this issue. The link that is missing from many of our programs is that clarity of communication that comes through working together to plan and teach resource-based programs. If you examine staffing reductions in the past few years, you will find that positions have been eliminated primarily in school districts where there is no stated aim for the program, where the role of the teacher-librarian is not understood, even by teacher-librarians, and where the teacher-librarian has traditionally provided spare periods for classroom teachers.

What has been eliminated, however, is not the teacher-librarian's position at all, since it never really existed; what has been eliminated is the position of "prep time" or relief teacher. In secondary schools, the same is true of the reference librarian who answers questions and helps kids individually but has not planned programs and is certainly not a teaching partner. Too many teacher-librarians still seem to think that they are language arts teachers working in an enriched language arts classroom, or that they are a children's or reference librarian simply providing public library services for students in schools.

If the program is a partnership, then we have to not only determine objectives for the program, but also who is best at implementing them. For example, one objective for this program may be that youngsters in the primary grades have a regular storytelling and story reading experience in the resource center. However, there is no indication that it is necessary that this be done by the teacher-librarian. In fact, if the teacher-librarian is part-time, it may be much more appropriate that the classroom teacher provide that experience in the resource centre during the time that the teacher-librarian is absent, if the activity requires only one teacher and an entire class.

We know, for example, that the promotion of voluntary reading can be done best through the classroom teacher. Youngsters will accept recommendations for recreational reading from their peers and then their classroom teacher long before the school librarian. This is indisputable; it is proven fact. In that case, if we put one-tenth of the energy that we now put into preparing booktalks and literature appreciation programs on our own into working with classroom teachers to promote voluntary reading in the classroom, our objective might be better realized, while we may not necessarily be the active participant with the students. Oh I know—all teacher-librarians are trained storytellers, expert in children's literature and literary appreciation. Nonsense! Most teacher-librarians have no more specialized training in these areas than most primary teachers. And besides, that expertise and knowledge of the resources should be shared with teachers, not jealously guarded.

In the school there are many factors affecting the development and extension of a program, even at a most basic level. Obviously, from what I have said so far, there must not only be an understanding of the role of the teacher-librarian, but also a strong commitment by the teacher-librarian to that role. The teacher-librarian must place a premium on planning. Emphasis on day-to-day operations almost always pushes planning into the background; putting out today's fire can take priority over planning. The conclusion one reaches here is that fire-fighting interferes with fire prevention. There is no question that planning takes time. There is also no question, however, that answering the same question twenty-seven times from twenty-seven different youngsters takes a lot more time, and is far less effective, and it certainly does not usually require the professional teacher's expertise.

COOPERATIVE PROGRAM PLANNING AND TEACHING

In planning a program of study, a teacher goes through a number of steps. Objectives are established for the unit. You and I both know that there are teachers who carefully think out their objectives and write them down. There are even more teachers who don't stop to think about objectives at all but know in the back of their mind what it is that they want to accomplish with the youngsters: content or subject matter to be taught is determined and put into sequence. We may, for example, study South America by looking at one country at a time. Perhaps instead we wish to look at themes, such as political leadership or social conditions. It may be that a chronological approach to an entire continent is preferable. The content can be organized in a large number of ways quite aside from what the textbook publisher has determined.

As professional teachers, we have a whole range of instructional strategies at our disposal in order to accomplish the objectives we have set for ourselves. We may set up activity centers in the classroom. Perhaps a Socratic question and answer approach is most useful for our purpose. It may be that we are going to use library resources and team teach with the teacher. Activities are planned for the youngsters, and we evaluate student performance and occasionally take the time to look at the effectiveness of the unit.

The major weakness in teacher-librarianship today is that we have intended to plug in at the learning activities phase of program planning. By the time the eighth youngster has asked the same question, it dawns on us that someone has given an assignment somewhere. We then simply reinforce our stereotype as handmaiden, run around and help the youngsters, and complain about not getting advance warning. Rarely do we pursue discussion with the teacher to prevent a recurrence. I would suggest that it is foolhardy, if not downright dishonest, to claim that we are helping teachers accomplish their objectives if we don't even know what they are, let alone have any role in helping to plan them.

We all know how well a ten-year-old can interpret the directions given to him or her by another adult and yet teacher-librarians persist in using the youngster as the professional link with the classroom teacher. We have to move our involvement back to planning with the teacher so that we have that clarity of communication and each knows what is expected, and where we are going. Only in this way can everyone work effectively toward accomplishment of the objectives. Stated another way, discussion with teachers should focus less on what we want the students to do and more on what we want them to learn, and only then on how we are going to organize for that learning.

By putting time into planning, there will be that clarity of communication about what the students are to learn, what previous skills and activities they have been involved in, what resources are appropriate, and how they are to be used; there will be determination of how student competence in these skills is going to be measured, and there will be some assessment as to the effectiveness of the unit itself.

If we believe that research and study skills or information skills, or whatever we want to call them are important then there must be a systematic approach to their development. They have to be specified and included in school district goals. We can no longer simply react to teachers and take a gentle, hodgepodge approach. We are really wasting our time teaching skills that are not going to be followed up and extended in succeeding years. We are also saying that these skills are not really important for all youngsters because some students can be taught how to make effective notes for five years in a row, while other students are not taught it ever.

Consequently, tied in with cooperative program planning and teaching, there must be a school-based, staff-developed skills continuum for research and study skill development. At the elementary level this is relatively easy to develop, and at the secondary level it is relatively easy to develop with different subject departments. The process of involving teachers in articulating specific information skills at different grade levels provides part of the framework or reference points for effective cooperative planning. For example, in planning a unit at the grade three level in science or at the grade ten level in social studies, it is much easier to refer with the teacher to the school's continuum of skills to determine which skills should be introduced or reinforced during that unit so that there is a systematic and developmental approach to research and study skills.

The research and study skills continuum overcomes many of the problems of a haphazard approach and also implicates the staff in the success of the program. With the research and study skills continuum, of course, it becomes quite easy to develop different units of study with classroom teachers at each grade level, but these units incorporate the same skills. Teachers are then able to choose topics and units for research and study skill development or to develop new units with the teacher-librarian but all students at the grade level are taught specific things and it's incorporated with classroom instruction. In this way the program becomes entrenched in the school and provides a foundation for continuing growth and development.

At this point, it becomes critical that the teacher-librarian write down the unit as it was developed with the classroom teacher, noting such things as the objectives, how the program was organized and scheduled, what activities were developed, what specialized resources were used, which materials were better for slower youngsters, and which were better for youngsters who needed more challenge, and what the two partners thought the strengths and weaknesses of the unit were and how it might be changed if it was done again.

This provides the important support systems. The first is, that when working with the teacher again on the same unit in a succeeding year, or even with different teachers on that unit, it is much easier to revise and adapt to new circumstances than to start from scratch. In this way, the resource center develops a large collection of resource-based units which integrate research and study skills for demonstration to teachers and for revision to meet program needs.

What happens too often today is that when the teacher-librarian leaves the school, the program essentially leaves with him or her. The new teacher-librarian goes through all the same processes of getting to know the staff, making overtures, starting to plan with one person, and so on. How much better it would be if the new teacher-librarian found that there had been a large number of units that had been developed and could work with teachers to revise, adapt, and then build on them rather than starting over.

Similarly, when the classroom teacher leaves, there are units which he or she has developed with the teacher-librarian which can be presented to a new teacher-librarian in a new situation, again revised and adapted, but forming a component of a program which is ongoing. Without this foundation for resource-based learning in the school, we are really no further ahead today than where we were forty-five years ago. Each year we virtually start all over again. What an incredible waste and what a loss of easily obtained commitment from teaching colleagues.

The prescription for survival and even growth is relatively simple — a stated aim for the program, a clearly defined role for the teacher-librarian, commitment by the teacher-librarian to that role, cooperative program planning and teaching as a philosophical framework, a school-based scope and sequence continuum of study and research skills, and units of study which are not only jointly planned and taught but also recorded for future use and improvement.

Guidelines for these can be established both at the district and the school level. There must be guidelines for flexible scheduling, for example, and guidelines for cooperative planning. It seems to me that the district has a responsibility to define these guidelines, but this seems to be a school-based decision. In Vancouver, we found that when there was a board policy mandating flexible scheduling at the elementary school level, the programs had a much better chance of support and teacher involvement. In other words, our teacher-librarians do not provide spare periods and resource center use occurs after planning between the teacher and teacher-librarian.

We also found, to the surprise of a great many, that the circulation of library materials increased dramatically, in fact it tripled in eight years, after rigidly-scheduled library classes were ended. And, as you know, if the purpose of the program is to provide spare periods, there are many, much cheaper ways of doing that and districts will certainly discover them quickly if they haven't thus far.

EDUCATION FOR SCHOOL LIBRARIANSHIP

The question that immediately comes to mind is "How do we get to this position?" Where we are badly let down, of course, is in the institutions training teacher-librarians. Obviously, there is a critical need for minimum qualifications for teacher-librarians. You simply cannot transfer a teacher from the classroom to the resource center and presume this knowledge of research and study skills, cooperative planning, team teaching, resource-based learning, and the selection and organization of materials. These are specialized skills that have to be developed in addition to teacher education and classroom experience. But there is no stated aim for the program in most faculties of education and library science, there is no outline of competencies to be developed, there is no cohesive statement on the role of the teacher-librarian, and yet this is where it all begins. Teacher-librarians are coming out of these programs having been convinced that every component of the resource center, from curricular leadership to cataloguing, is equally important. They have not been provided with a context of cooperative program planning and teaching and they have not been provided with the important, specialized skills to set priorities within that context, or to advocate strong support for the program.

Not only is there a stated aim, clarified role, and context for the program, but just the number of units assigned to each area of work is message enough for the prospective teacher-librarian. Ample time is often given over to cataloguing and organizing resources, for example, while cooperative program planning and teaching is buried in general courses on services, which includes not only storytelling, story reading, booktalks, but often facilities. Prospective teacher-librarians must have opportunities to learn the skills necessary to plan with colleagues and team teach and to provide leadership in program advocacy.

Those who persist in placing an emphasis on reading and telling stories to youngsters on a regularly scheduled basis in order to provide spare periods for classroom teachers will be the death of school librarianship. I would like to state that again. Those of you who believe that by reading and telling stories to youngsters on a regularly scheduled basis and teaching library skills out of any meaningful context should get out of teacher-librarianship and give the rest of us a chance of preserving and extending what is good and exciting in what we are doing. There are still too many teacher-librarians who are paid professional salaries for being effective homemakers, book exchangers, and all round martyrs.

PROGRAM ADVOCACY

If teacher-librarians do not have a clear understanding of their role, if they cannot speak with a unified voice, how on earth do we expect principals and teachers to understand what we are doing, work closely with us, and speak on our behalf? Until we develop an understanding of who we are and what we are about, the essential component of program advocacy becomes very difficult to implement with confidence. We are not both teachers and librarians; this is not a dual role—we are teachers who specialize in the effective use of learning resources, teachers who know what information skills are and how they might be integrated in instructional programs.

We must become advocates for our programs, there is no question of this. We must also speak in the language of the audience, namely in terms of education. We must speak with a clear, cohesive, and unified voice.

Strong programs in schools are not difficult to develop. But strong programs must rest on strong, philosophical foundations with stated goals and objectives if they are to be both valid and sustaining. This means that the programs must operate within a framework of cooperative program planning and teaching and a well understood and supported role for the teacher-librarian, with many referral points for entering the curriculum, such as through a continuum of research and study skills. A so-called strong program which takes place within the framework of scheduled library skills classes, or scheduled literature appreciation classes, or at the secondary level within the context of English classes only, is not a strong program at all. The resource center may be busy and the youngsters may seem productive, but the research is clear that these youngsters are not going to retain those skills of processing and using information and apply them in different contexts in their school career and beyond.

We might begin with our sense of professionalism. Some believe they are professional simply because they are teachers and/or librarians. In other words, professionalism is defined by the level of academic achievement. Others define professionalism by the long hours which they work, and not being a puncher of clocks in order to collect a check. I think that the word professionalism involves both of these things.

There is indeed a body of knowledge that it is necessary to master for one to be an effective teacher-librarian. There is also a framework or understanding of where the program is going and how it is going to get there that is essential. These are developed through the level of academic achievement and through long hours of work.

But there is also the question of commitment—the commitment of the teacher-librarian to teacher-librarianship. Professionalism is also, after all, an attribute. We have seen too many teacher-librarians who are not concerned about program erosion because they know they will always have some kind of position. There is no commitment to the program, there is no commitment to the profession, there is only a commitment to continued employment regardless of where that might be within the school or library system. I would submit that advocacy and commitment are what we will be looking for in teacher-librarians over the next few years if we expect the program to expand and survive.

John Naisbett in *Megatrends* outlines that we are moving into a world which will be information rich, a cliché which you have heard many times, but also a world which may be knowledge poor. The reason for this is that citizens will not be able to handle information effectively. Surely, this is what teacher-librarianship is all about. Helping youngsters to develop a commitment to informed decision-making, through the ability to locate, process, and use information effectively, is going to be critical to the continuation of democratic societies and to technological achievement.

We as teacher-librarians have a central role to play in this, as an integral component of public education. Teacher-librarians as I know them are essential to the public schools. With role clarification, a strong commitment to cooperative program planning and teaching, a framework for success through flexible scheduling and a school-based continuum of research and study skills, units jointly planned and recorded with teachers, teacher-librarians will be in the forefront in the resolution of educational problems in schools in the information age.

Graduates of our schools will be able to define important problems, locate pertinent information, extract it, analyze it, organize it, and use it effectively, whether from books or data bases. They will be well-prepared for the society of today and tomorrow. This is our potential! I would urge you, through your professional commitment, to make it your personal promise.

Contributors

Bev Anderson was a teacher-librarian, coordinator of program resources and an elementary school principal with the Calgary (Alberta) Board of Education.

Liz Austrom is district principal—curriculum resources with the Vancouver (British Columbia) School Board.

Nancy Black is coordinator of young adult services for the Saskatoon (Saskatchewan) Public Library.

Jean Brown is assistant professor in the learning resources division of the Faculty of Education at Memorial University in St. John's, Newfoundland, where she teaches courses in resource-based teaching and school librarianship at the undergraduate and graduate levels.

Susan Casey is teacher-librarian at Ian Bazalgette Junior High School in Calgary, Alberta.

Alixe Hambleton is associate professor at the University of Regina Faculty of Education in Saskatchewan.

Carol-Ann Haycock is president of the HRD (Human Resources Development) Group, a consulting and staff training group.

Ken Haycock is director of program services for the Vancouver (British Columbia) School Board and managing editor and publisher of *Emergency Librarian*.

James Henri is senior lecturer in the School of Information Studies at Riverina-Murray Institute of Higher Education in Wagga Wagga, New South Wales, Australia and is the coordinator of the post graduate diploma program in school librarianship.

Barbara Howlett is a secondary school teacher-librarian in Langley, British Columbia.

Ron Jobe teaches courses in English education at the University of British Columbia in Vancouver. Dr. Jobe is a former teacher-librarian and consultant with the Edmonton (Alberta) Public School Board.

Igor Kusyszyn is associate professor of psychology and associate director of the teaching skills program for the Counselling and Development Centre of York University in Toronto.

Roy Lundin is head of the department of librarianship and teaching studies and coordinator of continuing education at Brisbane College of Advanced Education in Kelvin Grove, Queensland, Australia.

Michael Marland is headmaster at the North Westminster Community School in the Inner London Education Authority in the United Kingdom.

William McKinnie is head of the P.G. Reid Resource Centre at Guelph Collegiate and Vocational Institute in Guelph, Ontario.

Mieko Nagakura is senior research officer at the National Institute for Educational Research in Tokyo, Japan.

Antoinette Oberg is an associate professor in the Faculty of Education at the University of Victoria in British Columbia.

John Patrick prepared this summary on critical thinking skills for the ERIC Clearinghouse for Social Studies/Social Science Education.

Ken Roberts is director of the Whitby (Ontario) Public Library.

Debra Simmons is teacher-librarian at Templeton Secondary School in Vancouver, British Columbia.

Iris Spurrell was a teacher-librarian and is now consultant for school library programs with the Calgary (Alberta) Board of Education.

Sharon Walisser was a teacher-librarian and is now a program and staff development consultant with the Vancouver (British Columbia) School Board.

Valerie White is coordinator of young adult services for the Calgary (Alberta) Public Library.

Sources

Attitudes of School Librarians Toward Networking and Teacher Utilization: A Comparative Study of Ten Countries. Mieko Nagakura. *EL* 10:5 (May-June, 1983), pp. 11-14.

Changing Teaching Practice to Meet Current Expectations: Implications for Teacher-Librarians. Jean Brown. *EL* 16:2 (November-December, 1988), pp. 9-14.

Communication Skills and Strategies for Teacher-Librarians. Barbara Howlett. *EL* 11:1 (September-October, 1983), pp. 14-19.

Cooperative Program Planning—A Model That Works. Carol-Ann Haycock. *EL* 16:2 (November-December, 1988), pp. 29-38.

Critical Thinking in the Social Studies. John Patrick. *EL* 14:3 (January-February, 1987), pp. 19-20.

Developing the School Resource Center Program—A Systematic Approach. Carol-Ann Haycock. *EL* 12:1 (September-October, 1984), pp. 9-16.

Developing a School-Based Research Strategy. Sharon Walisser. *EL* 13:1 (September-October, 1985), pp. 19-26.

Hard Times ... Hard Choices [editorial]. Ken Haycock. *EL* 9:5 (May-June, 1982), p. 5.

In Search of Effectiveness. Ken Haycock. *EL* 13:1 (September-October, 1985), p. 7.

Information Skills in the Curriculum: Developing a School-Based Continuum. Carol-Ann Haycock. *EL* 13:1 (September-October, 1985), pp. 11-17.

The Integrated Approach to School Library Programming. James Henri. *EL* 14:3 (January-February, 1987), pp. 9-14.

Libraries, Learning and the Whole School. Michael Marland. *EL* 15:2 (November-December, 1987), pp. 9-14.

The Library, the Computer, and Utopia. Debra Simmons. *EL* 10:3 (January-February, 1983), pp. 11-12.

Maximizing Learning in Small Groups. Igor Kusyszyn. *EL* 11:1 (September-October, 1983), pp. 20-22.

Micros: The New Status Symbol [editorial]. Ken Haycock. *EL* 10:3 (January-February, 1983), p. 5.

Networking—Essential to Survival. Ken Haycock. *EL* 12:5 (May-June, 1985), p. 7.

On Book Exchanges. Carol-Ann Haycock. *EL* 11:2 (November-December, 1983), p. 5.

Online Bibliographic Searching in Secondary School Resource Centers. William G. McKinnie. *EL* 10:3 (January-February, 1983), pp. 8-11.

The Role of the School Librarian as a Professional Teacher: A Position Paper. Ken Haycock. *EL* 8:5 (May-June, 1981), pp. 4-11.

School Assignments: A Public Library Responsibility. Nancy Black, Ken Roberts, Valerie White. *EL* 13:5 (May-June, 1986), pp. 25-26.

The School Librarian and the Classroom Teacher: Partners in Curriculum Planning. Antoinette Oberg. *EL* 14:1 (September-October, 1986), pp. 9-14.

School Libraries—Definitely Worth Their Keep. Bev Anderson. *EL* 10:5 (May-June, 1983), pp. 6-11.

Secondary School Assignments: Cooperatively Planned and Taught. Liz Austrom. *EL* 15:2 (November-December, 1987), pp. 15-31.

Secondary Schools and Critical Thinking. Ken Haycock. *EL* 14:3 (January-February, 1987), pp. 27-28.

Static in the Educational Intercom: Conflict and the School Librarian. Alixe Hambleton. *EL* 9:5 (May-June, 1982), pp. 18-20.

A Stations Approach to Learning: The Conversion of a Secondary School Skeptic. Debra Simmons. *EL* 14:3 (January-February, 1987), pp. 15-18.

Strengthening the Foundations for Teacher-Librarianship. Ken Haycock. *SLMQ* 13:2 (Spring, 1985), pp. 102-9.

Student Strategy for Research: A Developmental Approach. Iris Spurrell. *EL* 14:1 (September-October, 1986), pp. 15-19.

The Teacher-Librarian and Information Skills—An Across the Curriculum Approach. Roy Lundin. *EL* 11:1 (September-October, 1983), pp. 8-12.

Teacher-Librarian Collegiality: Strategies for Effective Influence. Ronald Jobe. *EL* 7:4-5 (March-June, 1980), pp. 5-8.

Ten Issues in School Librarianship [editorial]. Ken Haycock. *EL* 10:1 (September-October, 1982), p. 7.

Theory—Where Is My Reality? Susan Casey. *EL* 14:3 (January-February, 1987), pp. 21-24.

What Is a School Librarian? Towards Defining Professionalism. Ken Haycock. *EL* 6:5-6 (May-August, 1979), pp. 10-14.

What Works: Research about Teaching and Learning. U.S. Department of Education. *EL* 14:2 (November-December, 1986), pp. 22-25.

What Works: Summary of *EL* Research Findings to Date. *EL* 15:5 (May-June, 1988), p. 40.

Added Entry

Ken Haycock has also selected articles on the important theme of *Program Advocacy: Power, Publicity and the Teacher-Librarian*. This title is a companion volume to *The School Library Program in the Curriculum* and is also available from Libraries Unlimited. ISBN 0-87287-781-7.

The professional journal *Emergency Librarian* focuses on the role of the teacher-librarian in the school within the framework of cooperative program planning and teaching. Subscriptions are available for $45 or $40 prepaid from Dyad Services, Box C34069, Department 284, Seattle, Washington 98124-1069 [*in Canada*: Dyad Services, P.O. Box 46258, Station G, Vancouver, British Columbia V6R 4G6.]

ABOUT THE EDITOR

Ken Haycock is director of program services for the Vancouver (British Columbia) School Board where he is responsible for developing and delivering curriculum and staff development programs and resources for more than 5,000 employees in 110 schools. The Vancouver School Board has policies mandating the role of the teacher-librarian within the context of cooperative program planning and teaching and flexibly scheduled resource centers. Ken is a past president of both the Canadian Library Association and the Canadian School Library Association. He has received the Queen Elizabeth Silver Jubilee Medal for contributions to Canadian society, the Margaret Scott Award of Merit for contributions to teacher-librarianship, the Grolier award for research in school librarianship and was recognized by Phi Delta Kappa as one of the 75 leading young educators in North America. Mr. Haycock is managing editor and publisher of the school library journal *Emergency Librarian*.

Index